CHILDREN'S WORLD ATLAS

Consultant
Dr David Green

Written by
Simon Adams • Mary Atkinson • Sarah Phillips

DK

A Dorling Kindersley Book

Dorling Kindersley

LONDON, NEW YORK, MUNICH,
MELBOURNE, and DELHI

Project editors Lucy Hurst, Sadie Smith,
Shaila Awan, Amber Tokeley
Art editors Joe Conneally, Sheila Collins,
Rebecca Johns, Simon Oon, Andrew Nash
Senior editor Fran Jones
Senior art editor Floyd Sayers
Managing editor Andrew Macintyre
Managing art editor Jane Thomas
Picture research Carolyn Clerkin, Brenda Clynch
DK Pictures Sarah Mills
Production Jenny Jacoby
DTP designer Siu Yin Ho

Cartography Department
Senior Cartographic Editor Simon Mumford
Cartographer Ed Merritt
Digital Cartography Encompass Graphics Limited
Satellite images Rob Stokes
3D Globes Planetary Visions Ltd., London

This *Children's World Atlas* has been conceived by Dorling Kindersley Limited

First published in Great Britain in 2003
This revised edition first published in 2008 by
Dorling Kindersley Limited,
80 Strand, London WC2R 0RL

Copyright © 2003, 2008 Dorling Kindersley Limited
A Penguin Company

2 4 6 8 10 9 7 5 3
CD041 – 04/08

A CIP catalogue record for this book is
available from the British Library.

ISBN: 978-1-40533-160-9

Colour reproduction by Colourscan, Singapore, and
Media Development and Printing, UK
Printed and bound by Star Standard Industries Ltd, Singapore

**Discover more at
www.dk.com**

Contents

NORTH AMERICA   2

CENTRAL AND SOUTH AMERICA   20

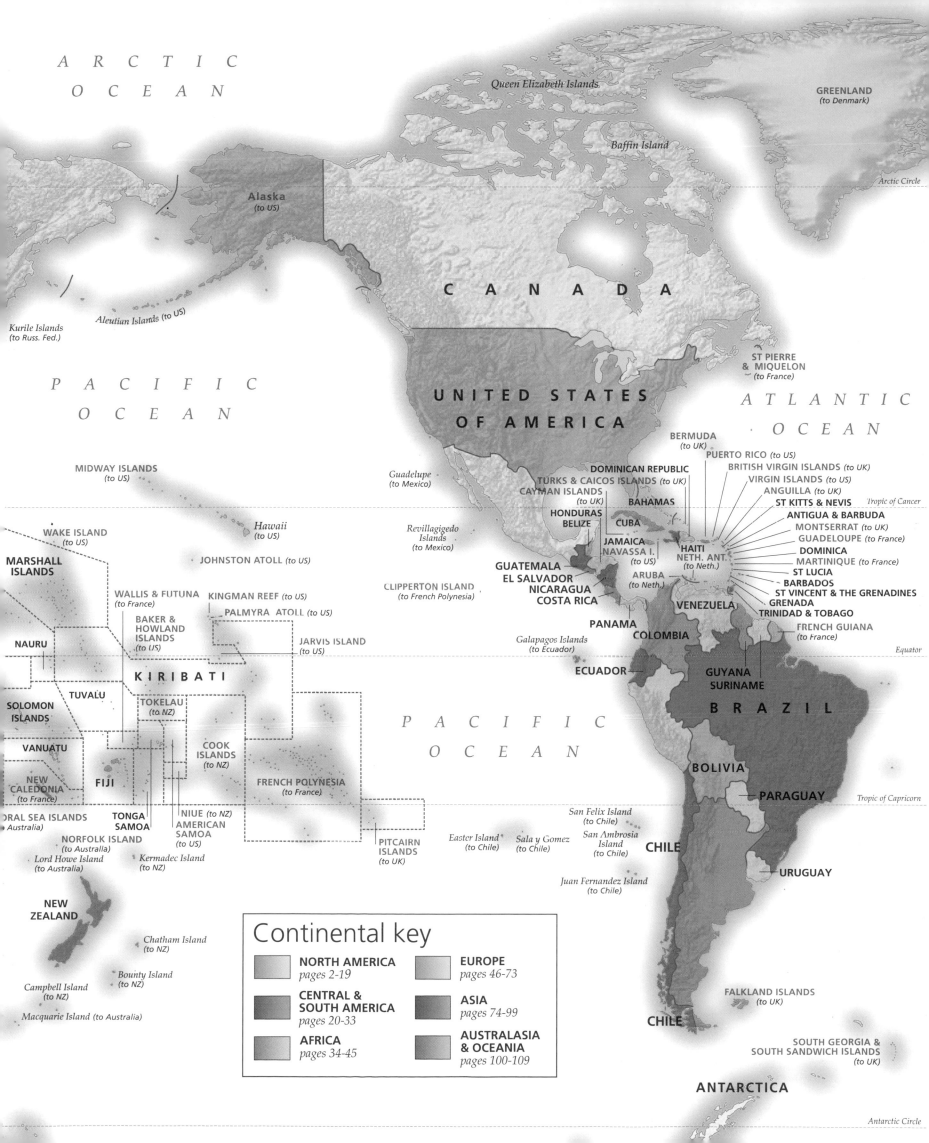

ARCTIC OCEAN

Queen Elizabeth Islands

GREENLAND
(to Denmark)

Baffin Island

Arctic Circle

Alaska
(to US)

CANADA

*Kurile Islands
(to Russ. Fed.)*

Aleutian Islands (to US)

PACIFIC OCEAN

UNITED STATES OF AMERICA

ATLANTIC OCEAN

ST PIERRE & MIQUELON
(to France)

BERMUDA
(to UK)

PUERTO RICO *(to US)*

MIDWAY ISLANDS
(to US)

*Guadelupe
(to Mexico)*

DOMINICAN REPUBLIC

BRITISH VIRGIN ISLANDS *(to UK)*

TURKS & CAICOS ISLANDS *(to UK)*

VIRGIN ISLANDS *(to US)*

CAYMAN ISLANDS
(to UK)

ANGUILLA *(to UK)*

BAHAMAS

ST KITTS & NEVIS

Tropic of Cancer

*Hawaii
(to US)*

HONDURAS
BELIZE

CUBA

ANTIGUA & BARBUDA

WAKE ISLAND
(to US)

*Revillagigedo
Islands
(to Mexico)*

MONTSERRAT *(to UK)*

GUADELOUPE *(to France)*

JAMAICA

MARSHALL
ISLANDS

JOHNSTON ATOLL *(to US)*

NAVASSA I.
(to US)

HAITI

DOMINICA

NETH. ANT.
(to Neth.)

MARTINIQUE *(to France)*

GUATEMALA

ST LUCIA

WALLIS & FUTUNA
(to France)

KINGMAN REEF *(to US)*

EL SALVADOR

ARUBA
(to Neth.)

BARBADOS

NICARAGUA

ST VINCENT & THE GRENADINES

PALMYRA ATOLL *(to US)*

COSTA RICA

GRENADA

BAKER &
HOWLAND
ISLANDS
(to US)

*CLIPPERTON ISLAND
(to French Polynesia)*

TRINIDAD & TOBAGO

JARVIS ISLAND
(to US)

PANAMA

VENEZUELA

FRENCH GUIANA
(to France)

NAURU

COLOMBIA

*Galapagos Islands
(to Ecuador)*

Equator

KIRIBATI

ECUADOR

GUYANA

SURINAME

TUVALU

TOKELAU
(to NZ)

BRAZIL

SOLOMON
ISLANDS

PACIFIC OCEAN

VANUATU

COOK
ISLANDS
(to NZ)

BOLIVIA

NEW
CALEDONIA
(to France)

FIJI

FRENCH POLYNESIA
(to France)

PARAGUAY

Tropic of Capricorn

NIUE *(to NZ)*

*San Felix Island
(to Chile)*

ORAL SEA ISLANDS
Australia)

TONGA
SAMOA

AMERICAN
SAMOA
(to US)

*Easter Island
(to Chile)*

*Sala y Gomez
(to Chile)*

*San Ambrosia
Island
(to Chile)*

CHILE

NORFOLK ISLAND
(to Australia)

*Kermadec Island
(to NZ)*

PITCAIRN
ISLANDS
(to UK)

*Lord Howe Island
(to Australia)*

URUGUAY

*Juan Fernandez Island
(to Chile)*

NEW
ZEALAND

*Chatham Island
(to NZ)*

*Bounty Island
(to NZ)*

*Campbell Island
(to NZ)*

Continental key

NORTH AMERICA *pages 2-19*		EUROPE *pages 46-73*
CENTRAL & SOUTH AMERICA *pages 20-33*		ASIA *pages 74-99*
AFRICA *pages 34-45*		AUSTRALASIA & OCEANIA *pages 100-109*

Macquarie Island (to Australia)

FALKLAND ISLANDS
(to UK)

CHILE

SOUTH GEORGIA &
SOUTH SANDWICH ISLANDS *(to UK)*

ANTARCTICA

Antarctic Circle

AFRICA

EUROPE 46

ASIA 74

AUSTRALASIA AND OCEANIA 100

Introducing Earth

TO US, THE EARTH SEEMS HUGE. Vast oceans stretch further than the eye can see and separate the giant landmasses that are home to billions of people, animals, and plants. However, Earth is just one of the nine planets that orbit the Sun – a huge, burning-hot star in the centre of our Solar System. The Solar System and all the stars in the night sky are part of our galaxy – the Milky Way, which contains as many as 200 billion stars. Beyond our galaxy are millions more galaxies. They all add together to make up the Universe.

Pluto

Neptune

Uranus

Saturn

Jupiter

Earth

Mars

Venus

Moon

Mercury

Sun

THE SOLAR SYSTEM

Planet Earth is part of a system of planets and their moons, as well as numerous asteroids and comets, which orbit around a huge star we call the Sun. The Sun itself consists of gas. Nuclear reactions inside its core produce the heat and light that make life on Earth possible. The Earth is the third of four small terrestrial (Earth-like) planets that orbit close to the Sun. Further out in our Solar System are four huge gas planets, while distant Pluto, the smallest planet, is made of rock and ice.

A PLANET'S "year" is the time it takes to orbit the Sun. Earth's year is 365.25 days, but distant Pluto takes as long as 90,588 days to complete its orbit.

Crust

Mantle of silicate

Iron and nickel outer core

Inner core

THE EARTH

Earth's distance from the Sun allows just the right amount of heat and light to support life. It is warm enough for water to exist in liquid form – in fact, two-thirds of the Earth's surface is covered with water. As well as water, the planet consists of seven landmasses, or continents, which include Antarctica.

THE EARTH'S STRUCTURE

The Earth is not a solid ball. It is made up of different layers, much like an onion. The outer layer, or crust, is a thin sheet of rock that forms the continents and the ocean floor. Beneath it is the mantle, a layer of hot and, in places, molten (liquid) rock about 3,000 km (1,900 miles) thick. At the centre of the Earth is a core of hot metal, which is liquid on the outside and solid on the inside.

OUR MOON

Unlike some other planets in the Solar System, the Earth has only one moon. The Moon is our nearest neighbour in space and circles the Earth once every 29.53 days. It is about a quarter of the size of Earth and is made of rock. Despite having no light of its own, it is clearly visible from Earth because it reflects sunlight.

MOVING EARTH

The continents that make up the Earth's surface are always on the move. Eight large and several smaller plates, which form the landmasses of the Earth – called tectonic plates – float on top of the mantle. Because the Earth's interior is extremely hot, magma wells up to the cooler surface and forces these plates to move and crack. This happens very slowly, but when it does, it releases huge forces that can create new land, form mountains, and cause earthquakes.

THE HIMALAYAS are a range of mountains that contain the world's highest peak, Mount Everest.

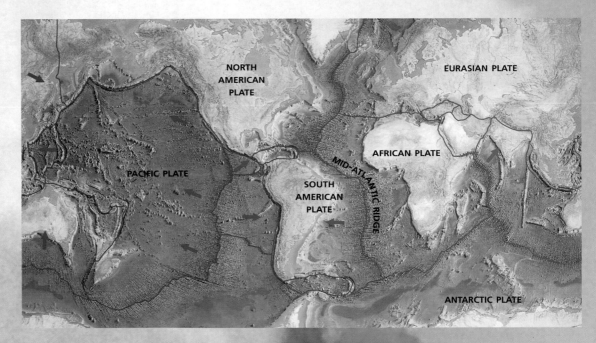

NORTH AMERICAN PLATE

EURASIAN PLATE

AFRICAN PLATE

MID-ATLANTIC RIDGE

PACIFIC PLATE

SOUTH AMERICAN PLATE

ANTARCTIC PLATE

MOUNTAIN BUILDING

Mountains form in three main ways. In the case of the Himalayas, Alps, and Rockies, two tectonic plates collided, causing the Earth's crust to buckle, crumple, and be forced upwards to create high mountains and deep valleys. But mountains can also be the result of a volcanic eruption, or caused by the edges of two plates fracturing into cracks called faults, pushing a chunk of land upwards to create a block mountain.

VOLCANOES

When two continental plates collide, one of them can be subducted, or pushed down, under the other into the Earth's hot mantle. The rocks of the subsiding plate melt, and may be forced up through the cracks to erupt onto the Earth's surface as a volcano. In addition, volcanoes may form when plates pull apart. Molten rock from the Earth's mantle rises up to fill the gap as the plates spread. Volcanoes can be separated into three different categories: active (continuously erupting), dormant (sleeping), or extinct.

THE HAWAIIAN volcano Kilauea is constantly erupting. Its name means "spewing" in Hawaiian.

Moving plates

The Earth's continental plates move in three ways: pulling apart, moving together, or sliding past one another. Where two plates pull apart, magma (molten rock) from the Earth's mantle wells up and fills the gap. If this happens on the ocean floor, it creates an underwater spreading ridge. If two plates collide, either they fuse to form a mountain range or one subsides under the other, causing volcanoes to appear. Where two plates slide past each other, a transform fault appears, and earthquakes can occur. Often a long crack or fault line appears on the Earth's surface.

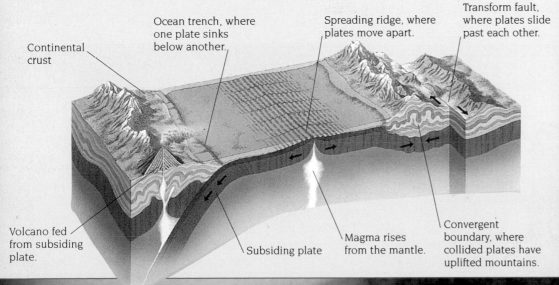

Ocean trench, where one plate sinks below another.

Spreading ridge, where plates move apart.

Transform fault, where plates slide past each other.

Continental crust

Volcano fed from subsiding plate.

Subsiding plate

Magma rises from the mantle.

Convergent boundary, where collided plates have uplifted mountains.

Climate and Vegetation

ON EARTH, A REGION'S WEATHER CAN CHANGE from day to day and even from hour to hour. But its climate – the average pattern of weather and temperature over a long period of time – remains fairly constant. Climate is affected by latitude (how far north or south of the Equator a region is), height above sea level, prevailing winds, and the circulation of ocean currents. An area's climate, as well as its landscape, affects the type of plant life, or vegetation, found there. Climate and vegetation also affect the lives of the animals, birds, and people that make the area their home.

Earth's axis is tilted at an angle of 23.5°.

Earth spins on its axis once every 23 hours, 56 minutes. We round this off to a 24-hour day.

Sun

Earth circles, or orbits, the Sun once every 365.25 days, a length of time known as a year.

THE FOUR SEASONS

SPRING

SUMMER

AUTUMN

WINTER

As the Earth orbits the Sun, its tilted axis gradually leans each hemisphere towards the Sun and then away from it. This causes the seasons. For example, summer occurs when a hemisphere leans towards the Sun and gets more sunlight, more heat, and longer days. Most regions of the world have four seasons, but some areas near the Equator are always hot and have only wet and dry seasons.

EARTH'S ORBIT

The Earth does not sit upright on its axis but tilts at an angle of 23.5°. It maintains this same tilt as it travels around the Sun on its 950 million-km (590 million-mile) journey – a journey that lasts for one year. The Earth also spins on its axis, turning once every 24 hours to give us night and day.

RAINFALL

This map of the world shows the amount of rain that falls in a year. The light brown areas receive so little rain that they tend to be either hot desert or cold polar regions. They are difficult places in which to live, and have little vegetation.
The blue areas receive a moderate amount of rainfall each year. The purple areas are mainly areas of rainforest, where high rainfall allows vegetation to flourish.

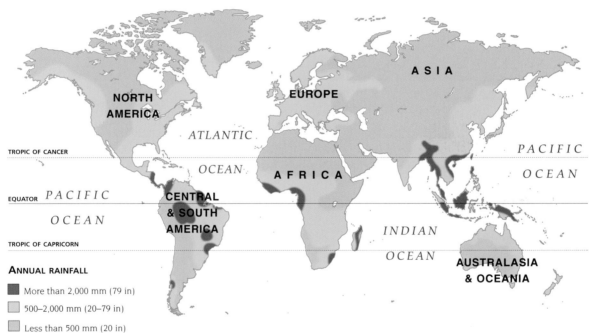

ASIA

NORTH AMERICA

EUROPE

ATLANTIC

TROPIC OF CANCER

OCEAN

PACIFIC

AFRICA

OCEAN

EQUATOR *PACIFIC*

CENTRAL & SOUTH AMERICA

OCEAN

INDIAN

TROPIC OF CAPRICORN

OCEAN

AUSTRALASIA & OCEANIA

ANNUAL RAINFALL

More than 2,000 mm (79 in)

500–2,000 mm (20–79 in)

Less than 500 mm (20 in)

PEOPLE AND CLIMATE

Some climates are easier to live in than others, but people can still adapt to a variety of different environments. These Moroccan girls (left) live in the Sahara desert. They are members of a nomadic tribe that travel from place to place in search of food and water. Other tribes have made their homes in humid rainforests, and others inhabit the icy polar regions.

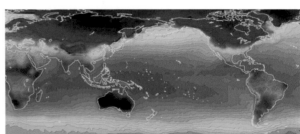

SATELLITE MAP of the world's average surface temperature in January.

WORLD TEMPERATURES

This map compares temperatures during January. The values range from –38°C (–36°F) in the purple regions, through blue, green, yellow, and red, to black, which is 40°C (104°F). As expected, temperatures are hotter near the Equator and cooler near the poles. Australia is tilted closer to the Sun during January, giving it a scorching summer.

VEGETATION ZONES

Several factors influence the vegetation (plant life) and animal life of a particular region – the climate, latitude, and physical landscape. After studying the different types of plant life, scientists have divided the Earth into nine main vegetation zones, or biomes. Over millions of years, plants and animals, as well as people, have adapted to life in these different zones, often developing special features that enable them to survive.

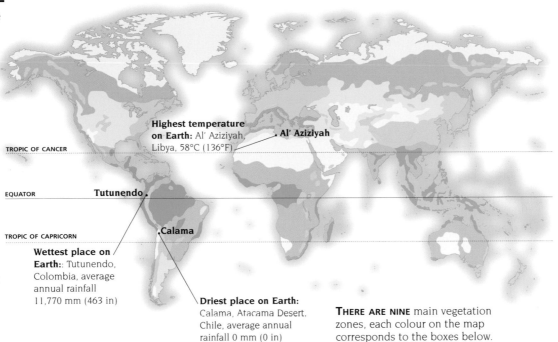

TROPIC OF CANCER

Highest temperature on Earth: Al' Aziziyah, Libya, 58°C (136°F)

● Al' Aziziyah

EQUATOR ● Tutunendo

TROPIC OF CAPRICORN

● Calama

Wettest place on Earth:: Tutunendo, Colombia, average annual rainfall 11,770 mm (463 in)

Driest place on Earth: Calama, Atacama Desert. Chile, average annual rainfall 0 mm (0 in)

THERE ARE NINE main vegetation zones, each colour on the map corresponds to the boxes below.

▢ POLAR AND TUNDRA

The freezing areas around the North and South Poles are covered with ice. South of the North Pole lies the tundra, where lower layers of soil stay frozen. Only hardy mosses, lichens, and shrubs can survive.

▢ MEDITERRANEAN

This vegetation zone refers not just to areas around the Mediterranean Sea in Europe, but also to places such as California, USA. With hot, dry summers and cool winters, vegetation such as olive and citrus trees are able to grow.

▢ TAIGA

The word taiga is Russian for "cold forest". It refers to the regions of northern Canada, Scandinavia, and Russia. These areas are home to forests of evergreens such as fir, spruce, and pine, all of which are able to withstand the cold, long, snow-filled winters.

▢ MOUNTAIN REGIONS

In mountain ranges, the higher the altitude, the colder it gets. Though vegetation can survive on the lower parts of the mountains, there is a point, called the tree line, above which it is too cold for trees to grow. Snow can be found on high peaks all year round.

▢ TEMPERATE FOREST

Temperate climates – not too hot or too cold occur in northern Europe, eastern North America, and eastern Asia. These areas often contain forests of deciduous trees, which lose their leaves in winter. Though many have been cut down, large woodland areas still survive.

▢ DRY GRASSLAND

Hot, dry summers and very cold winters, as well as sparse rainfall, give rise to areas too dry for trees to grow. These vast, dry grasslands are often found in the centre of continents, such as the prairies of North America. They are sometimes ploughed and used to grow wheat or raise cattle.

▢ TROPICAL RAINFOREST

The regions of tropical rainforest lie either side of the Equator, where the climate is hot and wet all year round. Up to 50,000 different species of trees, as well as millions of species of plants, animals, birds, and insects – 50 per cent of all animal and plant life – flourish in these humid conditions.

▢ HOT DESERT

The hottest places on Earth are deserts, though at night temperatures may plummet to below freezing. These dry regions get no rain for years at a time, so very little vegetation is found here. Cacti, evolved to cope without water for long periods, are usually the only plants that can survive here.

▢ TROPICAL GRASSLAND

Between tropical rainforests and hot deserts lie tropical grasslands, such as the pampas of South America and the African savannah. Tall grasses, low trees, and shrubs grow in these hot climates, which have only two seasons: wet and dry.

Population

EVERY SECOND, AROUND THE WORLD, four people are born and two people die. This means that over a year, the world's population increases by about 70 million people. In some of the richest countries of the world, population growth is slow. Elsewhere – especially in the poorer countries of Asia, Africa, and South America – the population is growing rapidly. Cities in such regions are growing fastest, and several now have populations of over 10 million people. When it comes to providing employment, housing, education and health care, such rapid growth rates can strain resources to the limit.

IN BURKINO FASO, less than 30 per cent of the population has access to a clean water supply, such as the water pump shown here.

THREATENED RESOURCES

As the world's population continues to rise, more people are chasing fewer natural resources. Only a small proportion of the Earth's land is suitable for growing food, while in some areas fresh water for drinking, cooking, and irrigating crops is scarce. Fossil fuels, such as oil and natural gas, will soon be in short supply, unless people begin to conserve energy or develop alternatives, such as solar power.

LIFE EXPECTANCY

A person's life expectancy is a measure of how long they are likely to live. This can vary dramatically from country to country, and depends on many factors including health care, nutrition, and access to fresh water. At present, the world's average life expectancy is 63 years.

FAMILY PLANNING

To help slow population growth, many countries now provide people with better health education and information, allowing them to plan the size of their families. Some governments even actively promote smaller families, as shown in this Chinese poster (above). But in many poorer parts of the world, a large family is often still necessary, so that the workload can be shared.

DISTRIBUTION OF PEOPLE

This map (above) shows the current populations of the major cities of the world. At the start of the 20th century, only one in ten people lived in a city. But over time people have been forced into the cities to find work, as factors such as poverty and loss of land have pushed them out of the countryside. Today, half the world's population lives in cities.

POPULATION GROWTH

In the past, the world's population grew slowly, but from about 1800, the pace began to quicken. Better diet, clean water, and improved health care helped to reduce the death rate. In advanced countries, children began to survive longer, so people started to have smaller families. However, because many people in the poorer countries still have large families, the rate of population growth has exploded.

Moscow 8.6 million
London 7 million
EUROPE
ASIA
NORTH AMERICA
Paris 9.3 million
Tehran 6.8 million
Lahore 5 million
Tianjin 8.8 million
New York 7.4 million
Beijing 10.9 million
Seoul 10.2 million
Istanbul 6.4 million
Karachi 9.3 million
Dhaka 6.1 million
Tokyo 7.8 million
Cairo 6.8 million
Delhi 8.4 million
Shanghai 13.5 million
Mexico City 16.7 million
AFRICA
Hong Kong 6.8 million
Bogotá 6 million
Mumbai (Bombay) 12.6 million
Kolkata (Calcutta) 11 million
Bangkok 5.6 million
Lima 6.5 million
SOUTH AMERICA
Chennai (Madras) 5.4 million
Jakarta 8.3 million
AUSTRALASIA & OCEANIA
Rio de Janeiro 10.2 million
Santiago 5.1 million
São Paulo 16.6 million
Buenos Aires 11.7 million

KEY:
■ Over 5 million people
○ 1–5 million people
· 50,000–1 million people

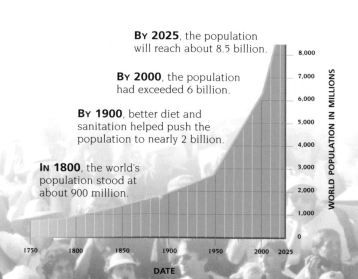

BY 2025, the population will reach about 8.5 billion.

BY 2000, the population had exceeded 6 billion.

BY 1900, better diet and sanitation helped push the population to nearly 2 billion.

IN 1800, the world's population stood at about 900 million.

WORLD POPULATION IN MILLIONS

8,000
7,000
6,000
5,000
4,000
3,000
2,000
1,000
0

1750 1800 1850 1900 1950 2000 2025

DATE

Mapping the World

ABOUT THE ATLAS

This atlas is divided into six continental sections – North America, Central and South America, Africa, Europe, Asia, and Australasia and Oceania. Each country, or group of countries, then has its own map that shows cities, towns, and main geographical features, such as rivers, lakes, and mountain ranges. Photographs and text provide detailed information about life in that country – its people, traditions, politics, and economy. Each continental section has a different colour border to help you locate that section. There is also a gazetteer and an index to help you access information.

FOREIGN NAMES

Features on the maps are generally labelled in the language of that country. For example, it would be:
Lake on English-speaking countries
Lago on Spanish-speaking countries
Lac on French-speaking countries
However, if a feature is well-known, or mentioned in the main text on the page, it will appear there in English so that readers can find it easily.

MAP LOCATOR

This map shows, in red, the location of each country, part of a country, or group of countries in relation to the continent in which it belongs. There is a locator for each map in the book.

PAGE CONTINUATION

The numbers that appear in a triangle at the top and side borders tell the reader the page of the neighbouring country, or region. For example, on USA: Midwest, the area that lies directly north of the Great Lakes is Eastern Canada – page 6 in the book.

USA: Midwest

LONGITUDE AND LATITUDE

Lines of longitude are vertical lines that run through the Poles. Lines of latitude are horizontal lines that run parallel to the Equator. These imaginary lines help locate places on a map.

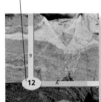

USING THE GRID REFERENCES

The letters and numbers around the outside of the page form a grid to help you find places on the map. For example, to find Wichita, look up its name in the gazetteer (pp 112–133), and you'll find the reference 12 G8. The first number is the page, the letter and number refer to the square made by following up or down from G and across from 8 to form G8.

SCALE

Each map features a scale that shows how distances on the map relate to kilometres and miles. The scale guide can be used to see how big a country is. Not all maps in the book are drawn to the same scale.

KEY TO MAP SYMBOLS

BORDERS

▬▬▬	International border: Border between countries which is mutually recognized.
▬▬▬	State border: Border used in some large countries to show internal divisions.
▬ ▬ ▬	Disputed border: Border used in practice, but not mutually agreed between two countries.
• • • •	Claimed border: Border which is not mutually recognized – where territory belonging to one country is claimed by another.
x—x—x	Ceasefire line
▪ ▪ ▪	Undefined boundary

PHYSICAL FEATURES

▲	Mountain
▽	Depression
▲	Volcano
⋊	Pass/Tunnel

DRAINAGE FEATURES

▬	Major river
▬	Minor river
- - - -	Seasonal river
┼	Dam
▬	Canal
ǀ	Waterfall
⌇⌇⌇	Seasonal lake

MISCELLANEOUS FEATURES

◇	Site of interest
∿∿∿	Ancient wall

COMMUNICATIONS

═══	Highway
▬▬	Major road
▬▬	Minor road
▬▬	Railway
✈	Airport

TOWNS & CITIES

◉	More than 500,000
◉	100,000 – 500,000
○	50,000 – 100,000
○	Less than 50,000
●	National capital
●	Internal administrative capital
◉	Polar research station

LATITUDE & LONGITUDE

▬	Lines of Latitude/Longitude
▬	Equator
- - - -	Tropics
25°	Degrees of Latitude/Longitude

NAMES

REGIONS

FRANCE	Country
JERSEY (to UK)	Dependent territory
KANSAS	Administrative region
Dordogne	Cultural region

TOWNS & CITIES

PARIS	National capital
SAN JUAN	Dependent territory capital city

NAMES continued

Seattle **Limón** Comayagua San José	Other towns & cities

PHYSICAL

Andes *Ardennes*	Landscape features
Balearic Islands	Island group
Majorca	Island
Lake Baikal	Lake/River /Canal
PACIFIC OCEAN *Gulf of Mexico* *Bay of Campeche*	Sea features
Chile Rise	Undersea feature

OTHER FEATURES

Tropic of Cancer	Graticule text

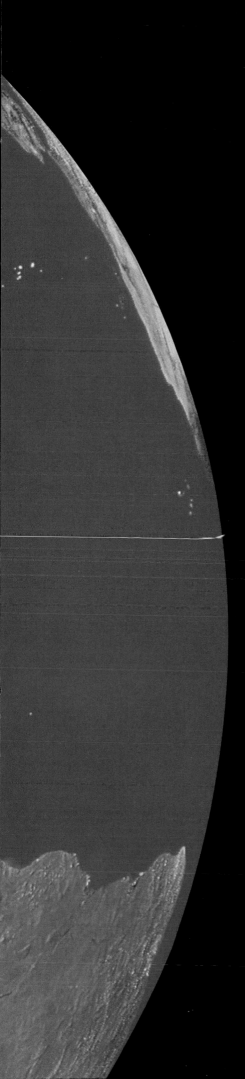

NORTH
AMERICA

NORTH AMERICA INCLUDES the United States of America,

Canada, and Mexico. Its population of 413 million is largely

based on immigrants, who arrived here from the 1500s onwards. North

America's varied landscape ranges from frozen tundra in the

north to hot desert and lush rain forest in the south.

Mexico is Spanish speaking and, despite vast oil and gas reserves, is relatively

poor. In contrast, the USA and Canada enjoy high standards of living and most

people speak English – except for the French-speakers in

Québec. They also have other features in common – they are

roughly the same size and share the longest undefended

land border in the world. However, the USA has a far larger

population and is the wealthiest nation on Earth. American technology, such

as computer software, has a global influence – as does its film and music.

A   B   C   D   E   F   G   H

Western Canada and Alaska

CANADA IS A HUGE COUNTRY and its western half stretches from the flat prairies in the east to the towering Rocky Mountains in the west, and from the relatively mild south to the permanently frozen area north of the Arctic Circle. Harsh conditions over much of the region mean that most of the population is concentrated in cities in the south, such as Vancouver, Calgary, and Winnipeg. The prairies – once a vast expanse of grassland – are now used mainly for growing wheat on huge mechanized farms. Oil and natural gas are found there as well. These natural resources are also important in Alaska, a part of the United States. The majority of Alaska's people moved there to work in these lucrative industries.

FORESTRY

Large parts of western Canada are covered in forests and lumbering is a major part of the local economy. The trees are used to make buildings, furniture, and paper. In the past, whole areas of trees were cleared but now sustainable methods such as selective cutting and replanting are practised.

FELLED trees are transported down a river near Vancouver.

TOTEM POLES

The native peoples of British Columbia use totem poles to record their clan history. Each carved and painted totem describes a real or mythical event and often features animals that the clan has a connection with, such as the eagle (left).

DOGSLED RACING

The state sport of Alaska is dogsled racing. Here, competitors take part in the annual Iditarod Trail Sled Dog Race, a gruelling run across the rugged landscape for drivers and their teams of dogs.

VANCOUVER

This city's vibrant cultural mix is typical of Canada's diversity. Many Chinese, as well as other ethnic groups, live here and reflect Vancouver's historic role as a destination for migrants. Its bustling economy, mild climate, and cultural links make it an attractive place to live.

Map labels

Chukchi Sea
ARCTIC OCEAN
Prince Patrick Island
Mould Bay
Beaufort Sea
Banks Island
Bering Strait
Wevok
Point Lay
Barrow
Kivalina
Gambell
Wales
Colville River
Prudhoe Bay
Umiat
Kaktovik
Sachs Harbour
Near Islands
Saint Lawrence Island
Deering
Norton Sound
Brooks Range
Rat Islands
Bering Sea
Alakanuk
Grayling
Yukon River
Kokrines
Fort Yukon
Aklavik
Inuvik
Tuktoyaktuk
Amundsen Gulf
Holma
Paulatuk
Andreanof Islands
Aleutian Islands
Nunivak Island
Pribilof Islands
Kwigillingok
ALASKA (to US)
Fairbanks
Fort McPherson
Atka
Platinum
Kuskokwim Mts
Alaska Range
Kugluktuk
Umnak Island
Dutch Harbor
Bristol Bay
Iliamna Lake
Mount McKinley 6194m
McKinley Park
Fort Good Hope
Mackenzie
Great Bear Lake
Echo
Unalaska Island
Unimak Island
Susitna
Anchorage
Hope
Gulkana
YUKON
Belkofski
Alaska Peninsula
Valdez
Chitina
TERRITORY
Rocky
NORTHWEST TERRITORIES
Shumagin Islands
Kodiak
Cordova
Mount Logan 5959m
Mountains
Kodiak Island
Katalla
Whitehorse
Tungsten
Fort Simpson
Edzo
Yellowknife
Great Slave Lake
PACIFIC OCEAN
Gulf of Alaska
Yakutat
Haines
Gustavus
Atlin
Fort Providence
Fort Liard
Hay River
Fort S
Juneau
Fort Nelson
Fort Verm
Kake
Alexander Archipelago
Port Alexander
Ware
BRITISH
Ketchikan
Fort St. John
McM
Prince Rupert
Queen Charlotte Islands
Kitimat
COLUMBIA
Fort St. John
ALBERTA
Grande Prairie
Ocean Falls
Queen Charlotte Sound
Prince George
Mount Waddington 4016m
Edmonton
Athabasca
Port Hardy
Red Deer
Campbell River
Kamloops
Calgary
Vancouver Island
Vancouver
Kelowna
Lethbridge
Nanaimo
Cranbrook
Milk River
Victoria
UNITED

109

4

A   B   C   D   E   F   G   H

NATIVE PEOPLES

The native peoples of Alaska are the Aleut, and those in the north of Canada are the Inuit. Native peoples are often called "First Nations" because they were the first to live in North America. Much of their land was later taken by European settlers. First Nation culture has revived and Nunavut is now a self-governing Inuit territory. The Inuit have adapted to the harsh environment and often combine modern technology with their traditional lifestyle.

INUIT children outside their summer camp on Baffin Island

Did you know?

▸ In 1867, the US bought Alaska from Russia for US$7.2 million, increasing the size of the USA by 20 per cent. Alaska is the largest US state.

▸ Grise Fiord is the most northerly community in the region, enduring freezing temperatures and four months of darkness every year.

▸ Canada has a population of 31 million people, but only 30 per cent of them live in western Canada, and most live near the US border.

▸ More than 100,000 British Columbians are direct descendants of the Chinese labourers who helped to build the Canadian Pacific Railway.

CENTRAL STATES

Large parts of Alberta, Saskatchewan, and Manitoba, have rich soils and form one of the greatest wheat-growing areas in the world. More wheat is grown here than Canadians can consume, so vast amounts are exported. Wheat is used to make flour for staple foods such as bread. Once harvested, wheat is stored in grain elevators, waiting to be transported by truck or train.

GRAIN ELEVATORS dominate the skyline of the prairies

GRIZZLY BEAR

ROCKY MOUNTAINS

The rugged Rocky Mountains stretch south through western Canada and into the USA. Every year they attract millions of visitors who enjoy walking, hiking, and canoeing in the dramatic scenery. Tourists sometimes see wildlife such as the grizzly bear, black bear, elk, moose, and wolf.

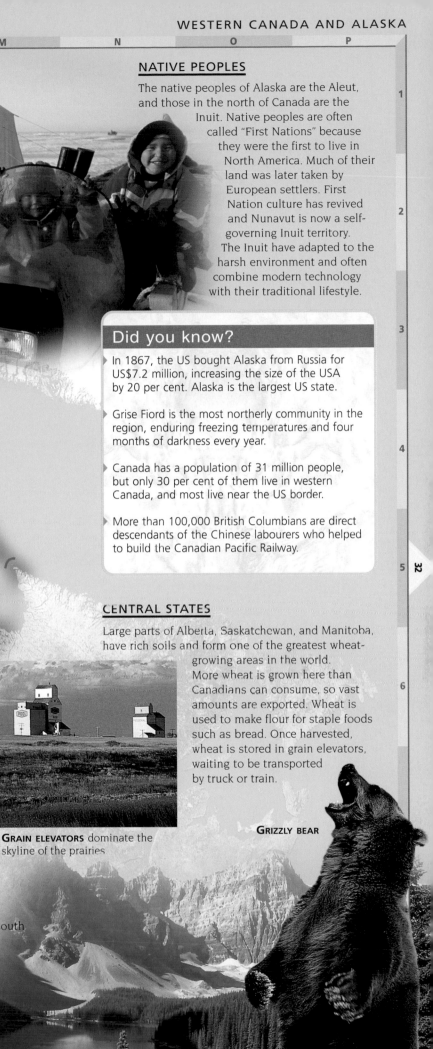

Eastern Canada

THE MOST INDUSTRIALIZED AND HEAVILY populated parts of Canada are in the east. Ottawa, the capital, is located here, along with other important cities, such as Toronto, Montreal, and Québec. Some of the earliest settlers were French and many people speak French as their first language. The Great Lakes – the largest system of lakes in the world – and the St Lawrence Seaway link the interior to the coast. The most easterly parts of Canada, the Atlantic Provinces, have rugged coastlines and dramatic scenery. However, soils are thin and so commercial agriculture is limited to a few areas. Fishing used to be the main activity, but fish stocks have been so depleted that few people are now employed in the industry. Despite a thriving tourist industry, the Atlantic Provinces struggle to keep their population, as many people migrate to the bustling cities further west.

MAPLE SAP is collected from cuts in the tree trunk.

MAPLE SYRUP

The colourful maple trees of Québec and Ontario are tapped for maple syrup, a major export, and a popular topping on pancakes for Canadians. The maple leaf is the national symbol of Canada and features on the nation's flag.

Did you know?

▸ In Québec, 82 per cent of people speak French as their first language.

▸ The province of Ontario got its name from native Iroquois. Translated, it means "glittering waters" and was inspired by the many lakes in the region.

▸ Canada produces 75 per cent of the world's maple syrup. Native peoples were the first to discover and extract the syrup. They passed their techniques on to early European settlers.

▸ Canadians have a high life expectancy – the average person lives to be nearly 80.

TORONTO

Toronto is Canada's most important economic centre. Located on Lake Ontario, close to the US border, it is not only an industrial and commercial centre but is also home to a wide diversity of ethnic and cultural groups. The Canadian National (CN) tower, which dominates the Toronto skyline, is the world's tallest freestanding structure and locals and tourists can get an impressive view of the city and Lake Ontario from the top.

CN TOWER

ICE HOCKEY

Sports and leisure are important to Canadians. A popular sport is ice hockey, which thousands of people enthusiastically play or watch. Teams of skaters use long, curved sticks to try and get a hard rubber disc, called a puck, into the opposing team's goal. Both the men's and women's national ice hockey teams won gold medals at the 2002 Olympics.

UNITED STATES OF AMERICA

Map labels

Charles Island
Ivujivik
Ungava Peninsula
Inukjuak
Hudson Bay
Fort Severn
Belcher Islands
Winisk
Severn
Winisk
James Bay
Akimiski Island
Sandy Lake
Attawapiskat
Attawapiskat
La Min
Rivière de Ruper
Fort Albany
Moosonee
Albany
Moose
Lac Seul
Armstrong
Hearst
Kapuskasing
Chibouga
Kenora
Dryden
Lake Nipigon
Longlac
Cochrane
Réser Go
Fort Frances
Atikokan
Nipigon
Marathon
Timmins
Amos
Rainy Lake
Thunder Bay
Tip Top Mountain △640m
Wawa
Foleyet
Rouyn-Noranda
Val-d'Or
Lake Superior
Kirkland Lake
Sault Ste.Marie
Sudbury
North Bay
Pembroke
Gati Hull
OTTAWA
Manitoulin Island
Georgian Bay
Lake Huron
Midland
Peterborough
Kingston
Brampton
Oshawa
Kitchener
Toronto
Lake Ontar
Sarnia
Hamilton
St. Catharines
London
Niagara Falls
Windsor
Leamington
Lake Erie

C A N
O N T A R I O
Q

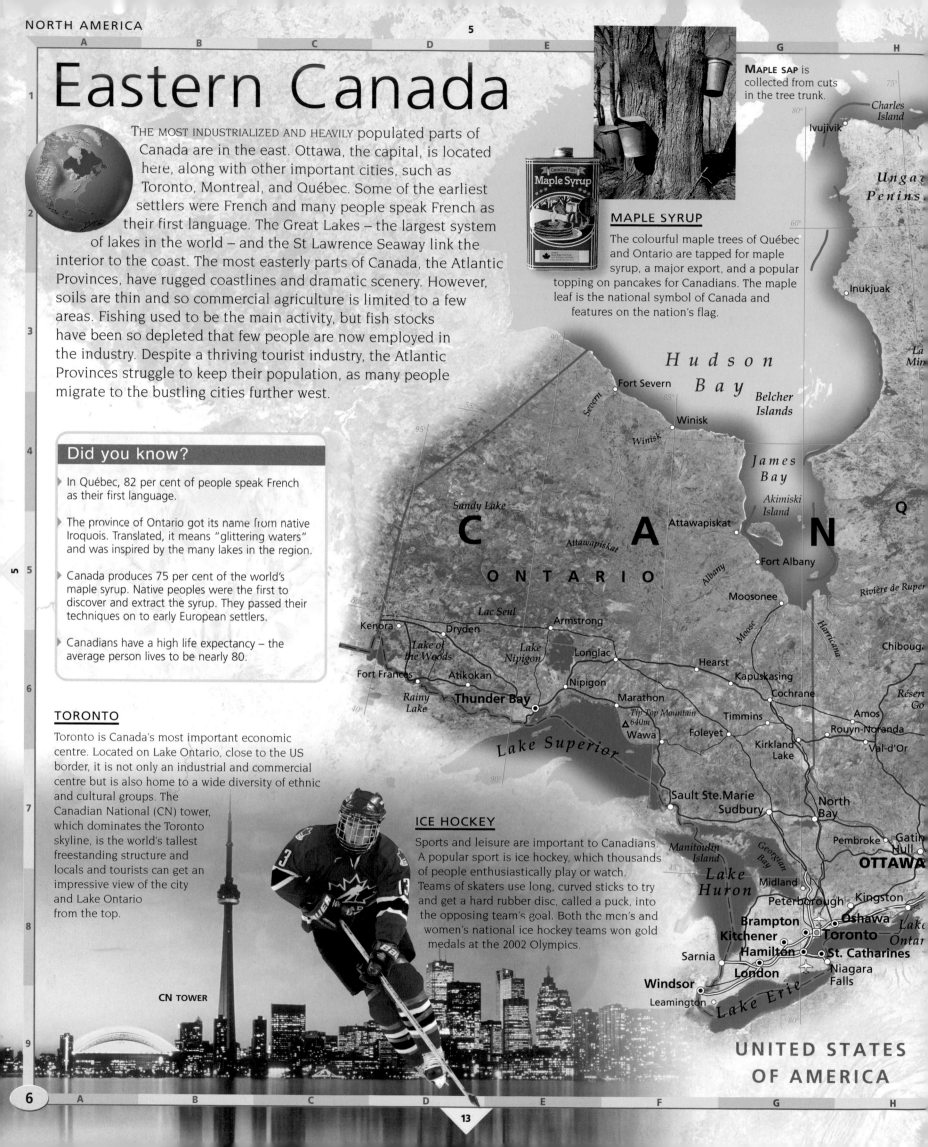

Atlantic Provinces

Nova Scotia, New Brunswick, Prince Edward Island, and Newfoundland and Labrador attract tourists for their landscape, wildlife, and quaint sea-side villages. Icebergs are a regular sight off the coast of Newfoundland and Labrador as they drift south from the Arctic.

FISHERIES

The Grand Banks, off the coast of Newfoundland, are shallow waters that once contained huge stocks of fish. Stocks have declined, however, due to overfishing and now catches are severely restricted. This has resulted in hardship for those who relied on fishing for their livelihood.

FRENCH signs in Québec city

FRENCH CANADA

Québec Province is the main French-speaking part of Canada. With a different language and cultural traditions from other parts of the country, there have been calls in the past for Québec to become independent from the rest of Canada.

ST LAWRENCE SEAWAY

Stretching far inland, the St Lawrence Seaway provides a link from the Great Lakes to the Atlantic. A series of huge locks descends from Lake Ontario to sea level, allowing ocean-going ships to transport their cargo as far inland as Lake Superior. Large amounts of iron ore, for example, are transported inland from Labrador to Ontario for processing. Corn, soy, and other agricultural products move in the opposite direction, from the prairies east to the markets of the world.

Map labels:

Baffin Island
Hudson Strait
Resolution Island
Akpatok Island
Button Islands
Ungava Bay
Kuujjuaq
Rivière à la Baleine
Caniapiscau
Nain
Hopedale
Makkovik
Cape Harrison
Cartwright
Scheffervile
NEWFOUNDLAND & LABRADOR
Smallwood Reservoir
Lake Melville
Churchill
Labrador Sea
St.Anthony
QUÉBEC
CANADA
Réservoir de Caniapiscau
Réservoir Manicouagan
Lac Mistassini
Laurentian Mountains
Havre-St-Pierre
Île d'Anticosti
Sept-Îles
Strait of Belle Isle
Gander
Grand Falls
St.John's
Newfoundland
Corner Brook
Cape Race
Baie-Comeau
Lac St-Jean
Gaspé
Péninsule de Gaspé
Matane
Rimouski
Gulf of St. Lawrence
Îles de la Madeleine
Channel-Port aux Basques
ST PIERRE & MIQUELON (to France)
Chicoutimi
Jonquière
St.Lawrence
Bathurst
Cabot Strait
La Tuque
Rivière-du-Loup
Edmundston
PRINCE EDWARD ISLAND
Glace Bay
Sydney
Cape Breton Island
Charlesbourg
NEW BRUNSWICK
Charlottetown
Québec
Moncton
Amherst
New Glasgow
Trois-Rivières
St-Georges
Oromocto
Truro
Fredericton
NOVA SCOTIA
Laval
Saint John
Dartmouth
Halifax
Sable Island
Montréal
Drummondville
Sherbrooke
Bay of Fundy
Liverpool
Yarmouth
ATLANTIC OCEAN

0 km 100 200
0 miles 100 200

USA: Northeast

THE NORTHEASTERN UNITED STATES is a heavily populated area that is steeped in history. This is traditionally the main immigration point into the States, with the Statue of Liberty lighting the way for those arriving into New York by boat. People from all over the world have settled in this region to live and work, creating a "melting pot" of cultures and ethnic groups. Important historical events, such as the signing of the Declaration of Independence and the Constitution, took place in Philadelphia. These documents set the foundations for American life today. It is also here that the capital and centre of government was established. Today, while industry and agriculture are still important, finance and commerce are the driving forces of the economy.

Lake Ontario

Hudson River

Appalachian Mountains

New York City

THRIVING CITY

New York is the largest city in the USA. Historically it grew because it has a good harbour and sits at the mouth of the Hudson River. Immigrants from overseas flooded into the city in the 19th and 20th centuries, boosting its population and economy. Today, it is the main financial centre, not just of the USA, but of the world.

Did you know?

▸ There are more than 100 universities and colleges in Boston.

▸ Every minute, about 180 million litres (40 million gallons) of water plunges over Niagara Falls, located on the border between the USA and Canada.

▸ The White House in Washington, DC, has been home to every president except George Washington, whom the city is named after.

▸ The stock exchange on Wall Street, New York City, is the world's largest. The street's name came from a wall built by Dutch settlers to keep the British out.

PITTSBURGH

Once a major steel-manufacturing centre with a polluted environment, Pittsburgh is now a thriving financial centre with a large number of corporate headquarters. Bridges span the three rivers that run through the city, connecting the core downtown area (above) to the suburbs.

CENTRE OF GOVERNMENT

All three branches of the federal government, the executive, legislative, and judicial, reside in Washington, DC. The United States Congress (the legislative branch) meets here in the Capitol building. Many of the city's residents work for the government.

THE SEAT of government is here at the Capitol building.

Map labels

CANADA

ONTARIO

St. Lawrence

Ogdensbu[rg]

Adirondac[k] Mountai[ns]

Watertown

Boonville

A[p]

Lake Ontario

Oswego

Rochester　Syracuse

Utica

Mohawk Ri[ver]

Niagara Falls　Lockport　Newark

NEW YORK

Niagara Falls　Buffalo　Avon

Oneonta

Hamburg　Dansville

Ithaca

Catsk[ill] Mount[ains]

Lake Erie

Dunkirk

Binghamton

Erie　Jamestown　Elmira

Sayre

Warren　Mansfield

Allegheny Plateau

Meadville　Wilcox

Scranton

Middlet[own]

Wilkes Barre

Milford

Mercer

PENNSYLVANIA

Lock Haven

Allegheny River

Du Bois

Milton

Stroudsberg

OHIO

State College

Butler

Indiana

Allentown

Aliquippa　Pittsburgh

Altoona

Reading　Trento[n]

Washington

Harrisburg

Appalachian Mountains

Philadelphia

Bedford

Carlisle　Lancaster

Uniontown

York　Wilmington

Cher[ry] Hill

Hagerstown　Aberdeen

Cumberland

Towson

Vineland

WEST VIRGINIA

Oakland

Baltimore

Columbia

Dover

VIRGINIA

Annapolis

DELAWA[RE]

WASHINGTON D.C.

Cambridge

Ocean City

MARYLAND

Salisbur[y]

Chesapeake Bay

75°

45°

40°

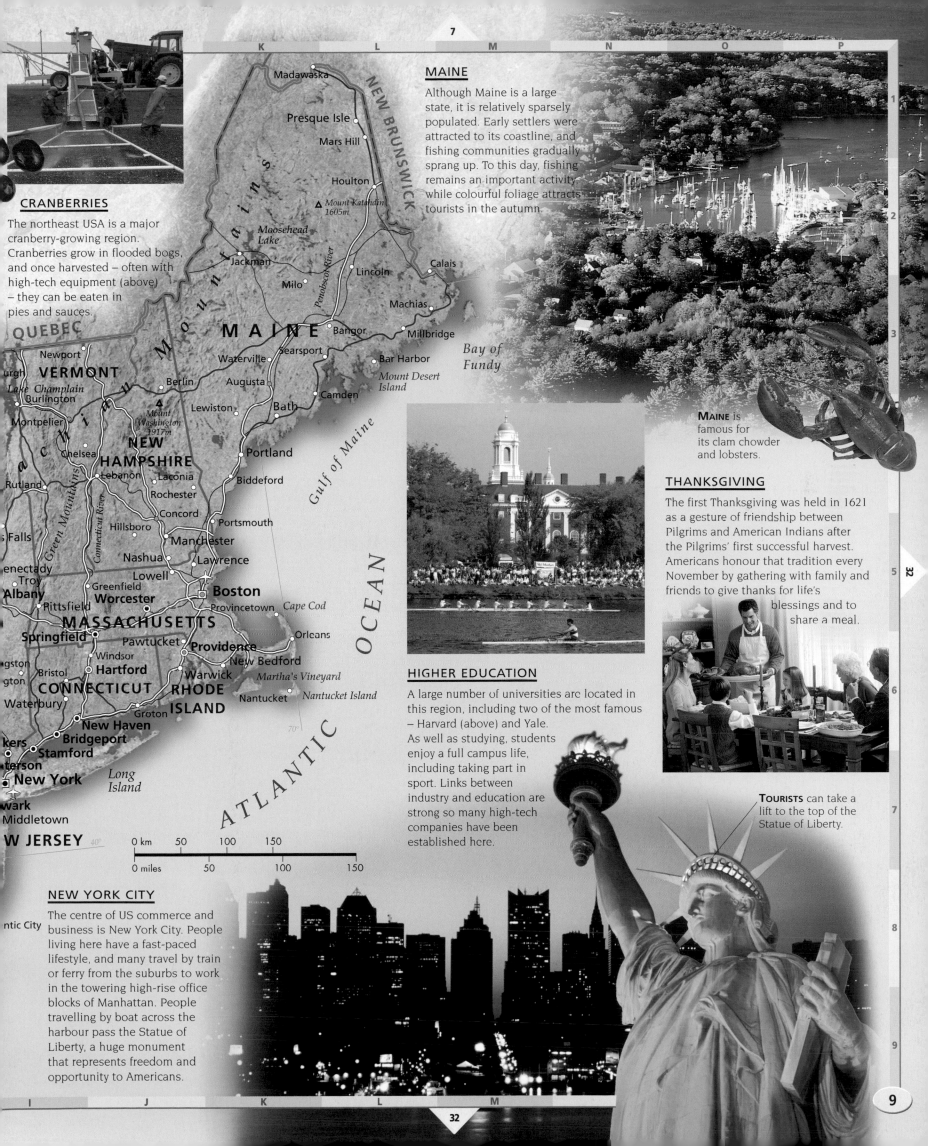

CRANBERRIES

The northeast USA is a major cranberry-growing region. Cranberries grow in flooded bogs, and once harvested – often with high-tech equipment (above) – they can be eaten in pies and sauces.

MAINE

Although Maine is a large state, it is relatively sparsely populated. Early settlers were attracted to its coastline, and fishing communities gradually sprang up. To this day, fishing remains an important activity, while colourful foliage attracts tourists in the autumn.

MAINE is famous for its clam chowder and lobsters.

THANKSGIVING

The first Thanksgiving was held in 1621 as a gesture of friendship between Pilgrims and American Indians after the Pilgrims' first successful harvest. Americans honour that tradition every November by gathering with family and friends to give thanks for life's blessings and to share a meal.

HIGHER EDUCATION

A large number of universities are located in this region, including two of the most famous – Harvard (above) and Yale. As well as studying, students enjoy a full campus life, including taking part in sport. Links between industry and education are strong so many high-tech companies have been established here.

TOURISTS can take a lift to the top of the Statue of Liberty.

NEW YORK CITY

The centre of US commerce and business is New York City. People living here have a fast-paced lifestyle, and many travel by train or ferry from the suburbs to work in the towering high-rise office blocks of Manhattan. People travelling by boat across the harbour pass the Statue of Liberty, a huge monument that represents freedom and opportunity to Americans.

Map labels: Madawaska, Presque Isle, Mars Hill, Houlton, Mount Katahdin 1605m, Moosehead Lake, Jackman, Milo, Lincoln, Calais, Machias, Millbridge, MAINE, Bangor, Searsport, Waterville, Bar Harbor, Bay of Fundy, Mount Desert Island, Augusta, Camden, Lewiston, Bath, Gulf of Maine, Portland, Biddeford, Portsmouth, Concord, Hillsboro, Manchester, Nashua, Lawrence, Lowell, Boston, Provincetown, Cape Cod, Orleans, Worcester, MASSACHUSETTS, Springfield, Pawtucket, Providence, New Bedford, Martha's Vineyard, Nantucket, Nantucket Island, Windsor, Hartford, Warwick, RHODE ISLAND, CONNECTICUT, Waterbury, Groton, New Haven, Bridgeport, Stamford, New York, Long Island, ATLANTIC OCEAN, Middletown, NEW JERSEY, Atlantic City, QUEBEC, NEW BRUNSWICK, Penobscot River, NEW HAMPSHIRE, VERMONT, Newport, Berlin, Lake Champlain, Burlington, Montpelier, Rutland, Mount Washington 1917m, Lebanon, Laconia, Rochester, Chelsea, Green Mountains, Connecticut River, Falls, Albany, Troy, Pittsfield, Greenfield, Bristol, New York

0 km   50   100   150
0 miles   50   100   150

32

USA: South

0 km 50 100 150 200

0 miles 50 100 150 200

THE SOUTHERN STATES OF THE USA have a varied landscape and an interesting mix of people, both culturally and economically. Some areas of the region are poor, especially the Appalachian Mountain communities, while other parts, such as the Florida coast, are wealthy and attract many people from other states and countries. The cultural mix includes people of Latin American origin, African Americans, Cajuns (French-Canadians), and European Americans, giving rise to diverse music styles, dialects, pastimes, and food. While coal mining in the Appalachian Mountains has declined in recent years, agriculture is still important, as are tourism and industry. Tourism is particularly important in Florida and in New Orleans near the mouth of the mighty Mississippi River.

COTTON CROPS

Cotton was once the mainstay crop of the south and was grown by African-American slaves. Today, cotton is still important for the economy of the region and is grown in large fields and harvested with huge machinery. Cotton has many uses, primarily as the raw material for textiles.

COTTON POD, OR BOLL

Did you know?

- The Mississippi is the largest river in North America, and the third largest in the world. It stretches 3,770 km (2,340 miles) from Lake Itasca in Minnesota to its mouth near New Orleans.

- Memphis, Tennessee, is named after the ancient Egyptian capital situated south of the Nile Delta.

- Half the nation's peanuts are grown in Georgia. Most of them are made into peanut butter.

MUSIC ORIGINS

The southern USA is famous for its music, much of which reflects the cultural mix of the region. New Orleans and other parts of Louisiana are the birthplaces of jazz and Cajun music, while bluegrass and country have origins in Nashville and Memphis. These music styles started here, but quickly spread throughout the country and developed even further in the cities.

JAZZ musician on Bourbon Street in New Orleans.

A CHEF holds a skillet of jambalaya, a Cajun dish.

CAJUN CULTURE

The Cajuns in this region are French-speaking people who were expelled from Canada in the 18th century. They mixed with other cultures in Louisiana, but their French influence can be seen in the music, food, and place names, such as Lafayette.

FLORIDA EVERGLADES

The increasing population of Florida means that the Everglades, swampy plains inhabited by alligators and other wildlife, are under threat as land is needed for houses and farms. However, the Everglades National Park protects part of this important ecosystem.

PENNSYLVANIA
40°

OHIO
Parkersburg · Clarksburg · Winchester
WEST VIRGINIA
Spruce Knob 1482m △
Arlington
smouth
Huntington · Harrisonburg · Dale City
River
Saint Albans · Charleston · Staunton · Fredericksburg
Beckley
James River
Richmond
Pikeville · Bluefield · VIRGINIA · Lynchburg · Petersburg
on · Pulaski · Roanoke · Cape Charles
dlesboro · Kingsport · Danville · Newport News · Norfolk
Bristol · Portsmouth · Virginia Beach
Greeneville
Roanoke River · Elizabeth City
oxville · Mount Mitchell 2037m △ · Winston Salem · Greensboro · Durham
Asheville · High Point · Cary · Raleigh · Rocky Mount · Greenville
NORTH CAROLINA
Gastonia · Goldsboro · New Bern · Pamlico Sound
sville · Charlotte · Fayetteville · Cape Hatteras 35°
Spartanburg · Rock Hill · Laurinburg
reenville · Union · Jacksonville · Onslow Bay
SOUTH CAROLINA
Greenwood · Florence · Wilmington
Athens · Clark Hill Lake · Columbia · Cape Fear
Lake Marion · Myrtle Beach
Augusta · Aiken · Long Bay
EORGIA · Orangeburg · Georgetown
Milledgeville · North Charleston
Macon · Statesboro · Charleston
Dublin · Vidalia · Hilton Head Island
ordele · Savannah
Savannah River · Hinesville
Tifton · ATLANTIC OCEAN
Waycross · Brunswick
Valdosta · Altamaha River
nasville · Okefenokee Swamp
Jacksonville
Lake City
Gainesville · Saint Augustine
Lake George
Ocala · Daytona Beach
De Land
Deltona
ring Hill · Orlando · Cape Canaveral
arwater · Lakeland · Melbourne
Largo · Lake Kissimmee
Tampa · Tampa Bay · Fort Pierce · Hutchinson Island
Saint Petersburg
Sarasota · FLORIDA · West Palm Beach
Port Charlotte · Lake Okeechobee · Boca Raton
Charlotte Harbor · Pompano Beach
Fort Myers · Fort Lauderdale
Naples · Big Cypress Swamp · Miami Beach
The Everglades · Miami
Cape Sable
Florida Bay · Key Largo
Florida Keys
Key West · Straits of Florida

KENTUCKY DERBY

Every year on the first Saturday of May, the Kentucky Derby takes place in Louisville. This horse race, and the festivities based around it, mark the beginning of spring for people in the area. The best horses and jockeys, as well as massive crowds of spectators from around the country, travel here for the event .

TOURISM

Tourism is an important industry in the south, especially for Florida. As well as warm weather and appealing scenery, tourists are attracted to the theme parks around Orlando. Jobs and income are generated by tourism, with many people working in retail outlets, restaurants, hotels, and theme parks.

KUMBA roller coaster at Busch Gardens is the fastest in Florida.

MARTIN LUTHER KING, JR.

Martin Luther King, Jr. (left) was born in Atlanta in 1929. In the 1960s, he led many peaceful protests to end the laws that discriminated against black Americans. King was assassinated in 1969 and has since been seen as a symbol of the struggle for racial equality. Many African Americans live in the southern USA where, before the Civil War (1861–65), their ancestors were forced to work on cotton plantations and farms.

MARTIN LUTHER KING, JR. speaking at the final rally of the March Against Fear, Mississippi, 1966

FLORIDA'S SUNSHINE COAST

Florida's sunny weather and sandy beaches have traditionally attracted many retired people, many of whom live in apartments along the coast in resorts such as Miami Beach (right). Florida also attracts young people, particularly to the vibrant city of Miami, where many immigrants from Central America, Cuba, and other Caribbean islands live, and Spanish is spoken by half the population. The Florida Keys, an island chain in the south of the peninsula, is also popular with tourists, and contains one of the largest living coral formations in North America.

USA: Midwest

THE AMERICAN MIDWEST is dominated by the Great Plains, once the home of cattle ranches, cowboys, and tribes of American Indian people. However, the discovery of gold in South Dakota brought a rush of settlers to the area. This, combined with a decline in buffalo numbers, led to the eventual displacement of the American Indians from the Plains. The area is prone to dramatic weather – with tornadoes, freezing blizzards, and blazing hot summers. To the west, vast areas of farmland generate more wheat and maize than anywhere else in the world. East of the Mississippi the landscape varies and, although farming is still important, this is the industrial centre of the country. Big cities, such as Chicago, Detroit, and Cleveland form the major manufacturing centres.

BUFFALO ON THE PLAINS

Up to 100 million buffalo once grazed on the Great Plains. They provided local American Indians with food for the family, and skin for clothes and teepees. But over-hunting and the destruction of their habitat by early European settlers drastically reduced the number of animals. Buffalo are now a protected species that live in reserves. This herd is from a reserve in South Dakota.

THE DAKOTA people used buffalo bones to make shields and tools. The animal's bladder made a bag for carrying water.

MOUNT RUSHMORE NATIONAL MEMORIAL

Mount Rushmore was created as a tribute to the American presidency. Four of the United States' greatest presidents – Lincoln, Roosevelt, Jefferson, and Washington – were carved into the granite cliff between 1927 and 1941. Teams of workers hung from saddles anchored to the mountain to complete the work, often enduring harsh winds or blazing sun. Today, it is a popular tourist attraction.

Each carved face is about 18 m (60 ft) high.

TORNADO ALLEY

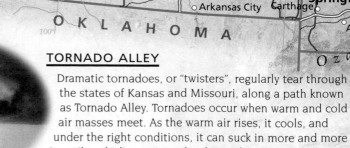

Dramatic tornadoes, or "twisters", regularly tear through the states of Kansas and Missouri, along a path known as Tornado Alley. Tornadoes occur when warm and cold air masses meet. As the warm air rises, it cools, and under the right conditions, it can suck in more and more air until a whirling twister develops. The more air that is drawn in, the greater the power of the tornado.

RURAL AMERICA

Although most Americans today live in cities and large towns, there are still many small towns with populations of less than 10,000 people. These towns are often in farming communities and are where people go to shop or to attend church. Children, such as these boys from Iowa (left), often have to be taken to and from school by special bus.

Did you know?

▸ The Great Lakes contain a fifth of the Earth's fresh water.

▸ Rock music began in the US in the 1950s. Many rock stars feature in the Cleveland Rock and Roll Hall of Fame.

GREAT LAKES

Several large cities are located on the shores of the Great Lakes, including Chicago on Lake Michigan. Burned to the ground in the late 19th century, it is now a leading industrial and financial centre and the third largest city in the country. The Great Lakes and their lakeside retreats are also a popular tourist destination for holidaymakers keen on watersports.

FOOTBALL

The first official game of American football was played between Princeton and Rutgers universities in New Jersey on 6 November, 1869. Since then, college and professional teams have been founded all over the country, and playing and watching football has become one of America's favourite pastimes.

AGRICULTURE

The Great Plains extend across the west of this region, and are important for agriculture. Rich soils support crops of wheat and maize, while livestock grazes on the extensive grassland. Millions of people live on the Great Plains, many on family-owned and run farms.

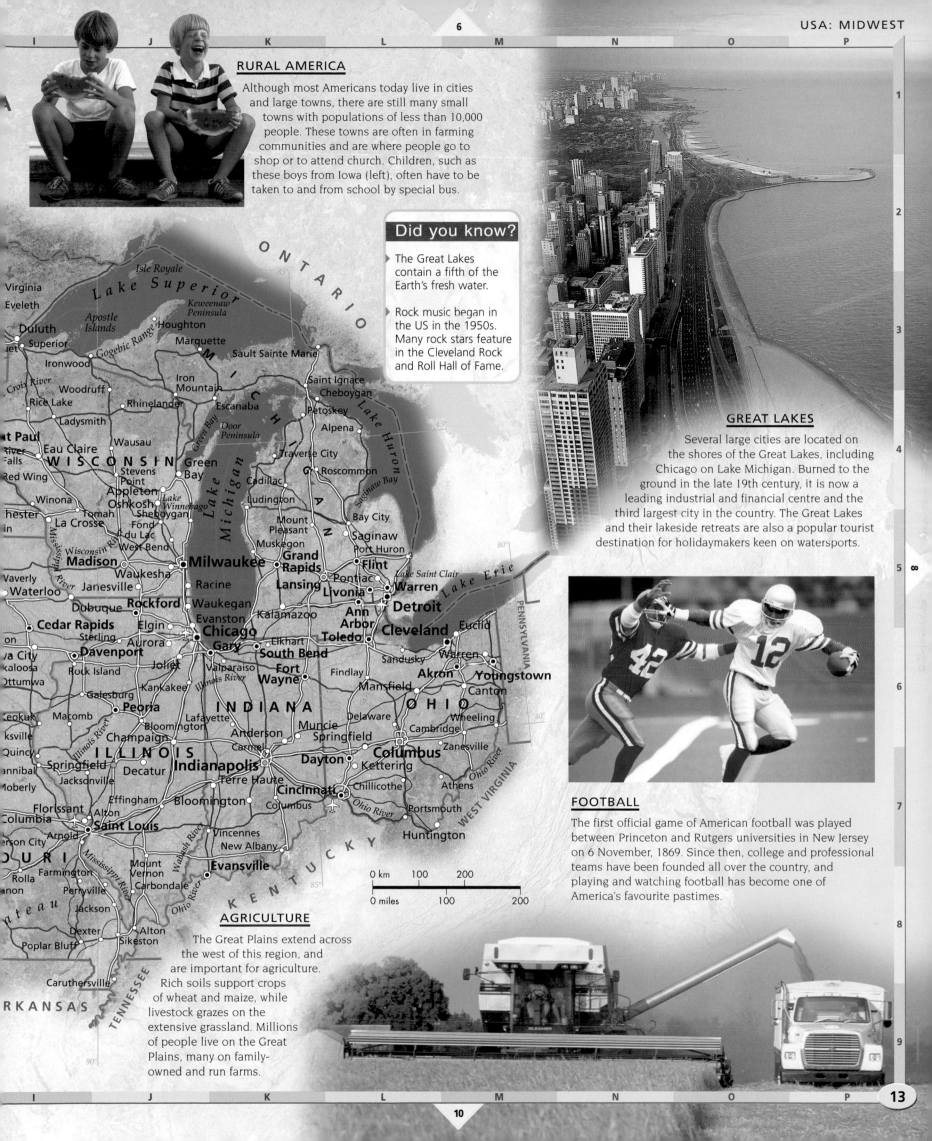

USA: West

THE ROCKY MOUNTAINS separate the coastal region from the drier inland states. Large and fast-growing cities, such as San Francisco, Los Angeles, and San Diego, hug the Pacific Coast, and have attracted many migrants because of good job opportunities. Inland, blazing desert and towering mountains provide some of the most dramatic landscapes in the country. National parks, such as Yellowstone in northwestern Wyoming and Montana, and Yosemite in central California, protect some of these wilderness areas. Further east, the foothills of the Rockies give way to vast plains grazed by large herds of cattle.

CALIFORNIA AGRICULTURE

California is warm, fertile, and, with irrigation, ideal for agriculture. Grapes are an important crop north of San Francisco in the Napa Valley. Further south, citrus crops, such as oranges also flourish. Premium farming land is under threat, however, as the population expands.

NORTHERN FORESTS

The coastal areas of Oregon and Washington contain large forests. These produce economically important timber, but much land is also left in its natural state and is popular with hikers. Most people here live in large cities like Seattle, and in the fertile inland valleys.

Did you know?

▶ The American Indian name for Death Valley is *Tomesha*, which means "land where the ground is on fire."

▶ The majority of the world's geysers and hot springs are in Yellowstone National Park.

LOS ANGELES

This sprawling city – the second largest in the USA – is home to migrants from all over the world, as well as from other states in the country. Sandwiched between the coast and the mountains, the city has massive air pollution problems. This mostly arises from the exhaust fumes from the high number of cars used by commuters on the city's highways.

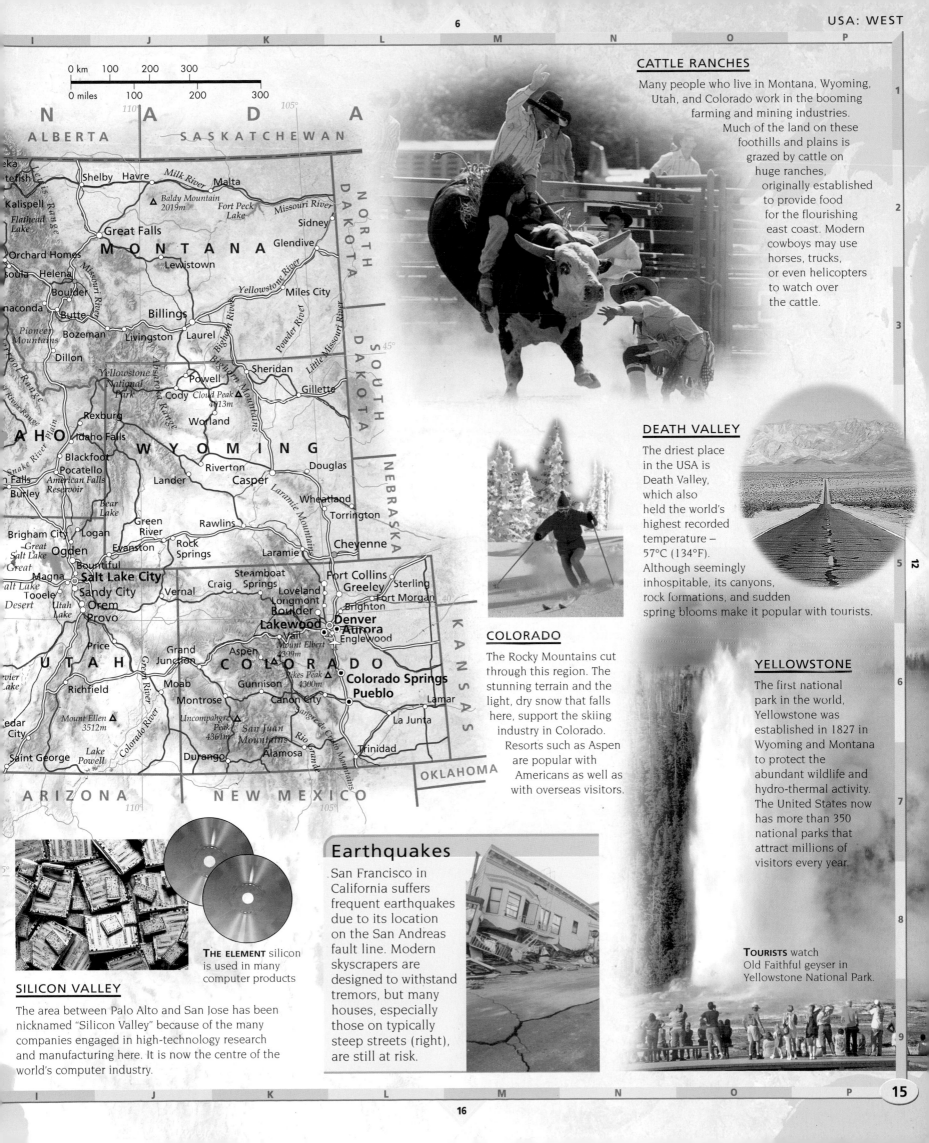

0 km   100   200   300

0 miles   100   200   300

N A D A

ALBERTA   SASKATCHEWAN

Milk River

Shelby   Havre   Malta

Baldy Mountain
2019m   Fort Peck
Lake   *Missouri River*

Great Falls   Sidney

M O N T A N A   Glendive

Orchard Homes

Lewistown

Helena   *Missouri River*

Boulder   *Yellowstone River*   Miles City

naconda   Butte   Billings

Pioneer
Mountains   Bozeman   Livingston   Laurel   *Bighorn River*   *Powder River*   *Little Missouri River*

Dillon

Sheridan

Powell   Cloud Peak
4013m   Gillette

Cody

IAHO   Worland

Rexburg

Idaho Falls   W Y O M I N G

Blackfoot

Pocatello   Riverton   Douglas

Falls   Lander   Casper   Wheatland

Burley   American Falls
Reservoir   *Laramie Mountains*   Torrington

Bear
Lake   Green
River   Rawlins

Brigham City   Logan   Rock
Springs   Laramie

Great
Salt Lake   Ogden   Evanston   Cheyenne

Bountiful   Steamboat
Springs   Fort Collins   Sterling

Magna   Salt Lake City   Craig   Loveland   Greeley

Tooele   Sandy City   Vernal   Longmont   Fort Morgan

Utah
Lake   Orem   Boulder   Brighton

Desert   Provo   Lakewood   Denver
Aurora

Price   Grand
Junction   Mount Elbert
4399m   Englewood

Aspen   C O L O R A D O

Richfield   Vail   Pikes Peak
4300m   Colorado Springs

Mount Ellen
3512m   Moab   Gunnison   Pueblo

Montrose   Canon City   Lamar

edar
City   Uncompahgre
Peak
4361m   *San Juan
Mountains*   *Rio Grande*   La Junta

Saint George   Lake
Powell   Durango   Alamosa   Trinidad

OKLAHOMA

A R I Z O N A   N E W   M E X I C O

*Flathead
Lake*

Kalispell

Flathead
Range

soula

NORTH   DAKOTA

SOUTH   DAKOTA

N E B R A S K A

K A N S A S

CATTLE RANCHES

Many people who live in Montana, Wyoming, Utah, and Colorado work in the booming farming and mining industries. Much of the land on these foothills and plains is grazed by cattle on huge ranches, originally established to provide food for the flourishing east coast. Modern cowboys may use horses, trucks, or even helicopters to watch over the cattle.

DEATH VALLEY

The driest place in the USA is Death Valley, which also held the world's highest recorded temperature – 57°C (134°F). Although seemingly inhospitable, its canyons, rock formations, and sudden spring blooms make it popular with tourists.

COLORADO

The Rocky Mountains cut through this region. The stunning terrain and the light, dry snow that falls here, support the skiing industry in Colorado. Resorts such as Aspen are popular with Americans as well as with overseas visitors.

YELLOWSTONE

The first national park in the world, Yellowstone was established in 1827 in Wyoming and Montana to protect the abundant wildlife and hydro-thermal activity. The United States now has more than 350 national parks that attract millions of visitors every year.

TOURISTS watch Old Faithful geyser in Yellowstone National Park.

SILICON VALLEY

THE ELEMENT silicon is used in many computer products

The area between Palo Alto and San Jose has been nicknamed "Silicon Valley" because of the many companies engaged in high-technology research and manufacturing here. It is now the centre of the world's computer industry.

Earthquakes

San Francisco in California suffers frequent earthquakes due to its location on the San Andreas fault line. Modern skyscrapers are designed to withstand tremors, but many houses, especially those on typically steep streets (right), are still at risk.

USA: Southwest

THE SOUTHWEST IS AN AREA of great contrasts. Much of Oklahoma and Texas consists of flat, rolling grasslands and huge farms, while both Arizona and New Mexico are hot, arid, and mountainous, with vast canyons and river valleys carving their way through the land. Since the discovery of oil in 1901, Texas has become the country's top oil producer after Alaska, with Houston as the centre of the billion-dollar industry. Tourism is also important to the southwest, as visitors flock to see the Grand Canyon, the Painted Desert, and other natural wonders. Buildings here reflect the mix of American Indians, Hispanic, European American, and modern American cultures.

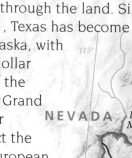

SUBURBS OF PHOENIX, ARIZONA

HOT PLACE TO LIVE

The climate across much of the southwest is hot and dry, with summer temperatures often reaching 38°C (100°F). Although water can be scarce, many people have a swimming pool in their garden so they can cool off.

DESERT LIFE

The Saguaro cactus (left) can reach up to 15 m (50 ft) tall, grow as many as 40 branches, and live for 200 years. Cacti, yucca, and other plants have all adapted to the hot, dry desert conditions found in the southwest. So, too, have many animals, including the deadly rattlesnake.

SAGUARO CACTI in the Sonoran Desert

THE GRAND CANYON

The Grand Canyon in northern Arizona is one of the natural wonders of the world. This incredibly deep gorge was slowly cut out of the rock by the Colorado River, beginning six million years ago. People can hike around its edge or venture down into the canyon to camp for the night.

AMERICAN-INDIAN CULTURES

American Indians, including Navajo, Hopi, and Apache, used to live across the southwest but are now concentrated in reservations set up by the US government. The largest of these is in Arizona and New Mexico, and is home to the Navajo people. The Navajo farm the land and produce crafts, like the woven blanket wrapped around these Navajo children (below).

KACHINA dolls are made by the Hopi.

Map labels:

UTAH · NEVADA · CALIFORNIA · Colorado · C O (Colorado)

Lake Powell · San Juan River · Page · Shiprock · Aztec · Bloomfield · Farmington · Wheeler 40 · Lake Mead · Grand Canyon · Chuska Mountains · Los Alamos · Espanc · Coconino Plateau · Tuba City · Plateau · Painted Desert · Gallup · Rocky · Santa Fe · Kingman · Humphreys Peak 3851m · Sanders · Corrales · Albuquerque · Hualapai Peak 2566m · Flagstaff · Mountains · Sedona · Grants · Lake Havasu City · Prescott · Holbrook · Belen · A R I Z O N A · Willa · Wickenburg · Show Low · Socorro · Colorado River · Glendale · Scottsdale · N E W M E · Signal Peak 1487m · Mesa · Globe · Black Range · Rio Grande · Phoenix · San Carlos · Elephant Butte Reservoir · Yuma · Casa Grande · Eloy · Clifton · Alamogordo · Somerton · Gila River · Safford · Sonoran Desert · Ajo · Las Cruces · Organ Peak 2704m · Tucson · Willcox · Deming · Sierra Vista · Benson · El Paso · Nogales · Bisbee · Fabens · Douglas · MEXICO · San Juan Mountains

Scale:
0 km 50 100 150 200
0 miles 50 100 150 200

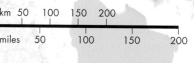

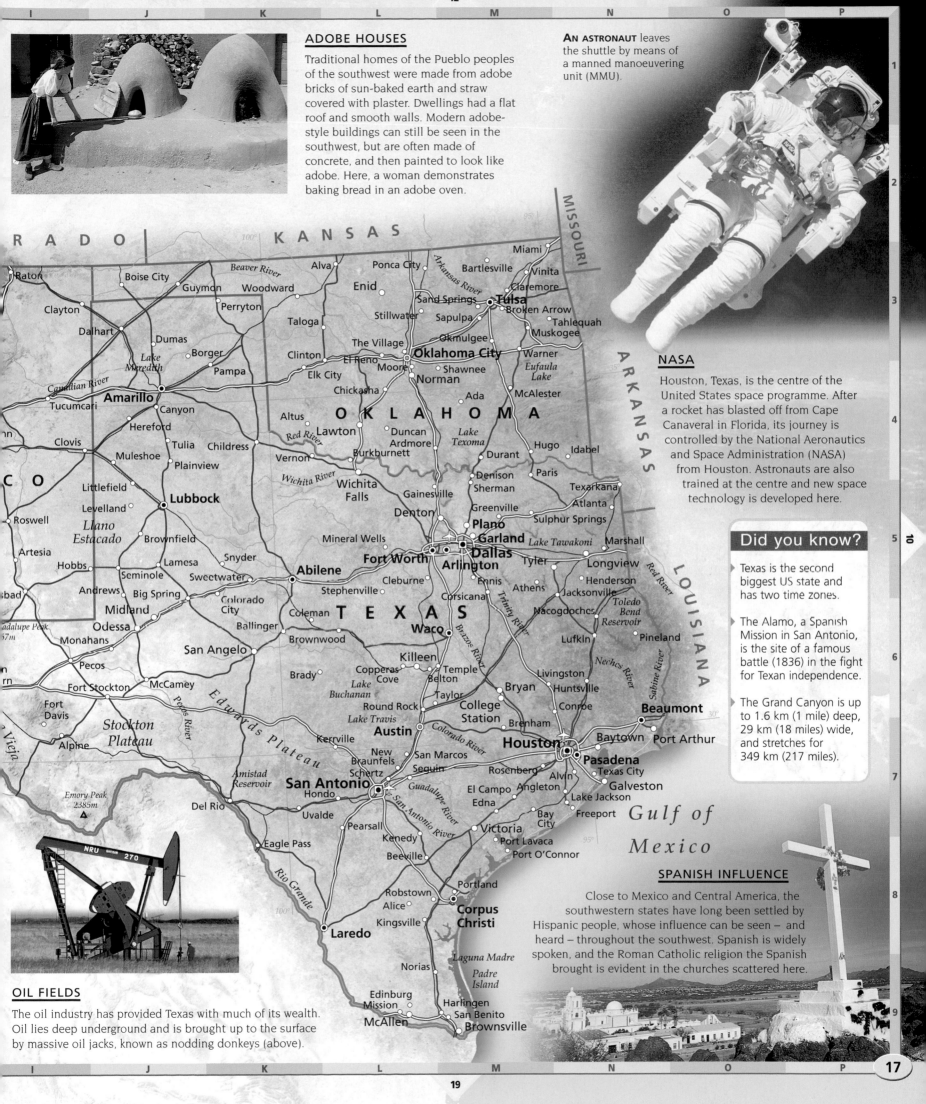

ADOBE HOUSES

Traditional homes of the Pueblo peoples of the southwest were made from adobe bricks of sun-baked earth and straw covered with plaster. Dwellings had a flat roof and smooth walls. Modern adobe-style buildings can still be seen in the southwest, but are often made of concrete, and then painted to look like adobe. Here, a woman demonstrates baking bread in an adobe oven.

AN ASTRONAUT leaves the shuttle by means of a manned manoeuvering unit (MMU).

NASA

Houston, Texas, is the centre of the United States space programme. After a rocket has blasted off from Cape Canaveral in Florida, its journey is controlled by the National Aeronautics and Space Administration (NASA) from Houston. Astronauts are also trained at the centre and new space technology is developed here.

Did you know?

▸ Texas is the second biggest US state and has two time zones.

▸ The Alamo, a Spanish Mission in San Antonio, is the site of a famous battle (1836) in the fight for Texan independence.

▸ The Grand Canyon is up to 1.6 km (1 mile) deep, 29 km (18 miles) wide, and stretches for 349 km (217 miles).

SPANISH INFLUENCE

Close to Mexico and Central America, the southwestern states have long been settled by Hispanic people, whose influence can be seen – and heard – throughout the southwest. Spanish is widely spoken, and the Roman Catholic religion the Spanish brought is evident in the churches scattered here.

OIL FIELDS

The oil industry has provided Texas with much of its wealth. Oil lies deep underground and is brought up to the surface by massive oil jacks, known as nodding donkeys (above).

Mexico

ONCE HOME TO THE great Aztec and Mayan civilizations, then the focus of Spanish conquistadors who came in search of wealth, the culture and architecture of Mexico today reflects its colourful past. The majority of Mexicans are *mestizo* (mixed race), of Spanish and native Indian descent. Mexico City, site of the ancient Aztec capital, is today one of the largest cities in the world, with a population of over 16 million. Despite oil and natural gas reserves, and a plentiful supply of labour, large numbers of Mexicans are still poor, especially in the rural areas and the urban slums.

ALONG THE BORDER

In 1994, Mexico signed the North American Free Trade Agreement (NAFTA), which effectively bound its economy to that of the USA. A large industrial area has developed along the Mexican border with the USA, and many American companies have relocated south of the border to benefit from the lower labour costs.

DAY OF THE DEAD

One of the biggest festivals in Mexico is the Day of the Dead. It is believed that once a year the souls of the dead can come back and visit their loved ones. In celebration of this, special food is prepared to welcome the souls, and offerings of flowers, candles, and incense are made at the gravesides.

LIFE IN THE CITY

Mexico City is the political, economic, and cultural hub of the country, and is home to some 16 million people. Its site, in a basin surrounded by a mountain, means that expansion is difficult. Air pollution from factories and cars cannot escape, so that on most days a thick layer of smog builds up over the city. Attempts to deal with the pollution, including banning cars from some parts, have had limited success.

THE VOLCANO
Popocatépetl is the highest peak around the city.

MEXICO CITY is contained within a ring of mountains.

WORKING ON THE LAND

Agriculture employs seven million people – about one-quarter of Mexico's work force. However, only 12 per cent of the land is suitable for farming because it is so mountainous and dry. The peasant communities of the south rely on farming for their food, while communities in the north are more industrialized. Here, the agave plant is being harvested near the town of Tequila.

Map labels

UNITED STATES O
Mexicali
Tijuana
Rosarito
Ensenada
San Luis
Colorado River
Desierto de Altar
Sierra San Pedro Mártir
Nogales
Agua Prieta
Ciudad Juárez
Samalayuca
Rio Grande
Rio Bravo del Norte
Cananea
Caborca
Magdalena
Cumpas
Nuevo Casas Grandes
El Sueco
Ojina
Rio Bavispe
San Pedro de la Cueva
El Sáuz
Rio Conchos
Isla Ángel de la Guarda
Hermosillo
Rio Yaqui
Chihuahua
Cuauhtémoc
Delicias
Isla Guadalupe
Bahía Sebastián Vizcaíno
Isla Tiburón
Ciudad Camargo
Isla Cedros
Guaymas
Empalme
Esperanza
Navojoa
San Francisco del Oro
Jiméne
Guerrero Negro
Ciudad Obregón
San Francisco del Oro
Hidalgo del Parral
Santa Barbara
San Ignacio
Huatabampo
Gómez Pal
Baja California
San Blas
Los Mochis
Gulf of California
Guasave
Guamúchil
M
Loreto
Sierra de la Giganta
Navolato
Culiacán
Durango
Isla Magdalena
Bahía de La Paz
El Dorado
Isla Santa Margarita
La Paz
PACIFIC OCEAN
Tropic of Cancer
Miraflores
Mazatlán
Santa Genoveva 2406m
Escuinapa
Acaponeta
Islas Marías
Tepic
Puerto Vallarta
Sierra Madre Occidental
Manza
115°
110°
105°
30°
25°
20°

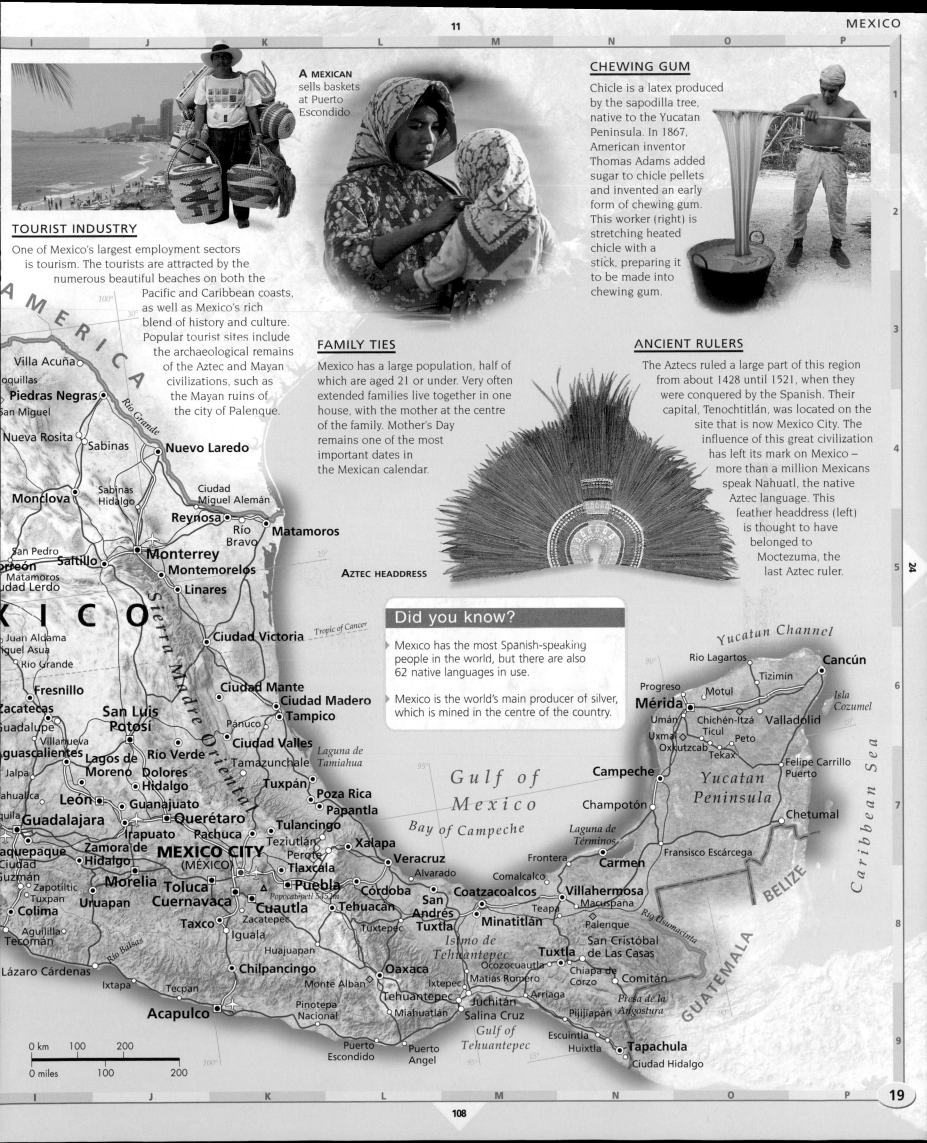

A MEXICAN sells baskets at Puerto Escondido

TOURIST INDUSTRY

One of Mexico's largest employment sectors is tourism. The tourists are attracted by the numerous beautiful beaches on both the Pacific and Caribbean coasts, as well as Mexico's rich blend of history and culture. Popular tourist sites include the archaeological remains of the Aztec and Mayan civilizations, such as the Mayan ruins of the city of Palenque.

CHEWING GUM

Chicle is a latex produced by the sapodilla tree, native to the Yucatan Peninsula. In 1867, American inventor Thomas Adams added sugar to chicle pellets and invented an early form of chewing gum. This worker (right) is stretching heated chicle with a stick, preparing it to be made into chewing gum.

FAMILY TIES

Mexico has a large population, half of which are aged 21 or under. Very often extended families live together in one house, with the mother at the centre of the family. Mother's Day remains one of the most important dates in the Mexican calendar.

ANCIENT RULERS

The Aztecs ruled a large part of this region from about 1428 until 1521, when they were conquered by the Spanish. Their capital, Tenochtitlán, was located on the site that is now Mexico City. The influence of this great civilization has left its mark on Mexico – more than a million Mexicans speak Nahuatl, the native Aztec language. This feather headdress (left) is thought to have belonged to Moctezuma, the last Aztec ruler.

AZTEC HEADDRESS

Did you know?

- Mexico has the most Spanish-speaking people in the world, but there are also 62 native languages in use.

- Mexico is the world's main producer of silver, which is mined in the centre of the country.

AMERICA

Villa Acuña
oquillas
Piedras Negras
San Miguel
Nueva Rosita
Sabinas
Nuevo Laredo
Río Grande
Sabinas Hidalgo
Ciudad Miguel Alemán
Monclova
Reynosa
Río Bravo
Matamoros
San Pedro
Saltillo
Monterrey
orreón
Montemorelos
Matamoros
udad Lerdo
Linares

MEXICO
Sierra Madre Oriental

Juan Aldama
iguel Asua
Río Grande
Ciudad Victoria
Tropic of Cancer
Yucatan Channel

Fresnillo
Ciudad Mante
Zacatecas
Ciudad Madero
San Luis Potosí
Tampico
uadalupe
Pánuco
Río Lagartos
Cancún
Villanueva
Ciudad Valles
Tizimín
guascalientes
Río Verde
Laguna de Tamiahua
Progreso
Motul
Isla Cozumel
Lagos de Moreno
Tamazunchale
Mérida
Jalpa
Dolores Hidalgo
Umán
Chichén-Itzá
Valladolid
ahuatica
Uxmal
Ticul
Peto
León
Guanajuato
Tuxpán
Oxkutzcab
Tekax
quila
Querétaro
Poza Rica
Campeche
Felipe Carrillo Puerto
Guadalajara
Papantla
Gulf of Mexico
Yucatan Peninsula
Irapuato
Pachuca
Tulancingo
Champotón
quepaque
Zamora de Hidalgo
Teziutlán
Bay of Campeche
Laguna de Términos
Chetumal
Ciudad uzmán
MEXICO CITY (MÉXICO)
Perote
Xalapa
Veracruz
Frontera
Fransisco Escárcega
Morelia
Toluca
Tlaxcala
Alvarado
Carmen
Zapotiltic
Popocatépetl 5452m
Puebla
Comalcalco
BELIZE
Tuxpan
Cuernavaca
Córdoba
San Andrés
Coatzacoalcos
Villahermosa
Uruapan
Cuautla
Tehuacán
Teapa
Macuspana
Colima
Zacatepec
Tuxtla
Minatitlán
Palenque
Río Usumacinta
Taxco
Tuxtepec
Islmo de Tehuantepec
Palenque
Aguililla
Iguala
San Cristóbal de Las Casas
Tecomán
Huajuapan
Tuxtla
Ocozocuautla
Chiapa de Corzo
Comitán
Lázaro Cárdenas
Chilpancingo
Oaxaca
Matías Romero
Río Balsas
Monte Albán
Ixtepec
Arriaga
Presa de la Angostura
Ixtapa
Tecpan
Tehuantepec
Juchitán
Pijijiapán
GUATEMALA
Acapulco
Pinotepa Nacional
Miahuatlán
Salina Cruz
Escuintla
Gulf of Tehuantepec
Puerto Escondido
Puerto Angel
Huixtla
Tapachula
Ciudad Hidalgo

0 km   100   200
0 miles   100   200

24

19

CENTRAL & SOUTH
AMERICA

FROM THE VOLCANOES of Central America to the towering

Andes Mountains and vast grassy plains of South America,

this region offers a vast range of landscapes. South America is triangle-

 shaped, tapering down from the warm Caribbean Sea

to the icy tip of Cape Horn. In the north lies the Amazon

rainforest, the largest tropical rainforest in the world. Some 420 million

people live in Central and South America, in 32 countries that vary in size

from small islands to the vast expanse of Brazil. The

languages, history, and cultures of this continent have

 been shaped by colonization. The main influence has

been Spanish, which is still widely spoken. Portugal has

left its stamp on Brazil, while English, French, and Dutch influences remain

evident in several countries on the mainland and in the Caribbean.

Central America

VOLCANOES, EARTHQUAKES, and hurricanes threaten the livelihoods of people in the seven countries of Central America. People have also struggled with poverty and civil war. In more recent years, however, peace and economic recovery have offered hope, and education is now free in all countries. Remains of the ancient Mayan civilization that flourished until the 16th century when the Spanish invaded, can be seen throughout the region. Large numbers of the native population died after the invasion, mostly from disease. Today, Spanish is the main language of the region.

Did you know?

- Lake Nicaragua is the only freshwater lake in the world that has sharks.

- In 1998, Hurricane Mitch swept through here with devastating results.

- Tropical rainforest covers half the land in Belize.

FAUNA AND FLORA

Ecotourism, which encourages visitors but aims to protect and preserve the environment, is increasingly important in the region. In Belize, tourists can dive in the clear, warm waters off the world's second largest barrier reef, and there are wildlife treks to many forest areas. Animals include jaguars, howler monkeys, and butterflies.

TEMPLE PYRAMIDS

Between AD 250–900, the Maya designed ceremonial centres filled with temples, courts, and plazas. Without metal, they shaped tools from the solid lava of volcanoes to carve the limestone buildings. The largest site is at Tikal (left), in Guatemala, where temple remains lie in a huge area of tropical rainforest.

Pyramid has nine sloping terraces.

Steps lead up to the temple at the top.

Volcanic region

Central America is an unstable area because it lies along the meeting point of two of the Earth's tectonic plates. There are at least 14 active volcnoes here, including Volcán de Pacáya (left). Although this makes it a dangerous place to live, the volcanic soil is very fertile and good for crops.

DECORATED CHURCHES

The Spanish colonizers of the 1500s, and the missionaries who came with them, converted the native population and established Roman Catholicism throughout Central America. They also built many fabulously decorated churches. The one shown here, El Merced, is built in a low, "squat" style to resist the ever-present threat of earthquakes. The majority of people still follow the Roman Catholic faith.

Map labels

MEXICO

Corozal
Caledonia
Orange Walk
Indian Church
San Pedro
Altun Ha
Hill Bank
Belize City
Carmelita
Santa Elena
BELMOPAN
Tikal
San Ignacio
Dangriga
BELIZE
Flores
San Benito
La Libertad
Monkey River Town
Dolores
Maya Mountains
Sayaxché
San Antonio
San Luis
Punta Gorda
Gulf of Honduras
Islas de la Bahía
Roatán
Barillas
Chisec
Puerto Cortés
Trujillo
Puerto Barrios
Tela
La Ceiba
Jacaltenango
GUATEMALA
Morales
San Pedro Sula
Tocoa
Savá
Huehuetenango
Chajul
Nebaj
Cobán
Lago de Izabal
Los Amates
El Progreso
San Esteban
Gualaco
Rabinal
Río Montagua
Yoro
La Unión
Catacar
Santa Cruz del Quiché
Sálama
Zacapa
Gualán
HONDURAS
San Marcos
Chiquimula
Copán
Santa Rosa de Copán
Siguatepeque
Guaimaca
Juticalpa
Campamento
Quezaltenango
Comayagua
GUATEMALA CITY
Volcán de Pacáya 2553m
La Esperanza
Danlí
Escuintla
Jutiapa
Metapán
TEGUCIGALPA
Santa Ana
Chalatenango
Jalapa
San José
Ahuachapán
SAN SALVADOR
San Vicente
Ocotal
Somoto
Sonsonate
Río Chamalecón
Condega
EL SALVADOR
Usulután
San Miguel
Choluteca
Estelí
Jinote
Somotillo
Ciudad Darío
Sébaco
Mata
Gulf of Fonseca
Chinandega
Muy
NICA
Corinto
Lago de Managua
León
Tipita
Juic
MANAGUA
Masa
Jinotepe
Nandaime
Gra
Belén
Rivas
PACIFIC OCEAN
La Cru
Golfo de Papagayo
Filade
Penín de Nic

FOOD MARKETS

Coffee, bananas, and sugar cane are all key exports from here to the food markets of the world. Most are cultivated on large plantations. However, food for the local population, such as potatoes, avocados, rice, and maize, is grown on small farms and sold at local markets.

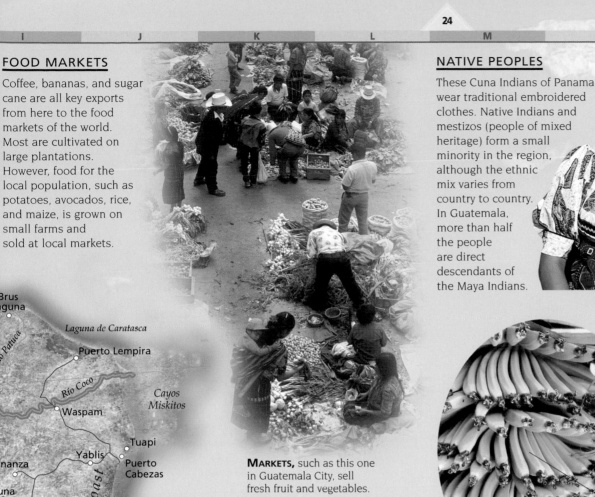

MARKETS, such as this one in Guatemala City, sell fresh fruit and vegetables.

NATIVE PEOPLES

These Cuna Indians of Panama wear traditional embroidered clothes. Native Indians and mestizos (people of mixed heritage) form a small minority in the region, although the ethnic mix varies from country to country. In Guatemala, more than half the people are direct descendants of the Maya Indians.

BANANA INDUSTRY

The hot, wet climate of Honduras is perfect for cultivating fruit, such as bananas. These are often grown on huge plantations, which employ local people who may work long hours for very little pay. Once cut down, the bananas are washed, inspected, and packed into boxes to be sent abroad. Bananas are a major export for Honduras.

As bananas grow, they begin to point upwards.

COFFEE BEANS

Costa Rica was the first country in Central America to grow coffee and, today, produces more than 160,000 tonnes each year. Coffee is harvested from the fruit of the coffee bush. Once picked, the beans are left to dry in the sun. This worker is raking the beans as they dry.

PANAMA CANAL

Forming a vital link between the Atlantic and Pacific Oceans, the Panama Canal is one of the world's busiest waterways. After sharing the canal with the US, Panama took full control in 1999. Over the years, trade has made Panama City a major financial centre.

Brus Laguna

Laguna de Caratasca

Puerto Lempira

Río Patuca

Río Coco

Cayos Miskitos

Waspam

Tuapi

Yablis

Puerto Cabezas

onanza

iuna

Prinzapolka

La Sirena

Barra de Río Grande

Laguna de Perlas

GUA

El Rama

Bluefields

go de caragua

Punta Gorda

San Carlos

San Juan del Norte

Upala

Río San Juan

Jagaces

Puerto Viejo

Cañas

Quesada

Siquirres

Alajuela

Heredia

Puntarenas

COSTA RICA

SAN JOSÉ

Cartago

Guabito

Limón

Cerro Chirripó Grande 3819m

Cordillera de Talamanca

Almirante

Quepos

Bahía de Coronado

Buenos Aires

Cortés

Palmar Sur

Boquete

Volcán Barú 3475m

Cordillera Central

Península de Osa

La Concepción

David

Golfo Dulce

Golfo de Nicoya

Caribbean Sea

Laguna de Chiriquí

Mosquito Gulf

Panama Canal

Lago Gatún

Balboa

Capira

Penonomé

Aguadulce

Santiago

Ocú

Chitré

Guarumal

Las Tablas

Golfo de Chiriquí

Península de Azuero

Isla de Coiba

Isla Cébaco

P A N A M A

Istmo de Panamá

Portobelo

El Porvenir

Colón

Cristóbal

Cordillera de San Blas

Ailigandí

Lago Bayano

San Miguelito

PANAMA CITY

Chimán

Puerto Obaldia

Gulf of Darien

La Palma

El Real

Garachiné

Yaviza

Jaqué

Archipiélago de las Perlas

Isla del Rey

Gulf of Panama

Serranía del Darién

COLOMBIA

km 50 100 150 200

miles 50 100 150 200

The Caribbean

UNITED STATES OF AMERICA

THIS REGION CONSISTS of thousands of islands stretching from Cuba in the west to Trinidad and Tobago in the east. European colonists wanted control of the islands in the 1500s, but the diseases they brought wiped out most of the local Carib and Arawak peoples. African slaves, imported to work on plantations, replaced local peoples and today most of the population are descended from those Africans. English, Spanish, and French are spoken in different countries, depending on which European power claimed the territory. Tourism and agriculture are major sources of employment.

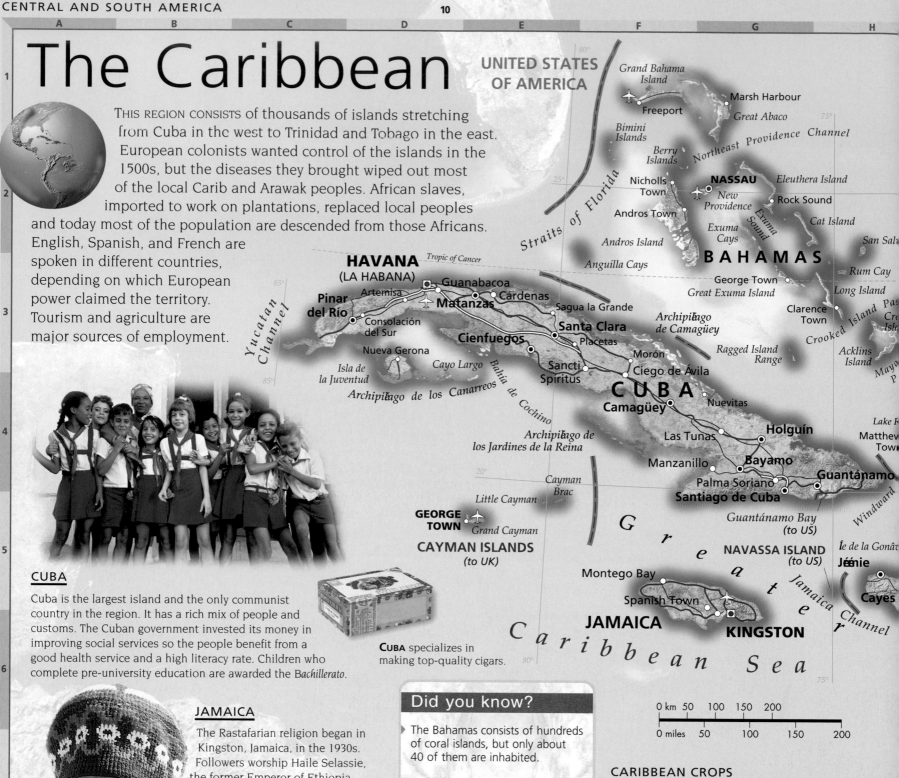

CUBA

Cuba is the largest island and the only communist country in the region. It has a rich mix of people and customs. The Cuban government invested its money in improving social services so the people benefit from a good health service and a high literacy rate. Children who complete pre-university education are awarded the *Bachillerato*.

CUBA specializes in making top-quality cigars.

JAMAICA

The Rastafarian religion began in Kingston, Jamaica, in the 1930s. Followers worship Haile Selassie, the former Emperor of Ethiopia (Ras Tafari), and believe that God will lead black people back to Ethiopia, the Promised Land. Jamaica is also home to reggae music, a rhythmic blend of African, European, and South American styles that can be heard across the island. The lyrics often tell of hardship and political struggle.

THE RASTAFARIAN religion forbids the cutting of hair.

Did you know?

▶ The Bahamas consists of hundreds of coral islands, but only about 40 of them are inhabited.

▶ The most densely populated country is Barbados.

▶ Steel bands, which use old oil drums as instruments, originated in Trinidad and Tobago.

▶ Rastafarians often wear red, green, and yellow because these are the colours of the Ethiopian flag.

CARIBBEAN CROPS

The semi-tropical climate here creates ideal conditions for many crops, especially sugar. The growing and processing of sugar is an important industry in Cuba, Jamaica, and many of the Lesser Antilles, providing jobs and income for the region. Fermented cane sugar is used to make rum and is a major export.

Sugar cane — Breadfruit — Sweet potato — Papaya — Okra

```
0 km  50   100   150   200
0 miles   50    100    150    200
```

Hurricanes

The Caribbean islands can be devastated by hurricanes between May and October each year. These powerful and damaging storms occur when a normal storm builds up energy as it moves across the Atlantic Ocean. Eventually, violent winds and torrential rain are released on the islands.

FAMILY LIFE

Family is very important here, and is usually the centre of everyday life. Some Caribbean people migrated to other countries, such as the UK, but return when they retire – often bringing considerable money back with them.

TROPICAL ISLES

White sands and warm seas attract vast numbers of visitors to these islands. Tourism is important to the economies of many countries including the Bahamas and the Dominican Republic. Many people work in tourism-related jobs, such as in hotels.

Tropic of Cancer

ayaguana
os Passage
tle Inagua
rat Inagua

TURKS & CAICOS ISLANDS
(to UK)
✈ COCKBURN TOWN

DOMINICAN REPUBLIC

Cap-
aïtien
Monte
Cristi
Puerto Plata
HAITI
Santiago
San Francisco de Macorís
Gonaïves
Cordillera Central
La Vega
La Romana
cmel
PORT-AU-PRINCE
SANTO DOMINGO
Isla Saona
Mona Passage
Isla Beata
Isla Mona

ntilles

70°
20°
70°

SAN JUAN
Caguas
Ponce
Mayagüez
PUERTO RICO
(to US)

VIRGIN ISLANDS
(to US)
65°

BRITISH VIRGIN ISLANDS
(to UK)
✈ ROAD TOWN
✈ CHARLOTTE AMALIE
St Croix

L e e w a r d I s l a n d s

ANGUILLA
(to UK)
THE VALLEY
Sint Maarten (to Netherlands)

ANTIGUA & BARBUDA
Barbuda
✈ BASSETERRE ✈ ST JOHN'S
Antigua
SAINT KITTS & NEVIS
✈ PLYMOUTH
MONTSERRAT
(to UK)
BASSE-TERRE
Basse-Terre
Grande Terre
GUADELOUPE
(to France)
Pointe-a-Pitre
Marie-Galante

L e s s e r A n t i l l e s
65°
15°

DOMINICA
✈ ROSEAU
Martinique
Pass
MARTINIQUE
(to France)
✈ FORT-DE-FRANCE
St Lucia Channel

A T L A N T I C   O C E A N
60°

ST LUCIA
✈ CASTRIES
Vieux Fort
Saint Vincent Passage

BARBADOS
✈ BRIDGETOWN

Saint Vincent
SAINT VINCENT & THE GRENADINES
✈ KINGSTOWN
The Grenadines

GRENADA ✈ ST GEORGE'S

W i n d w a r d   I s l a n d s

HAITI

Haiti was the first Caribbean country to become independent. However, political unrest, combined with poor soils, have made Haiti one of the poorest countries in the world. Health care and sanitation levels are poor and, as a result, life expectancy is low.

HAITIAN MAN selling flowers

Lesser Antilles

ARUBA
(to Netherlands)
✈ ORANJESTAD

NETHERLANDS ANTILLES
(to Netherlands)
Curaçao
Bonaire
✈ WILLEMSTAD

70°

COLOMBIA

VENEZUELA

A TIME TO CELEBRATE

The celebration of Divali (Hindu), Eid-ul-Fitr (Muslim), and Christmas (Christian) reflect the varied religions of people in Trinidad and Tobago. The woman above is dressed for Carnival in Port of Spain to mark the beginning of the Christian season of Lent.

Tobago
TRINIDAD & TOBAGO
PORT-OF-SPAIN
Trinidad
✈
Gulf of Paria
San Fernando
60°
10°
10°

Northwest South America

HIGH MOUNTAINS AND PLATEAUS, dense tropical rainforest, and coastal swamps are found in this region. In the 16th century, promises of untold riches attracted the Spanish to the countries here. They found the vast empire of the Incas, which stretched from what is now Peru into Northern Colombia. To the north and east, other colonizers arrived – Dutch, English, and French. Today, although the countries are independent, with the exception of French Guiana, Spanish remains the main language. The population is mainly a mix of native peoples and Europeans, except along the Caribbean coast where descendants of former African slaves live.

ANDES MOUNTAINS

The Andes, the world's longest mountain chain, extends 7,250 km (4,505 miles) down the western edge of South America. Barley, wheat, and potatoes grow well in highland areas, and are cultivated on the terraced hillsides.

FRENCH GUIANA

French Guiana is the only remaining colony in South America, and is governed by France. Tropical forests cover more than four-fifths of its land. In 1968, the European Space Agency established a launch site on the coast at Kourou, which is still used today.

CARACAS

Venezuela's population is growing rapidly and more than 87 per cent of the people now live in cities. The oil industry brings in considerable wealth, but many people are still poor. Although Caracas (left), Venezuela's capital city, is an important financial centre, it has many shantytowns.

24

22

ANGEL FALLS

Each year thousands of tourists visit the spectacular Angel Falls on the River Churún in eastern Venezuela. They were spotted by an American pilot, Jimmy Angel, in 1935, and later named after him. The water drops for 979 m (3,212 ft), making Angel Falls the highest uninterrupted waterfall in the world.

Did you know?

One-tenth of Suriname is now a nature reserve, established to protect the rainforests.

The railway from Lima climbs 4,818 m (15,806 ft) into the Andes and is the highest in the world.

Potatoes were first grown in the Peruvian Andes by the Incas. Flour was made from the dried potatoes.

THE INCAS

The Incas first lived in the mountainous area near Cusco in Peru. By the time of the Spanish invasion, the Inca Empire extended north into southern Colombia and south through Bolivia and into Argentina and Chile. The Quechua Indians were the most powerful group in the empire, and theirs was the official language. The Quechua and Aymará peoples now live on the high plains in the Andes.

QUECHUA woman from Peru

LIFE ON THE HIGH PLAINS

The Altiplano is a cold plateau at high altitude between two ranges of the Andes Mountains in southwest Bolivia and southern Peru. The native peoples who live here graze sheep and llamas on the windy plains, and grow potatoes and barley. They have generally retained their own language and customs.

MACHU PICCHU

The conquering Spaniards never found the remains of this important Inca city – it remained a secret until Hiram Bingham, an American archaeologist and explorer, discovered its ruins hidden in the forest in 1911. Situated on a high ridge northwest of Cusco, this magnificent ruined city covers 13 sq km (5 sq miles), and has small houses, temples, and stairways built around a central square.

MINERALS

Many countries in this area have extensive reserves of gold, silver, copper, and gems. Colombia produces more than half the world's emeralds. The Incas made good use of these resources and created many beautiful golden objects, such as this llama (below).

LAKE TITICACA

At 3,812 m (12,503 ft), Lake Titicaca is the highest navigable lake in the world. It is also South America's largest lake. The Uru people live here in houses built on huge, floating reed islands. They grow potatoes, hunt birds, and catch fish, using boats made from tightly bundled reeds (right).

Map labels

Piura
Ferreñafe
Chiclayo
Chachapoyas
Cajamarca
Tarapoto
San Pedro de Lloc
Trujillo
Chimbote
Huaraz
Huarmey
Chiquián
Huánuco
Pucallpa
Aguaytía
Cerro de Pasco
Huancayo
Ica
Nazca
Ayacucho
Ayaviri
Pisco
Lomas
Camaná
Moquegua
Callao
LIMA
Huacho
Quillabamba
Machu Picchu
Cusco
Juliaca
Puno
Arequipa
Tacna

PERU
Andes
Cordillera Occidental
Nevado Ampato 6310m

BRAZIL
Río Guaporé
Río Mamoré
Río San Miguel
Magdalena
Riberalta
Fortaleza
Cobija
Río Abuná
Río Madre de Dios
Río Beni
Puerto Maldonado
Reyes
Trinidad

BOLIVIA
San Matías
San José
Puerto Suárez
San Ignacio
Montero
Santa Cruz
Buena Vista
SUCRE
Aiquile
LA PAZ
Copacabana
Cochabamba
Oruro
Uncía
Potosí
Monteagudo
Lago Poopó
Sabaya
Villa Martín
Uyuni
Tupiza
Villazón
Tarija
Lago Titicaca
Nevado Sajama 6520m
Nevado Illimani 6561m
Altiplano

PARAGUAY
ARGENTINA
CHILE
Tropic of Capricorn

PACIFIC OCEAN

Río Ucayali
Río Huallaga
Río Juruá

0 km 100 200 300 400
0 miles 100 200 300 400

Brazil

THE VIBRANT CULTURE OF BRAZIL – with its fusion of music and dance – reflects the rich mix of its ethnic groups. The country also boasts immense natural resources with well-developed mining and manufacturing industries. Brazil grows all its own food, and exports large quantities of coffee, sugar cane, soya beans, oranges, and cotton. However, the wealth is not evenly distributed, with some people living in luxury, while most struggle with poverty. São Paulo is home to almost 10 million people, but poverty and lack of housing means that many live in shantytowns without running water or sanitation. Brazil was colonized in the 16th century by the Portuguese, who established their language and their Roman Catholic faith. It remains a deeply Catholic country with a strong emphasis on family life.

COFFEE

Brazil produces about one-quarter of the world's coffee, which is grown on large plantations in the states of Parana and São Paulo. However, as world coffee prices go up and down so much, Brazilians are now growing other crops for export as well.

AMAZON RAINFOREST

Covering more than one-third of Brazil, the rainforest is home to a huge variety of animal and plant life. At one time, more than 5 million native Indians also lived here, but now only about 200,000 remain. Over the years, vast areas of forest have been cut down to provide timber for export, to make way for farmland, or to mine minerals such as gold, silver, and iron. The Kaxinawa Indians (left) still cultivate root vegetables as a food crop.

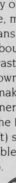

THE BRAZILIAN morpho butterfly has brilliant blue wings and lives in rainforests from Brazil to Venezuela.

BRASÍLIA

Brasília became Brazil's new capital (after Rio de Janeiro) in 1960 as part of a scheme to develop the interior. Situated on land that was once rainforest, the city is laid out in the shape of an aeroplane. Government buildings are in the "cockpit", residential areas are in the "wings".

FOOTBALL ENTHUSIASTS

Brazilians are passionate about football, which is played everywhere from beaches to shantytowns. There is fervent support for the national team, which has won the World Cup more times than any other country, most recently in 2002.

PEOPLE OF BRAZIL

Brazilians come from a variety of different ethnic groups, including descendants of the original native Indians the Portuguese colonizers, African slaves brought over to work in the sugar plantations, and European migrants.

Map labels

VENEZUELA
COLOMBIA
Guiana Highland
Uraricoera
Boa Vista
Caracaraí
Roraima
Equator
Pico da Neblina 3014m
Rio Negro
Repre Balbin
Rio Japurá
Rio Içá
Manaus
Tefé
Amazon
Coari
Rio Juruá
Rio Javari
Rio Madeira
Amazon Basin
PERU
Japiim
Feijó
Rio Purus
Acre
Humaitá
BR
Rio Abuná
Pôrto Velho
R
Guaporé
Rondônia
Chapada dos Paret
Vilhe
BOLIVIA

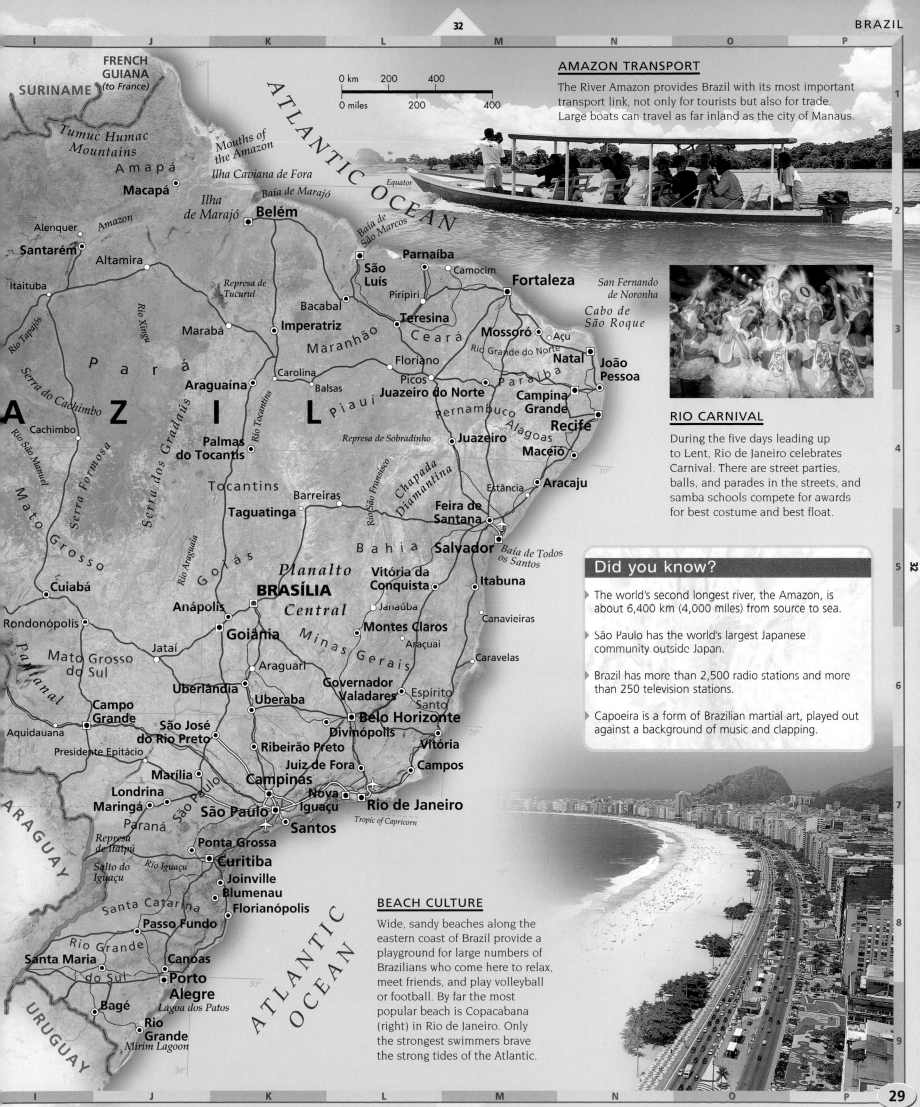

AMAZON TRANSPORT

The River Amazon provides Brazil with its most important transport link, not only for tourists but also for trade. Large boats can travel as far inland as the city of Manaus.

RIO CARNIVAL

During the five days leading up to Lent, Rio de Janeiro celebrates Carnival. There are street parties, balls, and parades in the streets, and samba schools compete for awards for best costume and best float.

Did you know?

▸ The world's second longest river, the Amazon, is about 6,400 km (4,000 miles) from source to sea.

▸ São Paulo has the world's largest Japanese community outside Japan.

▸ Brazil has more than 2,500 radio stations and more than 250 television stations.

▸ Capoeira is a form of Brazilian martial art, played out against a background of music and clapping.

BEACH CULTURE

Wide, sandy beaches along the eastern coast of Brazil provide a playground for large numbers of Brazilians who come here to relax, meet friends, and play volleyball or football. By far the most popular beach is Copacabana (right) in Rio de Janeiro. Only the strongest swimmers brave the strong tides of the Atlantic.

Southern South America

TOWERING MOUNTAINS, vast grassy plains, and hot deserts create a very diverse geographical landscape. The four countries in this region – Chile, Paraguay, Uruguay, and Argentina – were once Spanish colonies but gained their independence in the early 1800s. Each country has an elected government but their economies remain fragile. Most of the population speak Spanish and are mestizo – of mixed Spanish and native Indian descent – except for Argentina, where 97 per cent are descended from Europeans.

Atacama Desert

Sandwiched between the high Andes and the sea, the Atacama Desert in northern Chile is one of the hottest and driest areas in the world. Rain hardly ever falls here. This harsh landscape, however, is rich in copper deposits.

CHILEAN EDUCATION

Chile has the highest literacy rate (ability to read and write) in all of South America. Between the ages of 6 and 13 schooling is both free and compulsory.

ITAIPÚ DAM

The enormous Itaipú dam on the Paraná River in Paraguay is one of the world's largest hydro-electric projects. It can generate all the electricity Paraguay needs as well as large amounts for export.

MONTEVIDEO'S rich history shows in the mix of Colonial Spanish, Italian, and art deco styles of architecture.

URUGUAY'S CAPITAL

The capital of Uruguay, Montevideo, is home to nearly half the country's population. It is also the main port and economic centre. This lively capital lies on the east bank of the Río de la Plata, and is a popular holiday resort because of its white sandy beaches.

BRAZIL
BOLIVIA
PARAGUAY
ASUNCIÓN
URUGUAY
BUENOS AIRES
CHILE
SANTIAGO

Ciudad del Este
Eldoñado
Mirim Lagoon
Encarnación
Posadas
Rivera
Melo
Chuy
Coronel Oviedo
Caazapá
Yuty
Artigas
Tacuarembó
Villarrica
Santo Tomé
Río Negro
Pedro Juan Caballero
Pilar
San Juan Bautista
Corrientes
Mercedes
Salto
Florida
Concepción
Paraguay
Villarrica
Goya
Concordia
Paysandú
Trinidad
Mercedes
La Plata
Capitán Pablo Lagerenza
Fuerte Olimpo
Formosa
Monte Caseros
Paraná
Rosario
Gualeguaychú
Dolores
Zárate
General Eugenio A. Garay
Las Lomitas
Resistencia
Reconquista
Vera
Santa Fe
Pergamino
Junín
Mariscal Estigarribia
Río Bermejo
Añatuya
Rafaela
Rufino
Realicó
San Ramón de la Nueva Orán
San Miguel de Tucumán
Santiago del Estero
Frías
Córdoba
Villa María
San Luis
Villa Mercedes
San Salvador de Jujuy
Metan
Dean Funes
Jesús María
Río Cuarto
La Quiaca
Salta
La Rioja
San Fernando del Valle de Catamarca
Cafayate
San Juan
Mendoza
Godoy Cruz
Cordillera Occidental
Chuquicamata
Calama
Antofagasta
Taltal
Chañaral
Caldera
Copiapó
Vallenar
Domeyko
San Rafael
Arica
Iquique
Lagunas
Tocopilla
Mejillones
Atacama Desert
Cerro del Salado
Rancagua
Coquimbo
La Serena
Ovalle
Illapel
Salamanca
La Ligua
La Calera
Viña del Mar
Valparaíso
San Antonio
Monte Patria
Pichilemu
Curicó
Tropic of Capricorn
Pilcomayo
Cerro Gallán
Cerro Mercedario
Cerro Aconcagua
PERU

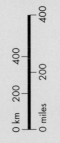

DANCING THE TANGO

Popular around the world today, the tango originated in the slums of Buenos Aires in the late 1800s. This passionate dance with its characteristic rhythm is accompanied by music on a type of concertina known as a *bandoneon*, together with piano and violin.

Did you know?

- The national drink in South America is *mate*. This healthy tea is made from a bitter herb, and drinking it with friends is a daily custom for most people.

- Across the region, four out of every five people live in cities.

- Chile has the largest concentration of astronomical observatories in the world because of its exceptionally clear skies.

BUENOS AIRES

More than one-third of Argentina's population lives in or around the capital Buenos Aires. A thriving port on the River Plate estuary, it is the largest city in Argentina. The colourful La Boca district (above) with its painted walls is home to the descendants of Italian immigrants.

A GAUCHO herds cattle in the Pampas region.

PAMPAS

Vast, treeless plains called the Pampas – which means "flat" in Spanish – cover much of southern and western Argentina. The Pampas are used to grow cereals and raise cattle. Gauchos Argentinian cowboys, work on large ranches, or *estancias*.

WINES FROM CHILE

About 90 per cent of Chileans live in the central region, where the rich soil is ideal for a wide range of agriculture. Vines were brought to Chile by the Spaniards, and the country now has an important wine-making industry that exports wine all over the world.

ANDES MOUNTAIN WEATHER

The Andes stretch the entire length of South America, and this has a major effect on the weather. As westerly air from the Pacific Ocean rises over the mountains, its moisture can fall as rain and snow. By the time it reaches the eastern side, the air is much drier and the landscape is more arid.

0 km 200 400
0 miles 200 400

ARGENTINA

CHILE

ATLANTIC OCEAN

PACIFIC OCEAN

Talcahuano
Chillán
Concepción
Los Angeles
Temuco
Valdivia
Osorno
Puerto Montt
Ancud
Castro
Isla de Chiloé
Puerto Varas
Loncoche
Lebu
Río Bío Bío
Santa Rosa
Azul
Olavarría
Tandil
Balcarce
Mar del Plata
Necochea
Tres Arroyos
Coronel Dorrego
Bahía Blanca
Punta Alta
Bahía Blanca
Choele Choel
Río Negro
Viedma
San Antonio Oeste
Golfo San Matías
Península Valdés
Golfo Nuevo
Rawson
Río Colorado
Cipolletti
Neuquén
Zapala
San Carlos de Bariloche
Maquinchao
Lago Nahuel Huapi
Esquel
Trelew
Río Chubit
Paso de Indios
Lago Musters
Sarmiento
Comodoro Rivadavia
Golfo San Jorge
Caleta Olivia
Puerto Deseado
Río Chico
Río Deseado
Puerto San Julián
Perito Moreno
Lago Buenos Aires
Chile Chico
Cochrane
Coihaique
Puerto Aisén
Archipiélago de los Chonos
Golfo de Penas
Golfo Corcovado
Cerro Corcovado
Cerro San Valentín 4058m
Isla Wellington
Cerro Melliza Sur 3050m
Cerro Paine 2670m
Río Santa Cruz
El Calafate
Río Gallegos
Puerto Natales
Punta Arenas
Porvenir
Tierra del Fuego
Ushuaia
Bahía Grande
Strait of Magellan
Isla de los Estados
Beagle Channel
Cape Horn (Cabo de Hornos)

Atlantic Ocean

THE WORLD'S SECOND LARGEST OCEAN, the Atlantic covers one-fifth of the Earth's surface. It separates the Americas from Europe and Africa. The world's youngest ocean, the Atlantic started to form about 180 million years ago, as the continental plates began to separate. This movement continues today, as the oceanic plates that meet at the Mid-Atlantic Ridge continue to pull apart. The Atlantic is a major source of fish, but due to overfishing, stocks are now low. Many shipping routes cross the Atlantic, and pollution is an international problem as ships dump chemicals and waste. There are substantial reserves of oil and gas in the Gulf of Mexico, off the coast of West Africa, and in the North Atlantic.

GREENLAND

The largest island in the world, Greenland is a self-governing part of Denmark. Most Greenlanders live on the southwest coast. Mainly Inuit, with some Danish-Norwegian influences, they make their living by seal hunting, fishing, and fur trapping.

Fishing for halibut

TOURISM

The volcanic islands and black beaches of the eastern Atlantic, especially the Canaries (left), Madeira, and the Azores, are popular with tourists, who are attracted by the scenery and sub-tropical climate.

Warm currents

The Gulf Stream flows up the east coast of North America and across the Atlantic. It brings warm water and a mild climate to northern Europe, which would otherwise be cooler.

MID-ATLANTIC RIDGE

Tristan da Cunha island

At the centre of the ridge is a valley at least 16 km (10 miles) wide.

UNDERWATER MOUNTAINS

The Mid-Atlantic Ridge is a great underwater mountain chain that runs the entire length of the Atlantic. It was formed by magma that oozed up from the seabed, cooled to create solid rock, and gradually built up to form a ridge. Some peaks are so high that they break the surface to form volcanic islands such as the country of Iceland.

WHALES

Many whales live in the Atlantic, migrating from summer feeding grounds in the cold polar regions to warmer waters in the Caribbean for the winter. They give birth and mate again before returning north.

Humpback whale breaching

ATLANTIC FISHING INDUSTRY

The Atlantic Ocean contains more than half the world's total stock of fish. Herring, anchovy, sardine, cod, flounder, and tuna are among the most important fish found here. However, overfishing, particularly of cod and tuna, has caused a significant decline in numbers.

FALKLANDS

Set in the windy South Atlantic off the coast of Argentina, the Falkland Islands belong to the UK but are also claimed by Argentina. Fishing and sheep farming are important. The land is rocky, mountainous, boggy, and almost treeless.

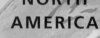

NORTH AMERICA

BERMU (to

Gulf of Mexico

Hatteras Plain

Greater Antilles

Puerto Trench

Caribbean Sea

Colombian Basin

Lesser An

Guatemala Basin

Panama Basin

Galapagos Islands (to Ecuador)

Peru-Chile Trench

Peru Basin

SOUTH

Andes

PACIFIC OCEAN

Peru-Chile Trench

Chile

Basin

Chile Rise

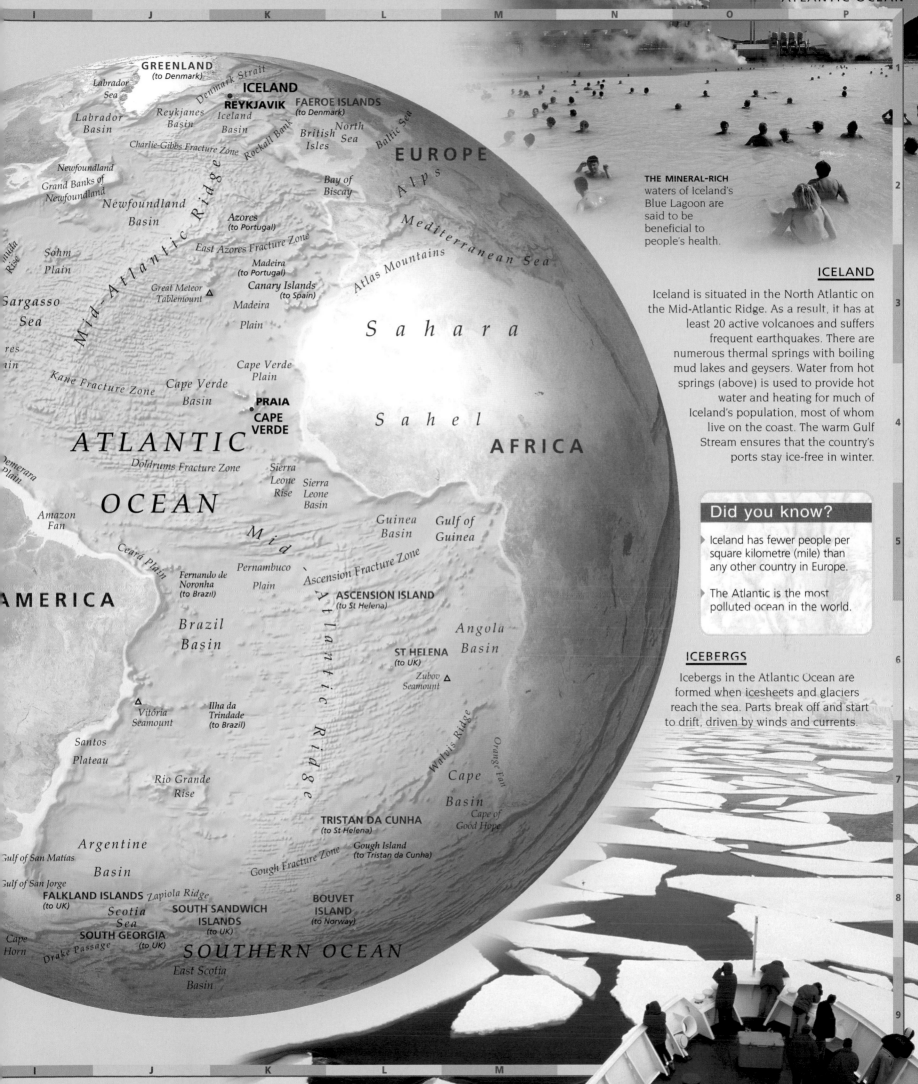

GREENLAND
(to Denmark)

Labrador
Sea

Labrador
Basin

Reykjanes
Basin

Denmark Strait

ICELAND

REYKJAVIK

Iceland
Basin

FAEROE ISLANDS
(to Denmark)

British
Isles

North
Sea

Baltic Sea

Charlie-Gibbs Fracture Zone

Rockall Bank

EUROPE

Bay of
Biscay

Alps

Mediterranean Sea

Newfoundland
Grand Banks of
Newfoundland

Newfoundland
Basin

Azores
(to Portugal)

East Azores Fracture Zone

Atlas Mountains

Bermuda
Rise

Sohm
Plain

Madeira
(to Portugal)

Canary Islands
(to Spain)

Sahara

Sargasso
Sea

Great Meteor
Tablemount

Madeira
Plain

Cape Verde
Plain

Sahel

res
ain

Kane Fracture Zone

Cape Verde
Basin

PRAIA
CAPE
VERDE

AFRICA

ATLANTIC

Doldrums Fracture Zone

Sierra
Leone
Rise

Sierra
Leone
Basin

Guinea
Basin

Gulf of
Guinea

Demerara
Plain

OCEAN

Mid-Atlantic Ridge

Amazon
Fan

Ceará Plain

Mid-

Pernambuco
Plain

Ascension Fracture Zone

AMERICA

Fernando de
Noronha
(to Brazil)

Atlantic Ridge

ASCENSION ISLAND
(to St Helena)

Angola
Basin

Brazil
Basin

ST HELENA
(to UK)

Zubov
Seamount

Vitória
Seamount

Ilha da
Trindade
(to Brazil)

Santos
Plateau

Walvis Ridge

Orange Fan

Rio Grande
Rise

Cape
Basin

Cape of
Good Hope

Argentine
Basin

Gulf of San Matías

TRISTAN DA CUNHA
(to St Helena)

Gulf of San Jorge

Gough Island
(to Tristan da Cunha)

Zapiola Ridge

FALKLAND ISLANDS
(to UK)

Gough Fracture Zone

BOUVET
ISLAND
(to Norway)

Scotia
Sea

SOUTH SANDWICH
ISLANDS
(to UK)

Cape
Horn

SOUTH GEORGIA
(to UK)

Drake Passage

SOUTHERN OCEAN

East Scotia
Basin

THE MINERAL-RICH
waters of Iceland's
Blue Lagoon are
said to be
beneficial to
people's health.

ICELAND

Iceland is situated in the North Atlantic on
the Mid-Atlantic Ridge. As a result, it has at
least 20 active volcanoes and suffers
frequent earthquakes. There are
numerous thermal springs with boiling
mud lakes and geysers. Water from hot
springs (above) is used to provide hot
water and heating for much of
Iceland's population, most of whom
live on the coast. The warm Gulf
Stream ensures that the country's
ports stay ice-free in winter.

Did you know?

▸ Iceland has fewer people per
square kilometre (mile) than
any other country in Europe.

▸ The Atlantic is the most
polluted ocean in the world.

ICEBERGS

Icebergs in the Atlantic Ocean are
formed when icesheets and glaciers
reach the sea. Parts break off and start
to drift, driven by winds and currents.

AFRICA

The second largest continent after Asia, Africa has plenty of record-breakers.

The Sahara is the world's largest desert, the Nile its longest river, Lake

Victoria its second-largest freshwater lake, and the Congo

river basin its second largest tropical rainforest. The

people of Africa are culturally and religiously diverse – those north of the

 Sahara are mainly Muslim, while people in the south follow

a variety of religions, including Christianity. With a rapidly

growing population of 793 million, spread across 52 countries, Africa also

contains some of the world's poorest countries. Many

economies depend heavily on exporting one crop or

product, and if prices fall, the country becomes poorer. Most people live on

 the land and are vulnerable to drought, floods, and famine,

with limited access to clean drinking water. However,

a growing number of people are moving to cities in search of a better life.

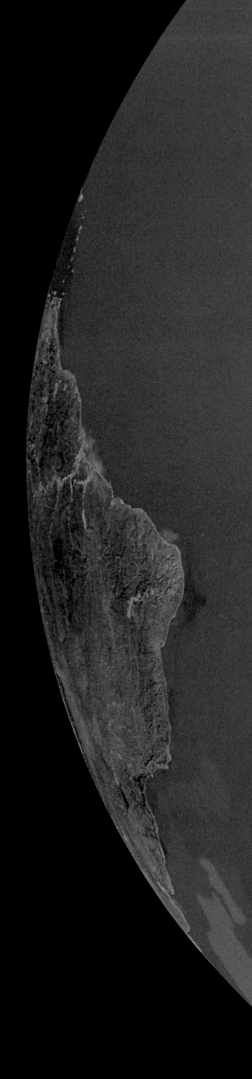

Northwest Africa

FOUR COUNTRIES, plus the disputed area of Western Sahara, make up this part of Africa. Algeria, Libya, and Tunisia have rich supplies of oil and natural gas that boost their economies. Morocco relies on tourism, phosphates used for chemicals and fertilizer, and agriculture. In the fertile valleys of the Atlas Mountains, farmers grow grapes, citrus fruit, dates, and olives. The area also attracts tourists to its colourful markets, historical sites, and sandy beaches. The Sahara Desert dominates the region, particularly in Algeria and Libya.

SUN AND SEA

Many tourists visit Tunisia and Morocco each year to enjoy the warm climate and sandy beaches. Tourism provides jobs for the local people and brings much-needed income.

ARAB INFLUENCE

Arab invasions during the 7th and 11th centuries have influenced the culture, religion (Islam), architecture, and language of northwest Africa. Today, Arabic is the main language, and more than 95 per cent of the people here are Muslim.

MOROCCAN MARKET

In a *souk*, or market, craftworkers sell handmade products to tourists. Goods are displayed in booths along the bustling streets.

MUSLIMS go to worship at the Hassan II mosque in Casablanca, Morocco.

BERBERS

The Berber people were the original inhabitants of northwest Africa. Most now live in the Atlas Mountains or the desert. Although most Berbers converted to Islam when the Arabs arrived, they kept their own language and way of life. In 2001, Algeria recognized Berber as an official language.

A BERBER WOMAN works on the land in the Atlas Mountains.

ATLANTIC OCEAN

Strait of Gibraltar
GIBRALTAR (to UK)
Ceuta (to Spain)
Tangier
Tetouan
Melilla (to Spain)
Ksar-el-Kebir
Chefchaouen
Salé Kénitra
RABAT Fès
Casablanca
Mohammedia
El-Jadida
Safi Khouribga Beni-Mellal
Essaouira
Marrakech
MOROCCO Ouarzazate Er-Rachidia
Agadir
Tiznit

Tizi Ouz
ALGIERS (ALGER)
Chlef Blida
Oran Mostaganem
Sidi Bel Abbès
Oujda Tlemcen Djelfa
Jerada Hauts Plateaux Chott ech Chergui
Atlas Saharien Laghoua
Figuig
Béchar Ghardaïa

Atlas Mountains

Grand Erg Occidental El Goléa

Hamada du Dra
Tan-Tan
LAÂYOUNE El Mahbas Tindouf
Smara
Boujdour Bou Craa
Galtat-Zemmour
WESTERN SAHARA (disputed territory under Moroccan occupation)
Ad Dakhla
MAURITANIA 'Erg Iguîdi
Adrar
A L G E
Plateau du Tademaït
I-n-Salah
Reggane
Erg Chech S
Tropic of Cancer Tanezrouft
Lagouira MALI

DATE PALMS

Dates are an important crop for Algeria and Tunisia. Date palms are often grown at oases, where water lies close to the surface of the desert. Here the clusters of dates are shown ripening beneath polythene. Leaves from the trees can be used for thatch and the trunk is cut for timber.

ANCIENT RUINS

Phoenicians, Romans, and Greeks from ancient times have all left their mark on this part of Africa. Today, tourists come to admire the historical sites along the coast. These ruins at Carthage, near Tunis, date from the 9th century BC, when the Romans controlled the whole of north African coast.

RUINS OF A ROMAN BATH AT CARTHAGE

Did you know?

▶ The stones from dates can be roasted and ground to make a traditional date coffee.

▶ Since Spain gave up control of Western Sahara in 1976, Morocco has been fighting a guerrilla group of desert tribesmen for control of the area.

Map labels

Mediterranean Sea
Bizerte
Annaba
Carthage
TUNIS
etif
Constantine
Sousse
Batna
Kairouan
Kasserine
Mahdia
Chott Melghir
Gafsa
Sfax
kra
Golfe de Gabès
Tozeur
Île de Jerba
TRIPOLI (ṬARĀBULUS)
Al Bayḍā'
Darnah
Chott el Jerid
Gabès
Médenine
Zuwārah
Al Khums
Al Marj
Ṭubruq
El Oued
TUNISIA
Az Zāwiyah
Miṣrātah
Benghazi (Banghāzī)
Al Jabal al Akhḍar
Touggourt
Yafran
Gharyān
Gulf of Sirte (Khalīj Surt)
Ouargla
Nālūt
Surt
Ajdābiyā
Wādī al Hamīm
Marsā al Burayqah
Al Jaghbūb
Marādah
Jālū
Great Sand Sea
E G Y P T
Waddān
L I B Y A
A
Bordj Omar Driss
Tiguentourine
Birāk
Sabhā
Ramlat Rabyānah
L i b y a n
Awbārī
Al 'Uwaynāt
Zawīlah
Al Khufrah
Tropic of Cancer
Tassili-n-Ajjer
h
a
r
a
Desert
Djanet
Idhān Murzuq
Ahaggar
▲ Tahat 2918m
Tamanrasset
▲ Pic Bette 2286m
C H A D
S U D A N
N I G E R

SURVIVAL IN THE SAHARA

The Sahara Desert covers almost one-third of Africa and is an inhospitable place to live with high daytime temperatures and freezing nights. The Tuareg are nomads for whom the desert is home. Traditionally, they keep camels for transport, and to provide meat, milk, and hides. Many Tuareg now live in the cities.

TUAREG NOMADS in the Sahara carry salt to trade in markets.

0 km 100 200
0 miles 100 200

LIBYAN OIL RESOURCES

The discovery of oil and gas in 1959 brought considerable wealth to Libya, and currently makes up 99 per cent of the country's exports. As a result, Libya's cities have grown as people have moved from rural areas to find work in the oil industry. Some of the money from oil is being spent on better healthcare and education for Libyans.

LIBYAN OIL FIELD

Northeast Africa

THIS REGION, KNOWN AS the Horn of Africa, contains the oldest civilizations in the continent, and some of its poorest countries. The borders that divide the countries today were mostly created by colonial rulers in the last hundred years. Pastoral nomads with their herds of animals often cross these borders in search of pasture. Most people still live in the countryside and farm the land, but increasing numbers are moving to cities. Tourism and agriculture are important sources of income for Egypt and Kenya, two of the richest and fastest-growing countries in the region. Elsewhere, tribal rivalries and disputes over land and resources have sometimes erupted into full-scale war and these, together with drought and poverty, have blighted the lives of millions of people in this region.

RIVER NILE

The Nile is the world's longest river. It flows north from Burundi to run along the Tanzania/Rwanda border, then through Uganda, Sudan, and Egypt to the coast. Most of Egypt's population lives around the valley and delta of the Nile, which provides the region's water. The river also provides irrigation for local crops, such as cotton.

SUEZ CANAL

The Suez Canal is one of the world's longest and most important artificial waterways. It links the Mediterranean Sea with the Gulf of Suez and the Red Sea, providing a crucial shortcut from Europe to India and East Asia. The tolls from the canal are a great source of income for Egypt.

LOSING FARMLAND

As the population grows in Ethiopia, more and more people cut down forests for firewood, or to cultivate new areas for food crops. The soil, no longer held firm by the trees, is easily blown or washed away, and valuable farmland is lost.

PLOUGHING fields in Ethiopia

ABU SIMBEL

Tourists come to Egypt to see the pyramids at Giza and the temples along the Nile, such as these two built at Abu Simbel, south of Aswan. Tourism brings in money to preserve these historical sites.

0 km   100   200   300   400
0 miles   100   200   300   400

Map labels

Mediterranean Sea
Red Sea
Gulf of Aden

EGYPT
SUDAN
LIBYA
CHAD
ERITREA
DJIBOUTI

Alexandria, El'Alamein, Sîdi Barrâni, Qattâra Depression -133m, Siwa, Bawîti, Qasr Farâfra, Sahara el Gharbiya (Western Desert), Great Sand Sea, Gilf Kebir Plateau, Jabal al 'Uwaynât 1907m

Port Said, Dumyât, Zagazig, El Gîza, CAIRO, Ismâ'iliya, Suez Canal, Suez, Gulf of Suez, Sinai, Gebel Mûsa 2285m, Beni Suef, El Minya, Mallawi, Asyût, Sohâg, Akhmîm, Qena, Luxor, Isna, Idfu, Aswân, Aswan Dam, Lake Nasser, El Khârga, Tropic of Cancer, Hurghada

Wadi Halfa, Akasha, Delgo, Argo, Dongola, Ed Debba, Merowe, Abu Hamed, Shereik, Atbara, Ed Damer, Shendi, Omdurman, KHARTOUM, Wad Medani, Sennar, Blue Nile, El Obeid, Umm Ruwaba, Sodiri, El'Atrun, Wâdi el Milk, Wâdi Howar, Darfur, Umm Bufu, Kebkabiya, El Fasher, El Geneina, Nyala

Nubian Desert, Wadi Oko, administered by Sudan, administered by Egypt

Port Sudan, Suakin, Tokar, Haiya, Kassala, Khashm el Girba, Gedaref, Teseney, ASMARA, Mek'elē, Māych'ew, Gonder, Lalibela, Massawa, Zula

Danakil Desert, Aseb, Caluula

Did you know?

The Masai tribe lives on the borders of Kenya and Tanzania. Between the ages of 14 and 30, young Masai men live in the bush and learn how to become great warriors.

Water makes up almost one-fifth of the surface area of Uganda.

RELIGIOUS BELIEFS

The Ethiopian Orthodox Union Church has been in existence since the 4th century AD. It is a branch of the Coptic Church, and mixes Christian beliefs, such as Catholic saints, with some traditional African spiritual beliefs.

COPTIC CROSS

TEA IN KENYA

Kenya is an important world producer of tea, which is grown on plantations in the highland areas (such as this one below). High rainfall here ensures a good crop. Coffee is also a valuable export.

KENYAN workers carefully select tea leaves for picking.

Map labels

SOMALIA
INDIAN OCEAN
ETHIOPIA
KENYA
UGANDA
TANZANIA
RWANDA
BURUNDI
DEM. REP. CONGO
CENTRAL AFRICAN REPUBLIC
MOZAMBIQUE
ZAMBIA
MALAWI
Great Rift Valley
Masai Steppe
Highlands
Sudd

MOGADISHU (MUQDISHO)
ADDIS ABABA (ĀDĪS ĀBEBA)
NAIROBI
DODOMA
DAR ES SALAAM
KAMPALA
KIGALI
BUJUMBURA
Zanzibar

Hargeysa, Doxo Nugaaleed, Sinujiif, Garoowe, Gaalkacyo, Gellinsoor, Dhuusa Marreeb, Buulobarde, Jawhar, Marka, Baraawe, Beledweyne, Xuddur, Baydhabo, Wanlaweyn, Baardheere, Jilib, Jamaame, Kismaayo, Buur Gaabo, Garsen, Afmadow, Garissa, Malindi, Mombasa, Pemba, Tanga, Zanzibar, Mafia, Lindi, Kilwa, Kivinje, Mohoro, Newala, Mtwara, Masasi, Tunduru, Songea, Nyamtumbo, Njombe, Mbeya, Iringa, Morogoro, Sao Hill, Sumbawanga, Kipili, Kasulu, Kigoma, Tabora, Singida, Nzega, Shinyanga, Nyantakara, Bukoba, Mwanza, Musoma, Bharamulo, Arusha, Moshi, Meru, Nyeri, Nakuru, Kisumu, Eldoret, Marsabit, Lodwar, Lokitaung, Kaabong, Lira, Gulu, Arua, Masindi, Mbale, Jinja, Entebbe, Masaka, Mbarara, Kabale, Gore, Agaro, Jima, Negele, Yabelo, Ĭrĕso, Awash, Nazrēt, Dire Dawa, Harer, Jijiga, Shilabo, Ogadén, Malakal, Bor, Amadi, Maridi, Yambio, Raga, Tambura, Rumbek, Tonj, Wau, Sumeh, Jur, Sue, Duk Faiwil, Kongor, Juba, Kapoeta, Kaabong

White Nile, Shebeli, Juba, Webi, Jubba, Awash, Hayk', Lake Turkana, Lake Albert, Lake Edward, Lake Kivu, Lake Victoria, Lake Tanganyika, Lake Rukwa, Lake Nyasa, Malagarasi, Great Ruaha, Rufiji, Rovuma, Kyoga Swamp, Elemi Triangle (administered by Kenya)

Equator

Mt. Kenya 5200m
Kilimanjaro 5895m

CAIRO

The largest city in Africa is Cairo, the capital of Egypt. The city has a population of nearly seven million. Here, Arab, African, and European influences exist alongside more traditional Egyptian customs.

BUSY STREET bazaar in Cairo

SUDANESE DINKA

There are more than 500 different tribes in Sudan, who speak over 100 languages and dialects. Like many tribal people here, the Dinka are nomadic – their cattle graze on the plains east of the Nile. Cattle are central to their lives – young Dinka men officially become adults with an initiation ceremony in which they are given an ox of their own.

YOUNG DINKA MAN

MOUNTAIN GORILLAS

The Volcanoes National Park in Rwanda is one of the few places where you can still see a mountain gorilla (right) in the wild. These animals are threatened with extinction because of poachers and the destruction of their habitat. Tanzania and Kenya also have many important game reserves, which preserve the wildlife of the savannah.

West Africa

0 km 100 200 300 400

0 miles 100 200 300 400

DRAMATICALLY DIFFERENT CLIMATE and landscapes influence life in West Africa. In the hot, dry, northern areas of the Sahara and Sahel, it is extremely difficult to grow crops. To the south, the climate is warm and wet, and crops such as cocoa and coffee are grown on large plantations. The region also has many valuable minerals. Despite these rich resources, most countries are very poor. Since independence from colonial powers, there has been much political unrest, often sparked by poverty and tribal rivalries in the region. West Africa is also divided by religion, with Islam dominant in the north and Christianity in the south.

GAMBIA

In recent years, tourism has become increasingly important to the economy of Gambia. Visitors come to see wildlife along the River Gambia and to visit the Atlantic coast beaches. These safari tourists are admiring a giant termite mound.

PEOPLE OF GHANA

Family ties and a sense of community are important to the people of Ghana, and ceremonies throughout each year mark the events of childbirth, puberty, marriage, and death. About half of Ghanaians are Ashanti people whose ancestors developed one of the richest and most notable civilizations in Africa.

DIAMONDS AND GOLD

West Africa has many valuable minerals, including diamonds, uranium, copper, and gold. In Sierra Leone, where diamonds (left) provid crucial income, the mines were a foc of fighting in the civil war between rebel groups and the governmen

Map labels

WESTERN SAHARA (disputed territory under Moroccan occupation)

'Aïn Ben Tili
Bîr Mogreïn
'Erg Iguîdi
Kâghet
El Hank
Erg
Che
Taoude
Tropic of Cancer
Fdérik
Zouérat
Touâjîl
Ouarâne
S   a
Nouâdhibou
Choûm
Atâr
Chinguetti
Akchâr
Akjoujt
Oujeft
El Mreyyé
MAURITANIA
NOUAKCHOTT
Idîni
Tidjikja
Tîchît
Araou
Boutilimit
Magta'
Lajjar
Boûmdeïd
Aoukâr
Oualâta
Rkîz
Rosso
Senegal
Aleg
Tâmchekket
Fagui
Richard Toll
Dagana
Kaédi
Kiffa
'Ayoûn el 'Atroûs
Néma
Goun
Saint Louis
Louga
Matam
Timbedgha
Amourj
Mékhé
SENEGAL
Sélibabi
Kobenni
Bassikounou
DAKAR
Thiès
Mbaké
Nioro
Mbour
Diourbel
Kayes
S
Ténenkou
Mo
Sokone
Kaolack
Kolokani
Niger
Baudia
BANJUL
Tambacounda
Toukoto
Ségou
Bani
GAMBIA
Gambia
Kita
Koulikoro
San
Bignona
Kolda
BAMAKO
Ziguinchor
Sédhiou
Bafatá
Bafing
Koutiala
BISSAU
Gaoual
GUINEA-BISSAU
Boké
Labé
Dinguiraye
Siguiri
Bougouni
Sikasso
Pita
Niger
Bobo-
GUINEA
Kankan
Dioulasso
Kindia
Mamou
Faranah
Tengréla
Tôkounou
Odienné
Ferkessédougou
CONAKRY
SIERRA
Kissidougou
Boundiali
Korhogo
Makeni
Beyla
CÔTE
LEONE
Bo
Kenema
D'IVOIRE
FREETOWN
Nzérékoré
(IVORY COAST)
Gbanga
Danané
Lac de
Kossou
Tubmanburg
YAMOUSSOUKRO
MONROVIA
Harbel
Gagnoa
Katiol
Zwedru
Divo
Buchanan
LIBERIA
Sassandra
Abidjan
Sassandra
Harper
San-Pédro

ATLANTIC OCEAN

FOOD CROPS

In regions with enough rain, root vegetables, such as yams and cassava, are grown for food. Peanuts, which also grow underground, are cultivated for export or to cook in traditional stew.

CASSAVA

PEANUTS

YAM

Did you know?

▶ Lake Volta in Ghana, formed by a dam, is the largest artifical lake in the world.

▶ Nigerian twins always have the same names. The firstborn is called Taiwo, the second is called Kehinde.

SPREADING SAHARA

As a result of droughts, overgrazing, and tree removal, the Sahara desert is spreading south into a region of semidesert known as the Sahel. People are now planting grass to try and halt the erosion.

LIBYA

ALGERIA

Tropic of Cancer

Erg I-n-Sâkâne

Tessalit

Adrar des Ifôghas

Ténéré du Tafassâsset

Séguédine

Assamakka

Iferouâne

Massif de l'Aïr

Ténéré

Monts Bagzane 2022m

Agadez

Grand Erg de Bilma

CHAD

Ngourti

MALI

NIGER

mbuktu (ombouctou)

Gao

Ansongo

Ménaka

Lac Niangay

Hombori

Tahoua

Keïta

Dakoro

Dilia

Nguigmi

Lake Chad

Ayorou

Tillabéri

Birnin Konni

Tessaoua

Zinder

Gouré

Guidimouni

Hadejia

Ouahigouya

NIAMEY

Dogondoutchi

Maradi

Nguru

URKINA

Kaya

Sokoto

Katsina

Hadejia

Maiduguri

OUAGADOUGOU

Jega

Gusau

Kano

Potiskum

dougou

Tada-Ngourma

Niger

Koko

Zaria

Gongola

Biu

FASO

Tenkodogo

Kandi

Yelwa

Kaduna

Bauchi

Kumo

olgatanga

Bawku

Sansanné-Mango

Natitingou

Kainji Reservoir

Jos

Gombi

Wa

Yendi

BENIN

NIGERIA

Jos Plateau

Yola

Tamale

Parakou

Minna

Shebshi Mountains

GHANA

Sokodé

Ilorin

Jebba

ABUJA

Lafia

ndoukou

Wenchi

Oyo

Ogbomosho

Owo

Lokoja

Makurdi

Gotel Mountains

Sunyani

Lake Volta

Ibadan

Ede

Benue

Wukari

CAMEROON

Kumasi

Abomey

PORTO-NOVO

Benin City

Enugu

ngourou

Nsawam

Kpalimé

Lagos

Onitsha

amankese

LOMÉ

Cotonou

Sapele

Owerri

isso

ACCRA

Bight of Benin

Warri

Uyo

Cape Coast

Gulf of Guinea

Port Harcourt

Aba

Calabar

Sekondi-Takoradi

Mouths of the Niger

WEST AFRICAN FARMERS

There are two types of farmer in West Africa. In the north, where it is hot and dry, nomadic herders have to keep moving from place to place in search of grazing land for their animals. In the south, where there is more rainfall, farmers may settle and grow food for their families and also for sale.

Herbs, shells, bones, and sticks are used by traditional healers.

MASKED DANCERS

Masks, such as this one from the Dan tribe of the Ivory Coast, are worn by dancers who take on different characters during tribal ceremonies. Round-eyed masks represent males, while straight-eyed masks are for females. However, the actual dancers are always men.

MEDICINE AND HEALING

Many people here seek advice from a traditional healer if they are ill. Often the healer is also a religious leader. Treatment may include the use of herbs or magical items to fight off the enemy spirit. Healers may also chant and dance to attract the good spirits.

Central Africa

ALL EIGHT COUNTRIES in Central Africa were European colonies with a painful history of slavery. Since the 1960s, independence has brought them mixed success. Rich mineral deposits and the discovery of offshore oil have provided income for Cameroon, Congo, and Gabon, while civil war and repressive governments have damaged other countries in the region. These include Chad and the Central African Republic, two of the world's poorest countries. Although the north is mainly arid, Africa's largest tropical rainforest dominates the south, with the powerful Congo River linking the interior with the coast. The tiny, volcanic country of Sao Tome and Principe lies off the coast of Gabon.

RELIGIOUS BELIEFS

Although Christianity is the main religion here, many people also follow traditional beliefs. These suggest that natural objects, such as mountains and rivers, have a spirit. Masks, like this Bambuku head, are sometimes used to scare off evil spirits.

VILLAGE LIFE

Most people in rural areas live in villages or small towns. Some grow crops, such as cotton or cassava, for sale, but many exist just by growing food just for their family.

Mud-brick home

FISHING IN LAKE CHAD

Lake Chad is an important source of food, but it is shrinking at an alarming rate. A shallow lake, it is now only about 6 m (20 ft) deep. Its surface area has also been reduced, due to droughts and the demand for water to irrigate the land.

PEOPLE OF CHAD

With almost half the country lying in the arid Sahara Desert, about 80 per cent of Chadians work on farmland near the River Chari in the south. Across Chad there are large numbers of ethnic groups, speaking over 100 languages. Women here live an average of just 53 years and have 6.5 children.

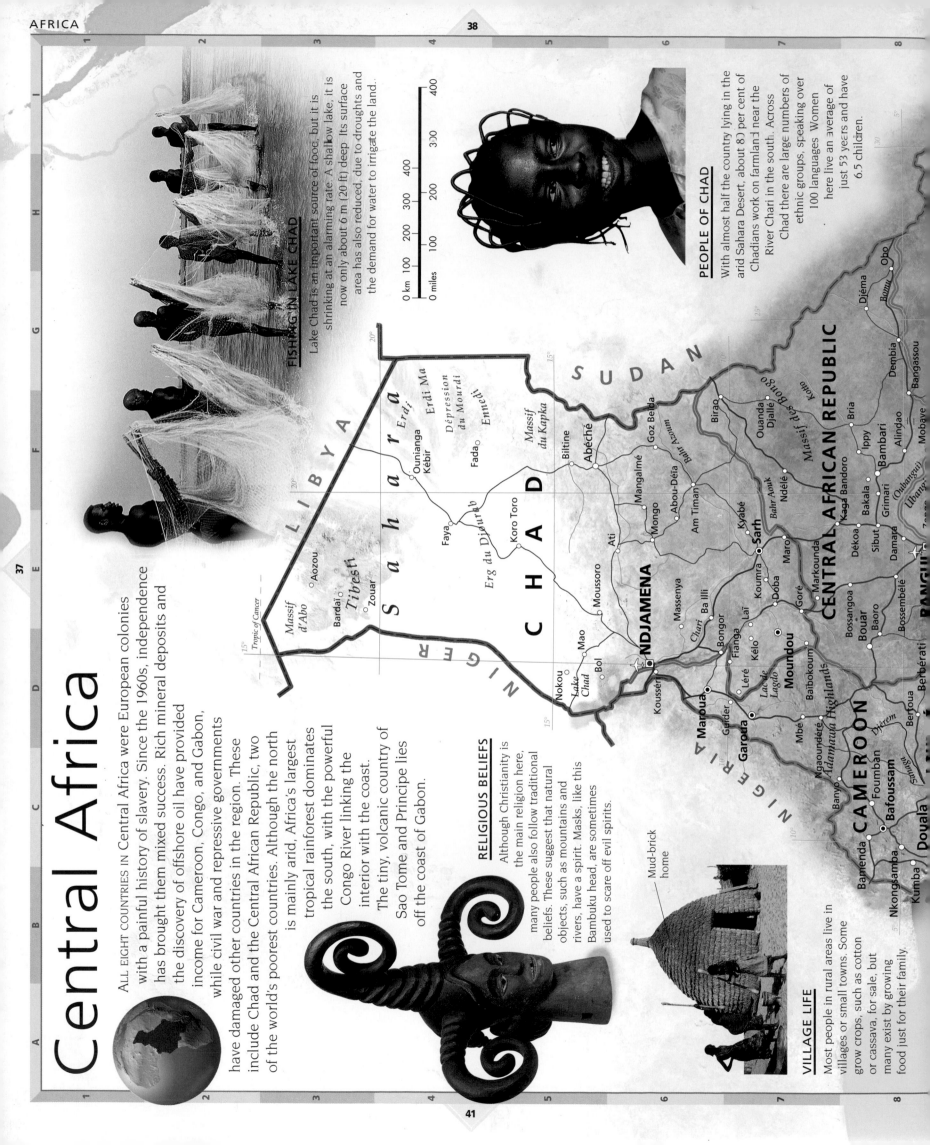

0 km 100 200 300 400
0 miles 100 200 300 400

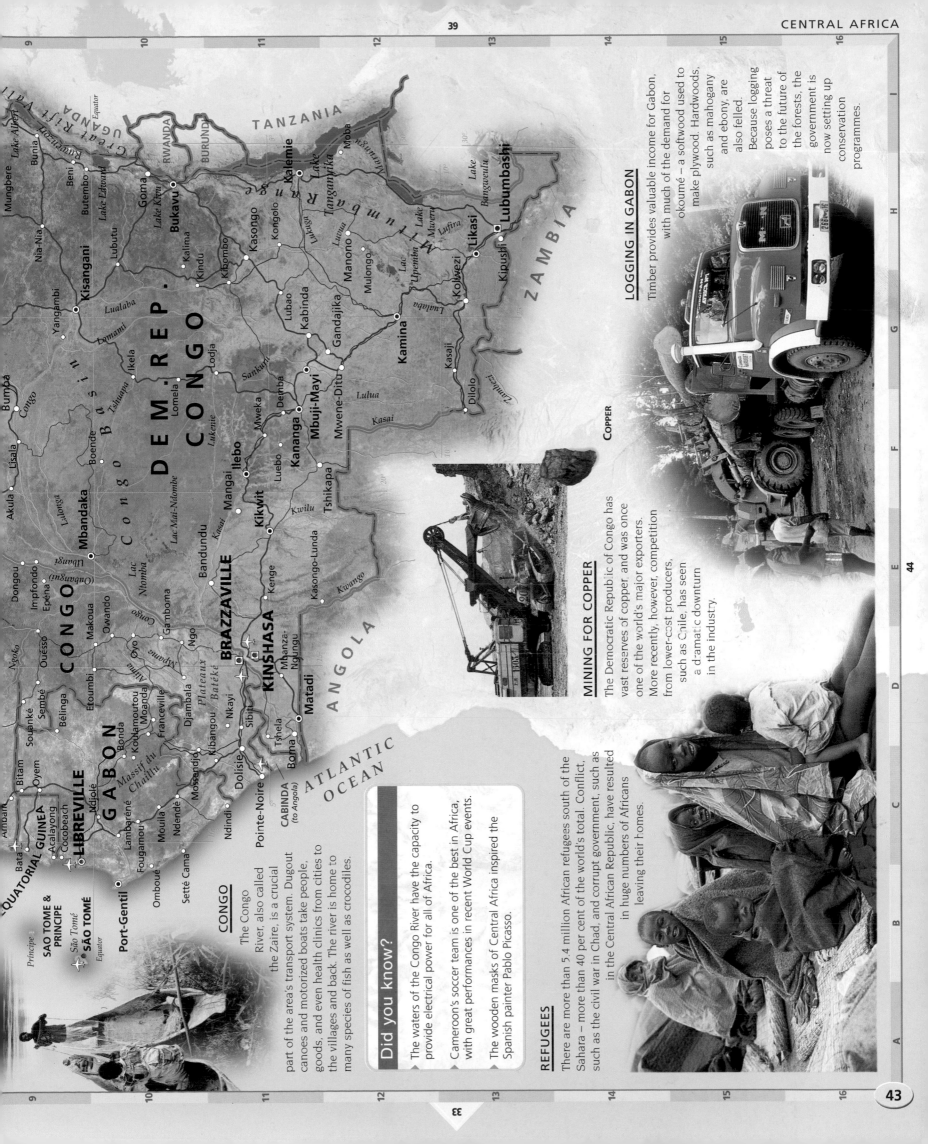

LOGGING IN GABON

Timber provides valuable income for Gabon, with much of the demand for okoumé – a softwood used to make plywood. Hardwoods, such as mahogany and ebony, are also felled. Because logging poses a threat to the future of the forests, the government is now setting up conservation programmes.

COPPER

MINING FOR COPPER

The Democratic Republic of Congo has vast reserves of copper, and was once one of the world's major exporters. More recently, however, competition from lower-cost producers, such as Chile, has seen a dramatic downturn in the industry.

CONGO

The Congo River, also called the Zaire, is a crucial part of the area's transport system. Dugout canoes and motorized boats take people, goods, and even health clinics from cities to the villages and back. The river is home to many species of fish as well as crocodiles.

Did you know?

▶ The waters of the Congo River have the capacity to provide electrical power for all of Africa.

▶ Cameroon's soccer team is one of the best in Africa, with great performances in recent World Cup events.

▶ The wooden masks of Central Africa inspired the Spanish painter Pablo Picasso.

REFUGEES

There are more than 5.4 million African refugees south of the Sahara – more than 40 per cent of the world's total. Conflict, such as the civil war in Chad, and corrupt government, such as in the Central African Republic, have resulted in huge numbers of Africans leaving their homes.

Map labels

TANZANIA

RWANDA

BURUNDI

Great Rift Valley

UGANDA

Ruwenzori

Lake Albert

Lake Edward

Lake Kivu

Mungbere

Bunia

Beni

Butembo

Nia-Nia

Goma

Bukavu

Equator

Kisangani

Lubutu

Kalima

Kindu

Kasongo

Kongolo

Kalemie

Lake Tanganyika

Moba

Lake Mweru

Lake Bangweulu

Lubumbashi

Kipushi

Likasi

Kolwezi

Lubudi

ZAMBIA

Lualaba

Yangambi

Lomami

DEM. REP. CONGO

Lomela

Ikela

Lodja

Sankuru

Kabinda

Manono

Mulongo

Kamina

Kasaji

Dilolo

Lualaba

Zambezi

Lufira

Luvua

Luapula

Congo Basin

Bumpa

Lisala

Akula

Lualonga

Boende

Mbandaka

Lac Mai-Ndombe

Mwka

Demba

Mbuji-Mayi

Mwene-Ditu

Gandajika

Kasaji

Lulua

Kasai

Mangai

Ilebo

Luebo

Kananga

Tshikapa

Kikwit

Kwilu

Kasongo-Lunda

Kwango

Bandundu

Kenge

Kasai

CONGO

Dongou

Impfondo

Epéna

Ouesso

Souanké

Sembé

Makoua

Owando

Oyo

Gamboma

Ngo

Plateaux Batéké

BRAZZAVILLE

KINSHASA

Matadi

Boma

Mbanza-Ngungu

ANGOLA

CABINDA (to Angola)

Pointe-Noire

Dolisie

Tshela

Sibiti

Nkayi

Kibangou

Djambala

Franceville

Koulamoutou

Moanda

Mossendjo

Massif du Chaillu

GABON

LIBREVILLE

Bitam

Oyem

Mékambo

Mdjole

Lambaréné

Fougamou

Mouila

Ndendé

Ndindi

Sette Cama

Omboué

Port-Gentil

EQUATORIAL GUINEA

Bata

Acalayong

Cocobeach

SÃO TOMÉ & PRINCIPE

SÃO TOMÉ

São Tomé

Príncipe

Equator

ATLANTIC OCEAN

Ubangi (Oubangui)

Congo

Sangha

Ngoko

Alima

Mpama

Ntomba

Lac

Southern Africa

FROM THE DRAMATIC Namib and Kalahari deserts in the west, to the tropical forests in the north, Southern Africa is a region of contrasts. Oil, diamonds, gold, and other precious metals are all mined here. There are huge inland plains that are home to a variety of wildlife, and large areas devoted to agriculture. But flooding and droughts, together with civil unrest, have hampered development so that despite an abundance of natural resources, many countries remain poor.

SAN BUSHMEN

SAN HUNTER uses a poison-tipped arrow.

One of the few groups of hunter-gatherers left in Africa, the San people roam the Kalahari Desert. Also known as Bush people, many San are now changing to a more settled life, often working on cattle ranches.

Did you know?

▶ The Okavango River does not run out to sea, like most rivers, but runs inland into the Kalahari Desert.

JOHANNESBURG

With a population of more than nine million, Johannesburg is the second largest city in Africa after Cairo. Many people have moved here from the surrounding countryside in search of work.

Tunnels transport water between dams.

Dams are marked in black.

LESOTHO

Water is a valuable resource in Southern Africa, and Lesotho makes good use of its mountainous land and numerous rivers. The Highlands Water Scheme uses dams and tunnels to transport water to neighbouring South Africa.

GOLD MINING

Gold, first discovered near Johannesburg in 1886, brought a great deal of wealth to the region. South Africa currently produces about one-third of the world's gold.

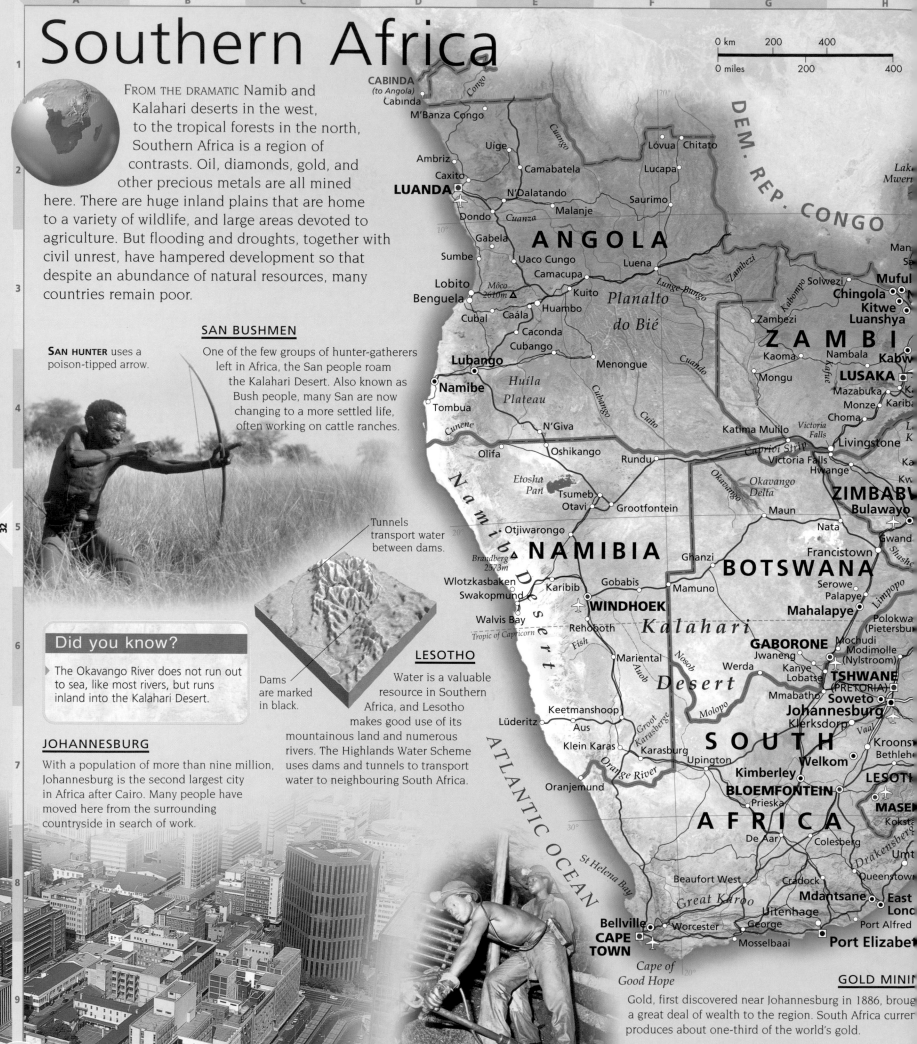

MOZAMBIQUE FLOODS

In Mozambique, floods in 2000 and again in 2001 ruined crops, swept away livestock, and left millions homeless and vulnerable. Many people now rely on foreign aid to stay alive.

TOBACCO PLANTATION

VICTORIA FALLS

At Victoria Falls, situated on the Zambia-Zimbabwe border, the mighty Zambezi River drops 128 m (420 ft) down a narrow chasm. The sound of the crashing water can be heard 40 km (25 miles) away.

WORKING ON THE LAND

In both Malawi and Mozambique, agriculture employs more than four out of every five workers. Important crops include cotton, tea, tobacco, and sugar.

Lake Rukwa

Mbala

T A N Z A N I A

Lake Nyasa

Isoka

MALAWI

Mzuzu

Mpika

Mocímboa da Praia

Negomane

erenje

LILONGWE

Rio Rovuma

Rio Lugenda

Rio Messalo

Mucojo

MORONI **COMOROS**

Grande Comore

Anjouan

Tanjona Bobaomby

Chipata

Salima

Monkey Bay

Rio Lúrio

Pemba

Mohéli

MAMOUDZOU

Antsiranana

Lúrio

MAYOTTE
(to France)

Ambanja

Albufeira de Cahora Bassa

Zomba

Nacala

Analalava

Sambava

Maromokotro 2376m

Antsohihy

Antalaha

ila do umbo

Blantyre

Tete

Milange

Nampula

Lumbo

Mahajanga

Maroantsetra

yamapanda

Nsanje

Mocuba

HARARE

Inyangani 2592m

Chitungwiza

Quelimane

Mutare

Chimoio

Fenoarivo

MADAGASCAN MAMMALS

Madagascar has an unusual range of mammals that developed in isolation after the island split from the African mainland. It is the only place where lemurs, members of the primate family, live in the wild.

Bemaraha

Masvingo

havane

Beira

Machanga

Morondava

Betafo

Ambositra

PORT LOUIS

Mananjary

Rio Save

Changane

Makay

Fianarantsoa

ST-DENIS

ina ssina)

Inhambane

Ihosy

Manakara

MAURITIUS

RING-TAILED LEMUR

RÉUNION
(to France)

Mascarene Islands

Quissico

Farafangana

APARTHEID

In 1994, Nelson Mandela (below) became the first black president to govern South Africa. This historic event marked the end of white rule and the first fair elections in the new "Rainbow Nation". Apartheid was a policy of racial segregation and restricted the rights of black people.

Xai-Xai

Toliara

Mangoky

Vangaindrano

Tropic of Capricorn

MAPUTO

MBABANE

SWAZILAND

Tanjona Vohimena

Amboasary

ee

termaritzburg

Durban

I N D I A N

O C E A N

WILDLIFE

Southern Africa is home to a huge variety of animals. Numerous parks have been created to protect the animals and their habitat. The Gaza-Kruger-Gonarezhou Transfrontier Park joins parks in Mozambique, South Africa, and Zimbabwe to form the largest conservation and ecotourism park in Africa.

MOZAMBIQUE

MADAGASCAR

Mozambique Channel

Toamasina

ANTANANARIVO

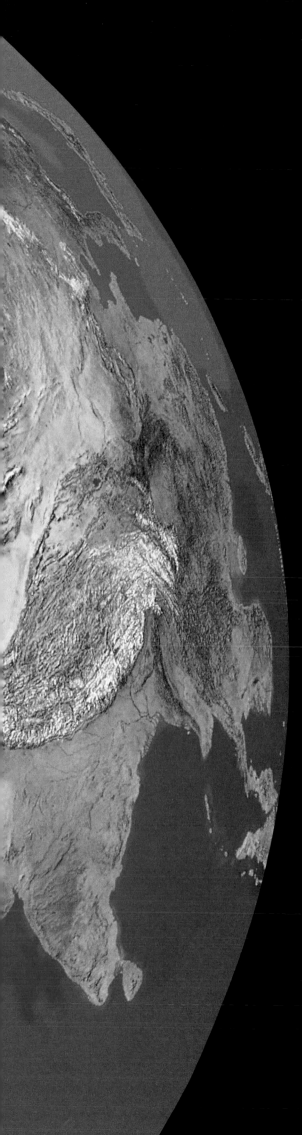

EUROPE

EUROPE IS THE SECOND smallest continent in the world, but it is one of the most densely populated, with more than 727 million people living in its 45 countries. Most Europeans

live in cities. They watch TV, use mobile phones, surf the Internet, drive cars, and in comparison with many other people in the world, are quite prosperous. The European climate is mild, although winters are cold in the north and east and summers

are hot in the south. Over the past 500 years, Europeans have conquered much of the world, setting up huge empires in every continent. These empires are now gone, but

their influences remain. Many people around the world still speak a European language, such as English, French, or Spanish, and European culture has been exported to many parts of the globe. As members of the European Union, many countries are forging closer economic and political links.

Scandinavia and Finland

THE THREE SCANDINAVIAN countries of Norway, Sweden, and Denmark, along with neighbouring Finland, are among the most northerly countries in Europe. Here the winters are long and cold. In the far north above the Arctic Circle, the Sun remains below the horizon for up to two months a year. Because of the harsh winter climate and the geographical isolation, Scandinavia has attracted little immigration, so the population is not very ethnically diverse. Finland is the most densely forested country in Europe, and wood accounts for 30 per cent of its exports. All four countries are highly industrialized and are among the wealthiest in the world.

URBAN POPULATIONS

Scandinavia has a high urban population. Many people live in towns and cities, with less than a fifth living in the countryside. Since it is an area covered in lakes, fjords, and surrounded by sea, many people also live near the water.

COPENHAGEN in Denmark is the largest city in Scandinavia.

SKIING

During the winter months, much of Scandinavia is covered with snow, so skiing is one of the easiest forms of transport. It is also a very popular sport.

SAMI man in traditional costume

LAPLAND

Northern Sweden and Finland are known as Lapland. Here the local Sami people survive the cold and inhospitable climate by herding reindeer, which they breed for their meat, milk, and skins.

INDUSTRIAL STRENGTH

Manufacturing is an important source of employment and wealth throughout Scandinavia. Many of the goods produced, such as cars in Sweden, electronic goods in Denmark (above), and mobile phones in Finland, are exported all over the world. In Denmark, many people also work in agriculture, fish processing, and brewing.

Did you know?

- *Ski* is Norwegian for "strip of wood".

- Two-thirds of all Danish people have surnames that end in "sen", such as Hansen, meaning "son".

- Sweden recycles more aluminium cans than any other country in the world.

THE SAUNA

The sauna, or steam bath, was invented in Finland about 1,000 years ago as a way of cleaning and relaxing the body. After a hot sauna, many Finns cool off by plunging into an icy pool (above) or a snowdrift.

NORWEGIAN FJORDS

The west coast of Norway has thousands of deep inlets, known as fjords, gouged out of the mountains by glaciers during the last Ice Age and then flooded by the sea. The fjords run inland between high mountains and are a favourite destination for cruise ships bringing tourists to admire the stunning scenery.

BUILDING WITH WOOD

Much of Norway and Sweden, and two-thirds of Finland, is covered by dense forests of birch, pine, spruce, and other trees. Many people work in the forestry industry, producing wood for the construction and furniture industries. This great natural resource is also used to build homes and churches, like this medieval stave church (left) in Norway.

SAVING THE ENVIRONMENT

The people of Scandinavia are very environmentally conscious and recycle as many household items as they can. Strict national laws protect the environment from industrial waste and pollution, although there is growing concern about the levels of pollution in the Baltic Sea.

The British Isles

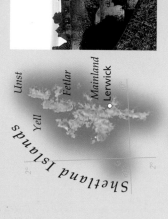

FOR SUCH A SMALL GROUP OF ISLANDS, the British Isles has a very rich history. This is evident from its legacy of ancient ruins, medieval castles, dramatic cathedrals, and grand country houses. Once a leading industrial and colonial power, British monarchs ruled an empire that circled the globe. As a result, English is still widely spoken around the world. Today, many traditional industries, such as shipbuilding, mining, and engineering, have declined, and the emphasis is now on banking and insurance, as well as pharmaceuticals. The British Isles consists of two countries: the United Kingdom of Great Britain and Northern Ireland (the UK), and the Republic of Ireland.

Did you know?

Edinburgh, in Scotland, is built on the core of an extinct volcano.

The Romans founded London in AD 43. They named it Londinium.

Wales has more than 200 castles.

IRELAND

Tourists visit Ireland every year, attracted by its unspoiled countryside and lively cities, such as Dublin (left). Once part of Britain, Ireland gained independence in 1922. It is now one of the fastest-growing economies in Europe.

HORSE BREEDING

Lush pastures and a mild climate have encouraged the breeding of thoroughbred racehorses in Ireland. Stud farms here raise some of the best racehorses in the world.

IRISH HORSE and rider on a training run

SCOTLAND

Scotland and England united as a single country in 1707. Today, however, Scotland is a self-governing part of the UK, with its own parliament and distinct legal and educational systems. Edinburgh, above, is a popular city with a magnificent castle. Each summer, it hosts an international arts festival

NORTH SEA ENERGY

Beneath the shallow seas around Britain, there are supplies of oil and natural gas. Large oil rigs raise oil and gas to the surface where it is pumped by pipeline to be refined on the mainland. Supplies are now beginning to run low and new, more distant areas are being explored.

MONEY MATTERS

The City of London is the UK's financial centre with more than 500 banks. Lloyd's Insurance Building (right) is one of the city's modern skyscrapers. Built of steel and glass, it has lifts on the outside.

Map labels

Shetland Islands
Unst
Yell
Fetlar
Mainland
Lerwick
Fair Isle
Sanday
Mainland
Kirkwall
Orkney Islands
Hoy
Thurso
John o'Groats
Wick
Elgin
Ben Hope 927 m
Ullapool
Inverness
Loch Ness
Aviemore
Spey
Moray Firth
Dee
Aberdeen
Peterhead
Fraserburgh
North Sea
North West Highlands
Grampian Mountains
SCOTLAND
Isle of Lewis
Stornoway
Harris
North Uist
South Uist
Barra
St Kilda
Outer Hebrides
The Minch
The Little Minch
Isle of Skye
Stromeferry
Mallaig
Fort William
Eigg
Rhum
Coll
Tiree
Isle of Mull
Oban
Firth of Lorn
Jura
Islay
Kintyre
Isle of Arran
Inner Hebrides
ATLANTIC OCEAN
Ben Nevis 1343 m
Loch Lomond
Forth
Stirling
Greenock
Paisley
Glasgow
Hamilton
Clyde
East Kilbride
Kilmarnock
Prestwick
Ayr
Dumfries
Stranraer
Southern Uplands
Forfar
Tay
Perth
Dundee
St Andrews
Arbroath
Montrose
Firth of Forth
Dunfermline
Edinburgh
Galashiels
Hawick
Cheviot Hills
Berwick-upon-Tweed
Newcastle upon Tyne
South Shields
Sunderland
Durham
Hartlepool
Carlisle
Penrith
Lake District
Workington
Whitehaven
Barrow-in-Furness
Kendal
Lancaster
Darlington
Tees
Northallerton
Middlesbrough
Whitby
Scarborough
Bridlington
Harrogate
Beverley
York
Ouse
Ribble
Pennines
UNITED KINGDOM
ISLE OF MAN
DOUGLAS
Coleraine
Londonderry
Stranorlar
Strabane
Omagh
Donegal
Donegal Bay
Lower Lough Erne
Enniskillen
Upper Lough Erne
Sligo
Colloney
Boyle
Cavan
Castlebar
Arless
Bangor
Newtownabbey
Belfast
NORTHERN IRELAND
Lough Neagh
Portadown
Armagh
Newry
Dundalk
Downpatrick
Newtownards

LONDON

The capital of the UK is London, a sprawling city on the banks of the River Thames. It is the political and financial centre of the country, as well as home to more than 7 million people. One of its most recent attractions is the London Eye – a giant ferris wheel, 135 m (443 ft) high.

When the pods reach the top, you can see all of the city beneath you.

STONEHENGE in southern England, was built from about 3000 BC onward.

BRITISH LANDMARKS

Tourism is a major industry in Britain. Visitors come from all over the world to see the many churches, castles, and ancient monuments, such as Stonehenge (above), and to admire the pretty villages. Many also come for the theatres, galleries, and shops in Britain's vibrant cities.

WALES

Wales was formally united with England in 1536, but retains its own language and traditions. Welsh is spoken widely in some parts, and public signs appear in both Welsh and English. Coal mining and steel production were important in the south, but have both declined. Rugby is the national game.

MULTICULTURAL SOCIETY

Britain once controlled a world empire with colonies in every continent. Many people – from the Indian subcontinent, Africa, and the Caribbean in particular – came here and brought their cultures with them. Today, about one in 20 British people are from ethnic minorities, but are integrated into British life.

WALES PLAYS IRELAND at rugby in the Millennium Stadium, Cardiff.

CHANNEL ISLANDS (to UK)
ST PETER PORT — Guernsey
ST HELIER — Jersey
Alderney, Sark

Map labels include: North Sea, Great Yarmouth, Lowestoft, Norwich, Ipswich, Felixstowe, Harwich, Colchester, Southend-on-Sea, Margate, Canterbury, Dover, Channel Tunnel, Maidstone, Folkestone, Hastings, Eastbourne, English Channel, Brighton, Hove, Crawley, Woking, Portsmouth, Havant, Bournemouth, Isle of Wight, Newport, Poole, Southampton, Eastleigh, Winchester, Guildford, Reading, Windsor, LONDON, Croydon, Watford, St Albans, Harlow, Stevenage, Luton, Milton Keynes, Bedford, Northampton, Oxford, Swindon, Cheltenham, Gloucester, Cotswold Hills, Thames, Bristol, Bath, Newport, Cardiff, Swansea, Llanelli, Port Talbot, Weston-super-Mare, Taunton, Exmoor, Tiverton, Exeter, Exmouth, Dartmoor, Torquay, Plymouth, Saltash, Bodmin, Newquay, St Austell, Truro, Falmouth, Penzance, Land's End, Isles of Scilly, Bideford, Barnstaple, Ilfracombe, Bridport, Weymouth, Lyme Bay, Yeovil, Salisbury, Stonehenge, Andover, WALES, Cambrian Mountains, Brecon Beacons, Snowdonia, Aberystwyth, Barmouth, Tywyn, Cardigan Bay, Carmarthen, Haverfordwest, Milford Haven, Fishguard, Holyhead, Bangor, Chester, Birkenhead, Crewe, Stoke-on-Trent, Stafford, Shrewsbury, Wolverhampton, Birmingham, Kidderminster, Worcester, Coventry, Nuneaton, Leicester, Derby, Nottingham, Sheffield, ENGLAND, Lincoln, Skegness, Boston, King's Lynn, The Wash, The Fens, Peterborough, Kettering, Newmarket, Cambridge, Mersey, Trent

Ireland labels: DUBLIN, Dun Laoghaire, Lucan, Liffey, Arklow, Wicklow, Wicklow Mts, Wexford, Leinster, Carlow, Kilkenny, Newbridge, Port Laoise, Athlone, Nenagh, Limerick, Shannon, Ennis, Galway, Galway Bay, Loughrea, Lough Derg, Munster, Cashel, Clonmel, Waterford, Youghal, Cork, Bantry, Killarney, Abbeyfeale, Tralee, Dingle Bay, Bantry Bay, Blackwater, Barrow, Rathkeale

Seas: Irish Sea, Celtic Sea, St George's Channel, Bristol Channel

Scale bar: 0 km 50 100, 0 miles 50 100

The Low Countries

THE NETHERLANDS, BELGIUM, AND LUXEMBOURG are known as the Low Countries because the land is so flat and low-lying. In the case of the Netherlands, much of the land is below sea level – Netherlands is Dutch for "under lands". The three countries are among the richest in Europe and, while farming still plays an important part, they all have strong, modern economies based on manufacturing and trade.

Luxembourg in particular is known as a tax haven and is a major centre for international finance. Their location at the mouth of the River Rhine and other major European rivers, places the three countries at the heart of western European trade and politics – all three were founder members of the European Economic Community (now the European Union or EU) established in 1957.

RECLAIMING THE LAND

Over the centuries, the Dutch have reclaimed land from the sea. They did this by building huge dykes, or dams, to keep out the sea, and then draining the surface water into canals. Windmills originally pumped out the water, but electric pumps are now used.

Land below sea level on main map

DUTCH PEOPLE

The Dutch once ruled a vast empire in Indonesia, the Caribbean, and South America. As a result, many nationalities now live here. Ethnic minorities make up about 45 per cent of the people and the majority of primary school children have a non-Dutch background.

Did you know?

Tulips were introduced into the Netherlands from Turkey in 1562. Black tulips were the most valuable.

Belgium combines two cultures: the French-speaking Walloons and the Dutch-speaking Flemings.

In Belgium, French fries, known as *frites*, are served in a paper cone or dish, with a dollop of mayonnaise. They are generally eaten using a small wooden fork.

ROTTERDAM

Every year, more than 30,000 sea-going ships and 110,000 barges call at the port of Rotterdam. Lying at the mouth of the River Rhine, this port is the largest in the world, and is where vast container ships from all over the world load or unload their cargoes. The smaller barges help to transport goods further inland. With the port's ultra-modern Vessel Traffic System (VTS) it's possible to track ships on a radar screen up to 60 km (37 miles) off the coast and 40 km (25 miles) inland.

DUTCH TULIP

CROPS

Fertile soil and good irrigation have helped the Netherlands become a major exporter of agricultural products, with vegetables and tomatoes forming important crops. It is also famous for its bulbs and cut flowers, notably tulips.

GERMANY

NETHERLANDS

Groningen
Delfzijl
Appingedam
Eenshaven
Loppersum
Zuidhorn
Zuidlaren
Vlagtwedde
Borger
Coevorden
Emmen
Haren
Leek
Beilen
Hoogeveen
Hardenberg
Den Ham
Schiermonnikoog
Leeuwarden
Assen
Dokkum
Drachten
Joure
Heerenveen
Steenwijk
Staphorst
Almelo
Tubbergen
Denekamp
Hengelo
Winsum
Wolvega
Meppel
Zwolle
Rijssen
Goor
Enschede
Menaldum
Harlingen
Sneek
Emmeloord
Deventer
Zutphen
Waddenzee
Ameland
Terschelling
Schiermonnikoog
West Friesian Islands (West Waddeneilanden)
Vlieland
Texel
Ijsselmeer
Flevoland
Opmeer
Hoorn
Emmeloord
Lelystad
Nunspeet
Vaassen
Apeldoorn
Schagen
Purmerend
Zaanstad
Almere
Zeewolde
Baarn
Alkmaar
Amstelveen
Amersfoort
Castricum
AMSTERDAM
Hilversum
Velsen-Noord
Haarlem
Noordwijk aan Zee
Assendelft
Leiden
Den Helder

AMSTERDAM

The old architecture and picturesque canals make Amsterdam one of the most visited cities in Europe. Occasionally the canals freeze over and city officials may decide it's safe for people to go skating. Amsterdam is also home to some of the world's best museums, including the Van Gogh Museum.

Cyclists have their own traffic lights – this one is green for "go".

CYCLING

The flatness of the land makes the Netherlands ideal for cycling, and more than half a million people cycle to school or work each day. Most of the roads have special cycle lanes, and bicycles are often the quickest form of transport to get around the crowded towns and cities. The use of bicycles also reduces car use and thus cuts down the amount of air pollution.

TRILINGUAL

The Grand Duchy of Luxembourg lies between Germany, France, and Belgium. As a result, the majority of the people are trilingual – German and French are widely spoken as is Letzebugesch, the national language. The capital, also known as Luxembourg, has more than 200 banks.

FLAGS of the member states of the European Union

BELGIAN QUALITY

Belgium is renowned for its beautiful historic buildings, and for its excellent food, especially chocolates. Belgians have been making top-quality chocolates for more than 100 years and pralines, a type of filled chocolate, are a speciality. Brussels even boasts a chocolate museum.

GERMANY

LUXEMBOURG

LUXEMBOURG

BELGIUM

BRUSSELS
(BRUSSEL/BRUXELLES)

FRANCE

North Sea

Ardennes

0 km 25 50 75
0 miles 25 50 75

France

IN DIRECT CONTRAST TO ITS mainly rural landscape, France is a modern nation with most people now living in towns and cities. It has flourishing industries and is the fifth richest economy in the world, after the USA, Japan, Germany, and the UK. A country of varied scenery, from gently rolling farmland in the north to a stretch of dry, warm Mediterranean coast in the south, France also shares two mountain ranges – the Pyrenees and the Alps. Each of the 22 regions within France, which includes the island of Corsica, has its own distinct identity and culture. The tiny countries of Andorra and Monaco lie next to France.

Did you know?

▶ Some of the world's finest perfumes come from southern France, where fields of lavender, roses, and jasmine are grown. As many as 300 oils may be used to make one perfume.

▶ Boules, the national game of France, is still played in village squares around the country.

▶ *Poisson d'avril*, or April fish, is the name given to anyone who is fooled on April 1st. Confectionery shops sell fish-shaped chocolate, and people send funny cards with fish on them.

NUCLEAR POWER

Three-quarters of France's electricity is produced by nuclear power plants (above), making the country largely self-sufficient in energy and one of the main producers of nuclear power in Europe. Hydro-electric plants are also an important source of power.

HIGH-SPEED TRAVEL

France has the world's fastest train, the TGV – *train à grande vitesse* – which travels at an average speed of 300 kmh (186 mph). The TGV network connects Paris with all the country's major regional cities, which makes it easier to commute or visit relatives. It also extends to Germany, Italy, Belgium, Switzerland, and through the Channel Tunnel to Britain.

STREETS OF PARIS

Tourists flock to Paris to visit its world-famous museums and art galleries, shop in its elegant stores, and soak up its vibrant atmosphere. Montmartre, which overlooks the city, is famous for its artists. Close by, ir the Place du Tertre (above), visitors can have their portrait painted.

GERMANY

LUXEMBOURG

BELGIUM

SWITZERLAND

Dunkerque
Tourcoing
Roubaix
Lille
Calais
Douai
Valenciennes
Hirson
Charleville-Mézières
St-Omer
Cambrai
Sedan
Thionville
Hagondange
Metz
Boulogne-sur-Mer
le Portel
Berck-Plage
Arras
Albert
Laon
Reims
Châlons-en-Champagne
Bar-le-Duc
Toul
Nancy
Strasbourg
St-Dié
Haguenau
Schiltighem
Sélestat
Colmar
Mulhouse
St-Louis
Saverne
Épinal
Vesoul
Belfort
Montbéliard
Audincourt
Besançon
Abbeville
Somme
Amiens
Picardie
Beauvais
Senlis
Noyon
Oise
Compiègne
Château-Thierry
St-Quentin
Marne
Troyes
Langres
Burgundy
Bourgogne
Dijon
Beaune
Dieppe
Seine
Rouen
Louviers
Évreux
Pontoise
Argenteuil
Nanterre
PARIS
Créteil
Versailles
Antony
Melun
Fontainebleau
Nemours
Montargis
Sens
Yonne
Auxerre
Cosne-Cours-sur-Loire
Nivernais
Nevers
Fécamp
Baie de la Seine
le Havre
Barentin
Lisieux
Alençon
Chartres
Île-de-France
Châteaudun
Orléans
Orléanais
Blois
Vierzon
Bourges
Berry
Cher
Cherbourg
Bayeux
St-Lô
Caen
Avranches
Grapville
Normandie (Normandy)
Maine
la Flèche
le Mans
Vendôme
Tours
Touraine
Loir
Châteaux
Châtellerault
Châteauroux
Coutances
St-Malo
Dinan
Dol
Fougères
Châteaubriant
Laval
Sarthe
Angers
Saumur
Cholet
Anjou
Thouars
Poitou
St-Brieuc
Plérin
Loudéac
Rennes
Vitré
Morlaix
Landerneau
Brittany (Bretagne)
Pontivy
Quimperlé
Hennebont
Vannes
Redon
Nantes
Rezé
Challans
la Roche-sur-Yon
les Sables
Brest
Quimper
Concarneau
Lorient
Auray
Belle Île
la Baule-Escoublac
St-Nazaire
Iroise
Île d'Ouessant
Île d'Yeu

Golfe de St-Malo

CHANNEL ISLANDS (to UK)

Channel Tunnel / Strait of Dover

FRENCH CHEESE

The French generally like strong-smelling cheese. Among the best known are Brie, Camembert, and Roquefort. Made from either cow, sheep, or goat's milk, cheese is often named after the French town or region where it is made.

Corsica (Corse)

Bastia
Monte Cinto 2706m △
△ Monte Incudine 2136m
Ajaccio
Sartène
Bonifacio
Strait of Bonifacio

AVIATION INDUSTRY

The French were pioneers of aviation. They co-built Concorde and, in 1970, joined forces with German, Spanish, and UK companies to produce short-to-medium-range aircraft that were both economic to run and carried up to 300 passengers. Called Airbus, these aircraft filled a vital gap in the market and changed the face of the aviation industry.

TOUR DE FRANCE

The Tour de France cycle race was first held in 1903 and is the most important sporting event in France. Every July, thousands of people line the route to support their favourite team or cheer on the winner. The race covers about 4,000 km (2,500 miles) and is divided up into 20 or more daily stages.

VINEYARDS

The Romans first planted grape vines in southern France about 2 000 years ago. Today, France is the world's major wine-producing country, selling a range of wines for the home market and for export. The type of wine produced depends on the soil, location, and climate where the vine is planted. Wines from Burgundy, Champagne, and the Rhône valley are sold worldwide.

HISTORIC HOMES

During the 15th and 16th centuries, French aristocrats built beautiful châteaux, such as Chenonceau (above), in the Loire Valley, Bordeaux, and other regions of France. These houses were elaborately decorated by the best artists and craftsmen. Today, most are state-owned and open to the public.

0 km   50   100   150
0 miles   50   100   150

Germany and the Alpine States

LYING AT THE VERY HEART OF EUROPE, Germany is one of the world's wealthiest nations. It is also Europe's leading industrial power. To its south lie the Alpine states of Switzerland, Austria, Liechtenstein, and Slovenia. The region is famed for its beautiful alpine scenery, mountains, and lakes. German is the main language in all but Slovenia, however, each of the five countries has its own distinct history, culture, and national identity. Indeed, since 1815, Switzerland has been recognized as a neutral nation, and has stayed out of all the wars that have affected Europe.

THE BERLIN WALL

After World War II, Germany was split, with a US-backed capitalist state in the west and a Russian-backed state in the east. Built in 1961, the wall was 155 km (96 miles) in length and was designed to stop East Germans from leaving for a better life in the West. The wall divided Berlin and separated families, friends, and a nation for 28 years. When Germany was reunited in 1990, the Berlin Wall was demolished.

CELEBRATIONS AT the Brandenburg Gate mark the 10th anniversary of the fall of the Berlin Wall.

GERMAN INDUSTRY

With its coal and iron mines, the Ruhr Valley was once the powerhouse of the German economy. Today's industry ranges from engineering to high-tech goods. Quality assembly and design make it the third largest car producer in the world.

FOOD AND DRINK

The annual Munich *Oktoberfest* is Germany's biggest beer festival. Entertainment includes parades and musicians.

GENEVA

The Swiss capital, Geneva, lies on the shores of Lake Geneva, Europe's largest alpine lake. This orderly city is a global centre for banking and finance. It is also a base for many international organizations, such as the Red Cross.

Map labels

Baltic Sea

POLAND

DENMARK

NETHERLANDS

BELGIUM

GERMANY

North Frisian Islands (Nordfriesische Inseln)

East Frisian Islands (Ostfriesische Inseln)

Helgoland Bay

Sassnitz, Rügen, Bergen, Stralsund, *Pomeranian Bay*, Greifswald, Wolgast, *Oderhaff*, Anklam, Pasewalk, Penzlau, Angermünde, Eberswalde-Finow, Bad Freienwalde, Frankfurt an der Oder, Guben, Cottbus, Senftenberg, Hoyerswerda, Görlitz, Löbau, Zittau

Rostock, Warnemünde, Demmin, Teterow, Neubrandenburg, Neustrelitz, Neuruppin, Oranienburg, Bernau, **BERLIN**, Ludwigsfelde, Eisenhüttenstadt, Lübben, Lübbenau, Finsterwalde, Bautzen, **Dresden**, Pirna

Puttgarden, Mecklenburger Bucht, Wismar, **Schwerin**, Parchim, Güstrow, Waren, Malchin, Wittstock, Wittenberge, Perleberg, Potsdam, Brandenburg, Riesa, **Chemnitz**, Döbeln, Hainichen, **Zwickau**, *Erzgebirge (Ore Mts.)*, Plauen

Kappeln, *Kieler Bucht*, Kiel, Eutin, **Lübeck**, Boizenburg, Ludwigslust, Salzwedel, Stendal, Halberstadt, Magdeburg, Schönebeck, Bernburg, Dessau, Halle-Neustadt, **Halle**, **Leipzig**, **Gera**, **Jena**, Hof, Münchberg, Marktredwitz

Fehmarn Belt, Fehmarn, Schleswig, Flensburg, Husum, Rendsburg, Heide, Neumünster, Oldenburg, Norderstedt, **Hamburg**, Lüneburg, Dannenberg, Uelzen, Braunschweig, **Wolfsburg**, Peine, Seesen, Northeim, Nordhausen, Eisleben, Weimar, **Erfurt**, Saalfeld, Suhl, Coburg, Kronach, Lichtenfels, Schweinfurt

Westerland, *Schleswig-Holstein*, Rendsburg, Kiel Canal, Elmshorn, Itzehoe, Stade, Rosengarten, Scheessel, Soltau, Celle, **Hannover**, Hildesheim, Hameln, **Göttingen**, Kassel, Melsungen, Bad Hersfeld, Fulda, Gotha, Warburg, *Vogelsberg*

Cuxhaven, **Bremerhaven**, Winsen, Verden, Bassum, Diepholz, **Osnabrück**, Herford, Bielefeld, **Paderborn**, Marsberg, Hünfeld, Marburg an der Lahn, Giessen, Wetzlar, *Hessen*, Wiesbaden, **Mainz**

Norden, Wilhelmshaven, **Oldenburg**, Delmenhorst, **Bremen**, Cloppenburg, Lingen, Rheine, Ahlen, **Dortmund**, Hamm, **Bochum**, Gütersloh, Olpe, **Siegen**, Neuwied, Koblenz, Boppard, Frankfurt am Main, Offenbach

Emden, Leer, Weener, Nordhorn, **Münster**, Borken, Dülmen, **Recklinghausen**, **Duisburg**, **Essen**, Krefeld, **Wuppertal**, Solingen, **Düsseldorf**, Leverkusen, **Cologne (Köln)**, Alsdorf, Blankenheim, *Eifel*, Aachen, Bonn, Bitburg, Wittlich

Rhine, *Ems*, *Weser*, *Elbe*, *Saale*, *Spree*, *Oder*

SWISS WATCHES

The Swiss invented the first wristwatch, the first quartz watch, and the first water-resistant watch. With their worldwide reputation for quality and style, timepieces make up the country's third largest export.

Did you know?

Switzerland has four official languages – German, French, Italian, and Romansch.

Liechtenstein is so small that it only has 19 km (12 miles) of single-track railway.

From 1961–89, 171 people died trying to climb the Berlin Wall.

ALPS

The Alps run from southeast France and spread eastwards through Switzerland and northern Italy into Austria and Slovenia. A popular tourist destination, the Alps are famous for dramatic scenery and winter sports.

SLOVENIA

After centuries of rule by overlords, Slovenia became independent in 1991. Although the population is only two million, the national culture is strong. The famous Lipizzaner show horses are named after the Slovenian farm where they were first bred.

THE HIGH AND GRACEFUL stride of the Lipizzaner horses makes them excel in competitions.

VIENNA

Vienna is a city of baroque buildings, palaces, and famous concert halls. Grand balls with traditional waltzes are still customary. These are a reminder of when the city was the centre of the Austro-Hungarian Empire that controlled large parts of east and central Europe.

THE OPERA BALL in Vienna

Spain and Portugal

THE COUNTRIES OF SPAIN AND PORTUGAL share an area of land called the Iberian Peninsula. In the north, this land is cut off from the rest of Europe by the Pyrenees Mountains, while to the south, it is separated from Africa by the Strait of Gibraltar. The region was once ruled by Islamic people from North Africa, known as the Moors. Evidence of their occupation can still be seen from buildings in the cities of Andalucía. The Moors were eventually defeated in 1492, and for a while, Portugal came under Spanish control, as did much of Europe. During the 20th century, both countries were ruled by brutal dictatorships, which were overthrown in the 1970s. They are now modern democracies.

Did you know?

▶ In Spain, it is customary for families to eat dinner late in the evening, usually around 9 p.m. So after school, children eat a snack called *merienda*.

▶ Bullfights, known as *touradas*, are still popular in Portugal, despite opposition from local and international animal welfare groups.

HARVESTING CORK

Cork is made from the outer bark of the evergreen cork oak tree. The bark is carefully stripped off, flattened, laid out in sheets, and then left to dry. The cork is used for many products, such as stoppers for wine bottles, matting, and tiles. Portugal is the world's leading exporter of cork.

LISBON

The capital city of Portugal is Lisbon, which is situated at the mouth of the River Tagus on a series of steep hills and valleys. In 1755, two-thirds of the city was completely destroyed by an earthquake and tidal wave, but was rebuilt with beautiful squares and public buildings. Many explorers set sail from Lisbon in their quest to find new lands.

TRAMS are a feature of Lisbon streets, and a popular form of transport for both the locals and tourists.

FISHING

Spain and Portugal have well-developed fishing industries – with large-scale fleets and many smaller local fleets. However, overfishing along Portugal's coastline and out in the North Atlantic, plus a massive oil spill off the coast of Galicia in 2002, have put many people's livelihoods at risk.

SPANISH CITIES

The majority of Spanish people live in towns and cities. Madrid is the largest Spanish city and the capital of Spain. Bilbao, where this magnificent modern museum (left) can be found, is the capital of the Basque region. It is a flourishing industrial city, home to Spain's most important port.

THE GUGGENHEIM MUSEUM, opened in 1997

PAMPLONA BULL RUN is an annual fiesta that takes place in July.

FIESTAS

In Spain, many towns hold their own fiestas, or festivals, to celebrate a special event in their history or the birthday of their patron saint. These fiestas differ from one region to another. One of the most famous is held in Pamplona, where the brave run with the bulls.

HOLY WEEK

Easter in Spain is marked by solemn celebrations, known as the Holy Week Processions. These processions vary according to the region, but generally, men wear robes and hoods and carry heavy crosses to show penitence.

FLAMENCO DANCING was created by the gypsies of Andalucía and dates back to the 15th century.

COASTAL RESORTS

Every year, millions of northern Europeans head south for the beaches of southern Spain and Portugal, or for the Spanish Balearic Islands. They are attracted by the warm climate as well as affordable hotels and restaurants.

REGIONAL SPAIN

There are 17 Spanish regions, each with their own distinct cultures and traditions. For example, the south is Andalucía, with traces of Moorish influences and home of flamenco dancing.

Italy

THE BOOT-SHAPED COUNTRY of Italy stretches from the mountainous north down to the Mediterranean Sea. For much of its history, Italy consisted of city-states – such as Florence and Venice – and was only united in 1870. Regional differences in Italy are huge, as each region has its own cuisine, customs, and dialect, and is geographically quite distinct. As a result, many Italians identify themselves first by region and then by country. The national division, however, is between the rich north and the poorer south, a rugged region with several active volcanoes and the occasional severe earthquake. The mainland of Italy includes two tiny independent states – San Marino and Vatican City.

COLOSSEUM

One of Rome's greatest sights is the Colosseum, which opened in AD 80. Deadly gladiatorial combats and animal fights were staged here before crowds of up to 55,000 people.

The oval-shaped Colosseum stood at 189 m (620 ft) high.

HOME OF OPERA

The idea of setting drama to music originated in Italy during the 16th century. Since then, Italian composers, such as Rossini, Verdi, and Puccini, have made opera the most popular musical form in Italy. Many cities have their own opera houses.

ANDREA BOCELLI

CARNIVAL MASKS

Did you know?

The *Sartiglia* of Oristano is a festival in Sardinia. Before the tournament, masked horsemen must pierce the centre of a silver star with their swords while riding past at high speed.

Vatican City has a permanent population of only about 1,000 people, although a further 3,400 come to work in the city-state each day.

More than 600 different types of pasta are eaten in Italy.

CITY OF CANALS

The beautiful city of Venice is made up of 118 islands, 177 canals, and 400 bridges. The only way to get around is to walk or take a boat: a *vaporetto*, *motoscafo*, or *motonave*. The most familiar boat, however, is the gondola. Each year, in the days before Ash Wednesday, Venice hosts a carnival when the city celebrates with fireworks, and everyone wears spectacular masks.

FOOTBALL FANS

Italians are mad about football and fanatically follow the performance of teams such as Juventus, Milan, Roma, and Lazio. Italian teams have regularly won major European championships, and the national team has won the World Cup three times – in 1934, 1938, and 1982.

Adriatic Sea

Brindisi
Lecce
Maglie
Taranto
Manduria
Gallipoli

Strait of Otranto

Bari
Molfetta
Barletta
Manfredonia
Bitonto
Andria
Altamura
Foggia
San Severo
Cerignola
Matera
P u g l i a
Potenza
Golfo di Taranto

Ciro Marino
Crotone
Catanzaro
Siderno

Ionian Sea

La
Sila
Rossano

Campobasso
Isernia
Benevento
Avellino
Campania
Torre del Greco
Salerno
Battipaglia
Appennino Lucano
Lauria
Castrovillari
Sala
Consilina
Sapri
Cosenza
Amantea
Lamezia
**Reggio
di Calabria**
Palmi

*Strait of
Messina*

Naples
(Napoli)
Caserta
Isola
di Capri
*Gulf of
Salerno*
Agropoli

*Tyrrhenian
Sea*

Isole Eolie
Isola Stromboli
Isola Liparı

Messina
Catania
*Mount Etna
3340m*
Simeto

Caltanissetta
Cefalù
Siracusa
Modica

Palermo
S i c i l y
(S i c i l i a)
Agrigento
Gela
Vittoria
Ragusa
Pozzallo

Trapani
Marsala
Alcamo
Castelvetrano

Strait of Sicily

Gozo
MALTA
VALLETTA
Malta

Malta Channel

Isole
Pelagie

Isola di
Pantelleria

M e d i t e r r a n e a n   S e a

(ROMA)
Anzio
Latina
Terracina
Gaeta
*Golfo di
Gaeta*
Isole
Ponziane

*Sardinia
(Sardegna)*
Isola Asinara
la Maddalena
Tempio Pausania
Olbia
Porto Torres
Sassari
Alghero
Ozieri
Siniscola
Nuoro
Macomer
*Punta La Marmora
1834m*
Villacidro
Oristano
Iglesias
Cagliari
Carbonia
Quartu
Sant' Elena

Scale

0 km   50   100
0 miles   50   100

HOME LIFE

Family life is important in Italy, and most people live at home until they marry. This is partly due to lack of cheap housing. Lunch (*pranzo*) is often the main meal of the day.

OLIVE HARVEST

Italy is the world's largest producer of olive oil, followed by Spain and Greece. The oil is produced by first pressing the fruits of the olive tree between steel or stone rollers, then squeezing oil from the pulp using a press. Olive trees flourish in the fertile soils and the mild, frost-free climate of southern Italy.

Olives are gathered in large nets

VATICAN CITY

This tiny state in Rome is the centre of the Roman Catholic church and home to the Pope. As well as St Peter's basilica and the surrounding buildings and gardens, the Vatican boasts Michelangelo's Sistine Chapel. The state has its own flag, postage stamps, and coins.

SWISS GUARDS, in their red, yellow, and blue striped costumes, stand at the gates into Vatican City.

RENAISSANCE ITALY

Florence (below) sits either side of the River Arno. During the 14th century, a new movement in art and architecture, known as the Renaissance, or rebirth, began in Italy. Painters and sculptors, such as Leonardo da Vinci, Michelangelo, and Raphael created beautiful works of art often based on religious themes. Many of these can still be seen in the galleries and churches of Florence.

Central Europe

FOUR COUNTRIES LIE at the heart of Central Europe – Poland, the Czech Republic, Slovakia, and Hungary. The region is characterized by wide plains, broken by gentle hills and the Carpathian Mountain range in the south. In the late 1980s, these countries broke from years of communist rule. The new democratic governments were faced with the problems of trying to modernize their country. These changes are ongoing, but in some of the countries, such as the Czech Republic, there are signs of improvement and a rise in living standards.

GOLDEN PRAGUE

Prague, capital of the Czech Republic, is one of Europe's most beautiful cities. It contains many old buildings with golden roofs and grand squares. Unlike other Central European cities, Prague escaped serious damage during both world wars, and thus retains much of its charm.

PART OF PRAGUE'S colourful history is preserved in buildings around the Old Town Square.

FAMILY FARMS

Poland has one of the largest agricultural sectors in Europe, with more than a quarter of the workforce employed on the land. Most farms are still small, family-run businesses, growing grains, sugar beet, and potatoes. Large numbers of pigs and other animals are also kept.

TRADITIONAL TRADES

The countries of Central Europe, except Slovakia, are heavily industrialized. Vast coal mines, steel works (above), and engineering works dominate the urban landscape. Although some of these sites are old and poorly equipped, these countries are trying to update machinery and introduce measures to improve standards on environmental pollution.

RELIGION

The Roman Catholic Church is very strong throughout Central Europe. Attending mass on Sunday and observing religious holidays, such as Christmas and Easter, are important features of family life.

BELARUS

KALININGRAD
(to Russian Federation)

Baltic Sea

Gulf of Danzig

Vistula Lagoon

Pomeranian Bay

GERMANY

POLAND

Suwałki
Augustów
Goldap
Kuźnica
Sokółka
Białystok
Łapy
Biała Podlaska
Międzyrzec Podlaski
Radzyń Podlaski
Włodawa
Chełm
Krasnystaw
Zamość
Tomaszów Lubelski
Lubelski
Bielsk Podlaski
Siemiatycze
Siedlce
Lublin
Bartoszyce
Kętrzyn
Gizycko
Ełk
Pisz
Łomża
Zambrów
Bug
Łuków
Garwolin
Ryki
Puławy
Ostrowiec
Świętokrzyski
Sandomierz
Tarnobrzeg
Stalowa Wola
Suwałki
Gołdap
Grajewo
Narew
Góra Kalwaria
Pruszków
WARSAW
(WARSZAWA)
Radom
Skarżysko-Kamienna
Starachowice
Kielce
Jędrzejów
Zawiercie
Lidzbark
Warmiński
Dobre Miasto
Biskupiec
Olsztyn
Szczytno
Nidzica
Mława
Ostrołęka
Ostrów
Pułtusk
Maków
Mazowiecki
Ciechanów
Płońsk
Wyszków
Nowy Dwór Mazowiecki
Tomaszów
Mazowiecki
Piotrków
Trybunalski
Radomsko
Częstochowa
Braniewo
Elbląg
Malbork
Ostróda
Iława
Kwidzyn
Grudziądz
Brodnica
Rypin
Sierpc
Płock
Włocławek
Kutno
Łódź
Zgierz
Pabianice
Bełchatów
Wieluń
Kłobuck
Opole
Bytom
Gdynia
Gdańsk
Tczew
Rumia
Wejherowo
Wladysławowo
Kartuzy
Kościerzyna
Chojnice
Świecie
Chełmża
Toruń
Lipno
Inowrocław
Mogilno
Gniezno
Konin
Koło
Sieradz
Kalisz
Ostrów
Wielkopolski
Kępno
Wrocław
Brzeg
Oława
Ząbkowice Śląskie
Ustka
Słupsk
Lębork
Bytów
Słanowo
Sławno
Koszalin
Kołobrzeg
Białogard
Świdwin
Nowogard
Stargard Szczeciński
Wałcz
Piła
Trzcianka
Chodzież
Oborniki
Poznań
Września
Pleszew
Leszno
Rawicz
Głogów
Lublin
Legnica
Jelenia Góra
Świdnica
Wałbrzych
Goleniów
Świnoujście
Szczecin
Pyrzyce
Myślibórz
Gorzów
Wielkopolski
Międzyrzecz
Świebodzin
Sulechów
Zielona Góra
Nowa Sól
Żagań
Żary
Szprotawa
Lubań
Zgorzelec
Liberec
Wisła
Warta
Notec
Oder
Oder

Mazury

Śnieżka
1602m

Sudety

Wyżyna Lubelska

M a ł o p o l s k a

Déčin
Ústí nad Labem
Teplice
Chomutov
Most
Karlovy Vary
Lovosice
Turnov

Traditional folk culture is still preserved in Slovakia, and is seen as an essential part of regional identity. Throughout the year, especially during the summer months, folk festivals are held in many towns. The people dress up in their colourful regional folk costumes, play traditional instruments, and sing and dance.

LANDSCAPE OF SLOVAKIA

Slovakia is divided between a fertile, lowland south and a more rugged, mountainous north. The country is far more rural than its industrial neighbour, the Czech Republic. Most Slovaks live in small towns and mountain villages. The Tatra Mountains in the north are popular with skiers and hikers, who bring in much-needed tourist income.

Did you know?

- In 1993, Czechoslovakia was divided into two countries – the Czech Republic and Slovakia.

- Budapest was once two cities – Buda on the right bank of the River Danube, and Pest on the left bank.

- Poland has the oldest operating salt mine, now a World Heritage Site, in Wieliczka near Kraków. The layers of salt go down 327 m (1,073 ft).

INDUSTRIAL LIFE

The Czech Republic is Central Europe's most industrialized country. It is renowned for its centuries-old glass industry. The region also produces some of the world's best-known beers. Pilsener lager, for example, originated in the town of Plzeň, while Budweiser beer has been brewed at České Budějovice for over a century.

HOT SPRINGS

A land of fertile plains, Hungary is also famous for its numerous hot springs. In the capital city of Budapest, there are more than 100 hot springs. The warm waters rise naturally from the ground, and the spas and baths are centred on these springs. They are as popular today as they were centuries ago, when the Romans used the hot springs on the Buda side of the city

SZÉCHENYI BATHS has the hottest spa water in Budapest.

Southeast Europe

UNTIL 1991 CROATIA, Bosnia and Herzegovina, Serbia, Montenegro, and Macedonia were all part of Yugoslavia. Ethnic tensions between the Serbs and other peoples in Yugoslavia caused a series of bloody wars that broke the country up. Peace was eventually restored in 1999, but all five countries have suffered intense economic problems as a result. So, too, has Albania since its communist government collapsed. The six nations do, however, have huge potential, with considerable agricultural and mineral resources. In the north, the River Danube is an important trading route for both Croatia and Serbia, while Croatia has a flourishing tourist industry along its beautiful Adriatic coast.

THE ADRIATIC

The long Adriatic coastline of Croatia is one of the most beautiful in Europe. The wooded hillsides, pretty beaches, such as Markarska (right), islands, and historic towns once attracted tourists from all over Europe. Now that the country is no longer involved in the war, tourists are returning, contributing vital income to the national economy.

SPORTING ACHIEVEMENT

Croatia is a great sporting nation. Skier Janica Kostelic became Croatia's first triple Olympic champion, after winning three gold medals at the 2002 Winter Games. In January 2003, Janica and her brother, Ivica, both won World Cup Alpine Races.

JANICA KOSTELIC

Did you know?

▶ The Dalmatian dog is named after the coastal region of Dalmatia in Croatia, its first known home.

▶ In the mountains of Albania, announcements of a death, birth, or marriage are passed from one house to another by a gunshot or a shout that echoes through the mountains.

▶ Bosnia and Herzegovina hosts the Sarajevo annual film festival.

GROWING FOOD

The most fertile area in this region lies along the River Danube in northern Serbia and eastern Croatia. Here, vegetables, fruit, maize, and cereals are grown, as well as grapes for wine-making. Most farms are small-scale family businesses, growing a wide range of crops.

FAMILY-RUN ALLOTMENTS

DIFFERENT SCRIPTS

Croatian and Serbian languages are very similar but the people of Croatia, a predominantly Roman Catholic country, write in Roman script, as do Bosnians. Serbians are mainly Eastern Orthodox, and write using both Roman and Russian Cyrillic script.

MAGAZINE WITH CYRILLIC SCRIPT

MAGAZINE WITH ROMAN SCRIPT

Traditional folk culture is still preserved in Slovakia, and is seen as an essential part of regional identity. Throughout the year, especially during the summer months, folk festivals are held in many towns. The people dress up in their colourful regional folk costumes, play traditional instruments, and sing and dance.

LANDSCAPE OF SLOVAKIA

Slovakia is divided between a fertile, lowland south and a more rugged, mountainous north. The country is far more rural than its industrial neighbour, the Czech Republic. Most Slovaks live in small towns and mountain villages. The Tatra Mountains in the north are popular with skiers and hikers, who bring in much-needed tourist income.

Did you know?

- In 1993, Czechoslovakia was divided into two countries – the Czech Republic and Slovakia.
- Budapest was once two cities – Buda on the right bank of the River Danube, and Pest on the left bank.
- Poland has the oldest operating salt mine, now a World Heritage Site, in Wieliczka near Kraków. The layers of salt go down 327 m (1,073 ft).

INDUSTRIAL LIFE

The Czech Republic is Central Europe's most industrialized country. It is renowned for its centuries-old glass industry. The region also produces some of the world's best-known beers. Pilsener lager, for example, originated in the town of Plzeň, while Budweiser beer has been brewed at České Budějovice for over a century.

HOT SPRINGS

A land of fertile plains, Hungary is also famous for its numerous hot springs. In the capital city of Budapest, there are more than 100 hot springs. The warm waters rise naturally from the ground, and the spas and baths are centred on these springs. They are as popular today as they were centuries ago, when the Romans used the hot springs on the Buda side of the city.

SZÉCHENYI BATHS has the hottest spa water in Budapest.

Southeast Europe

UNTIL 1991 CROATIA, Bosnia and Herzegovina, Serbia, Montenegro, and Macedonia were all part of Yugoslavia. Ethnic tensions between the Serbs and other peoples in Yugoslavia caused a series of bloody wars that broke the country up. Peace was eventually restored in 1999, but all five countries have suffered intense economic problems as a result. So, too, has Albania since its communist government collapsed. The six nations do, however, have huge potential, with considerable agricultural and mineral resources. In the north, the River Danube is an important trading route for both Croatia and Serbia, while Croatia has a flourishing tourist industry along its beautiful Adriatic coast.

SPORTING ACHIEVEMENT

Croatia is a great sporting nation. Skier Janica Kostelic became Croatia's first triple Olympic champion, after winning three gold medals at the 2002 Winter Games. In January 2003, Janica and her brother, Ivica, both won World Cup Alpine Races.

JANICA KOSTELIC

THE ADRIATIC

The long Adriatic coastline of Croatia is one of the most beautiful in Europe. The wooded hillsides, pretty beaches, such as Markarska (right), islands, and historic towns once attracted tourists from all over Europe. Now that the country is no longer involved in the war, tourists are returning, contributing vital income to the national economy.

Did you know?

▶ The Dalmatian dog is named after the coastal region of Dalmatia in Croatia, its first known home.

▶ In the mountains of Albania, announcements of a death, birth, or marriage are passed from one house to another by a gunshot or a shout that echoes through the mountains.

▶ Bosnia and Herzegovina hosts the Sarajevo annual film festival.

GROWING FOOD

The most fertile area in this region lies along the River Danube in northern Serbia and eastern Croatia. Here, vegetables, fruit, maize, and cereals are grown, as well as grapes for wine-making. Most farms are small-scale family businesses, growing a wide range of crops.

FAMILY-RUN ALLOTMENTS

DIFFERENT SCRIPTS

Croatian and Serbian languages are very similar but the people of Croatia, a predominantly Roman Catholic country, write in Roman script, as do Bosnians. Serbians are mainly Eastern Orthodox, and write using both Roman and Russian Cyrillic script.

MAGAZINE WITH ROMAN SCRIPT

MAGAZINE WITH CYRILLIC SCRIPT

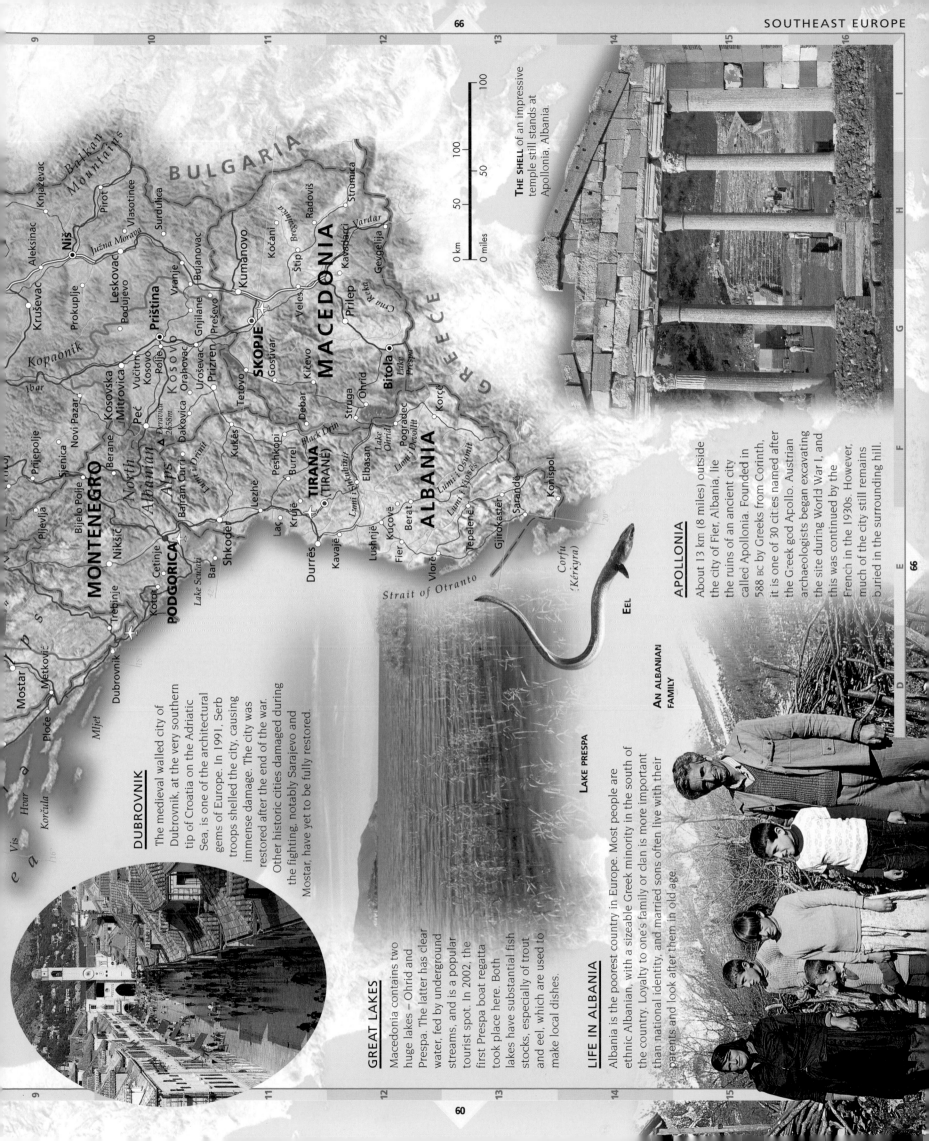

THE SHELL of an impressive temple still stands at Apollonia, Albania.

0 km — 50 — 100
0 miles — 50 — 100

APOLLONIA

About 13 km (8 miles) outside the city of Fier, Albania, lie the ruins of an ancient city called Apollonia. Founded in 588 BC by Greeks from Corinth, it is one of 30 cities named after the Greek god Apollo. Austrian archaeologists began excavating the site during World War I, and this was continued by the French in the 1930s. However, much of the city still remains buried in the surrounding hill.

AN ALBANIAN FAMILY

EEL

LAKE PRESPA

DUBROVNIK

The medieval walled city of Dubrovnik, at the very southern tip of Croatia on the Adriatic Sea, is one of the architectural gems of Europe. In 1991, Serb troops shelled the city, causing immense damage. The city was restored after the end of the war. Other historic cities damaged during the fighting, notably Sarajevo and Mostar, have yet to be fully restored.

GREAT LAKES

Macedonia contains two huge lakes – Ohrid and Prespa. The latter has clear water, fed by underground streams, and is a popular tourist spot. In 2002, the first Prespa boat regatta took place here. Both lakes have substantial fish stocks, especially of trout and eel, which are used to make local dishes.

LIFE IN ALBANIA

Albania is the poorest country in Europe. Most people are ethnic Albanian, with a sizeable Greek minority in the south of the country. Loyalty to one's family or clan is more important than national identity, and married sons often live with their parents and look after them in old age.

Bulgaria and Greece

FOR MORE THAN FOUR CENTURIES Bulgaria and Greece were ruled by the Ottoman Turks. Bulgaria gained independence in 1908, while southern Greece became independent in 1832, and was joined by northern Greece in 1913. After World War II, Bulgaria became a communist state, and Greece was ruled by the military from 1967 until 1974. Both states are now democracies, although Bulgaria remains relatively poor and underdeveloped in comparison with Greece, which is a member of the European Union. Although they share a common border, the two countries are quite different. The Greek mainland is mountainous with only one-third of the land suitable for cultivation. By contrast, Bulgaria is more fertile with a strong agricultural tradition. Tourism is an important source of income to both countries, with visitors flocking to the Black Sea resorts in Bulgaria, to the Greek mainland to see the ancient ruins, and to the Greek islands in search of sandy beaches.

BULGARIAN AGRICULTURE

Wheat, maize, and other cereals grow in the fertile Danube river valley in the north of the country. Tobacco (right) grows in the Maritsa river valley in the southeast, while grapes for the wine industry flourish on the slopes of the Balkan Mountains. The festival of Kukerov Dan, with traditional processions, celebrates the start of the agricultural year.

CITY LIFE

Bulgarians make up about 85 per cent of the total population of the country. The rest are Turkish, Macedonian, or Roma. Most people live in apartment blocks in the main towns and cities. They are more likely to use public transport as not all households have a car.

TRAMS provide an efficient way for people to get around the city of Sofia.

Did you know?

- Every June, Bulgaria holds a Festival of the Roses to celebrate the flowers harvested for their oils.

- First held in Athens in 1896, the modern Olympic Games were staged there again in 2004.

- Melbourne in Australia has the second largest number of Greek speakers in the world after Athens.

ARCHITECTURE

Bulgaria contains many fine old churches, monasteries, and mosques, despite the damage done to the country during World War II. Rila Monastery (above) was founded by a hermit monk who took to the mountains in search of solitude in 927 AD. After a fire in 1833, Rila was rebuilt and the magnificent church now boasts three great domes, a museum, and 1,200 frescoes.

LANGUAGE

The 24 characters in the Greek alphabet date from the 8th century BC, when the first texts were written in classical Greek. Since then, the language has evolved and is now spoken by 11 million people around the world.

Κέντρο Centre
Λαμία Lamia
Θεσσαλονίκη Thessaloniki

Black Sea

ROMANIA

SERBIA

MACEDONIA

BULGARIA

TURKEY

Silistra · Dobrich · Varna · Zlatni Pyasŭtsi · Kavarna · Durankulak · Varnenski Zaliv
Ruse · Razgrad · Shumen · Burgas · Burgaski Zaliv
Pleven · Veliko Tŭrnovo · Sliven · Stara Zagora · Plovdiv
SOFIA (SOFIYA) · Pernik · Kyustendil · Blagoevgrad
Salonica

GREEK WEDDING

About 94 per cent of Greeks follow the Greek Orthodox religion, and weddings follow the rites of the Orthodox Church. At the ceremony, it is traditional for the best man to place wreaths of orange blossom, linked by a silk ribbon, on the heads of the bride and the groom (above).

ATHENS

The capital city of Greece is dominated by the Parthenon, a temple built in 447–438 BC on a rocky hill known as the Acropolis. Modern-day Athens is a sprawling city where the large number of cars cause serious air pollution.

GREEK ISLANDS

More than 2,000 islands lie off the mainland of Greece. The Cyclades and Dodecanese in the Aegean Sea are often rocky and arid, while the Ionian Islands, such as Zakynthos (below), are more fertile. Tourists often travel from one island to another by ferry or hovercraft.

CORINTH CANAL

The Corinth Canal was built to provide a shortcut for ships between the Aegean and Ionian Seas. Dug through solid limestone, the steep-sided canal was begun in 1882 by the French and completed in 1893 by the Greeks.

EARTHQUAKES

The idyllic landscape of the Greek Islands, such as Santorini (left), can be rocked by earthquakes. This is because the islands and mainland of Greece, as well as Bulgaria, sit on a plate boundary. There is now a Greek Seismic Code that outlines regulations on all new buildings.

Aegean Sea

Dodecanese (Dodekánisos)

Rhodes (Ródos)
Lindos
Rhodes (Ródos)
Chálki
Kásos
Kárpathos
Kárpathos
Kattavia
Saría
Sými
Kos
Kos
Tílos
Nísyros
Léros
Agiá Marína
Agathonísi
Árkoi
Leipsoí
Pátmos
Kálimnos
Astypálaia
Ákra Floúda
Amorgós
Amorgós
Anáfi
Thíra
Thíra
Náxos
Náxos
Íos
Íos
Páros
Páros
Folégandros
Síkinos

Ikaría
Sámos
Sámos
Thérma

Mýkonos
Tínos
Tínos
Ándros
Ándros
Ermoúpoli
Sýros
Kýthnos
Kýthnos
Kástro
Sérifos
Sífnos
Mílos
Mílos

Cyclades (Kykládes)

Sea of Crete (Kritikó Pélagos)

Crete (Kríti)
Irákleio
Neápoli
Sitéia
Ágios Nikólaos
Ierápetra
Myrtos
Kántanos
Tympáki
Zarós
Spíli
Sfákia
Pánormos
Kastélli
Chaniá
Lefká Óri
Díki Óri
Gávdos

Mediterranean Sea

Mírtoo Pelagos

Mediterranean Sea

Límnos
Ágios Efstrátios
Mýrina
Límnos
Akrotírio Pínnes
Akrotírio Drépano
Leshos (Lésvos)
Mytilíni
Kalloní
Ántissa
Plomári
Chíos
Chíos
Psará
Antípsara
Skyros
Skíros

Euboea (Évvoia)
Kými
Kárystos
Marathónas
Kálamos
Kéa
Kéa
Thíra
Kéfalos

Northern Sporades (Vóreioi Sporádes)
Kyrá Panagía
Alónnisos
Skiáthos
Skópelos
Strofyliá
Chalkída
Aliveri

ATHENS (ATHÍNA)
Keratéa
Lávrio
Mándra
Megara
Piraeus (Peiraiás) (Peiraiás)
Aígina
Palaiá Epídavros
Póros
Ýdra
Ermióni
Náfplio
Árgos
Leonídi
Neápoli
Kýthira
Kýthira
Karavás
Gýtheio
Areópoli
Gerolimenas
Daímon á
Geráki
Koróni
Kalamáta
Spárti
Messíni
Kyparissía
Pylos
Zacháro
Pyrgos

GREECE

Pindus Mountains (Pindos)

Lárisa
Litóchoro
Olympus
Vólos
Agiá
Stómio
Thermaic Gulf
Velvendós
Kozán
Grevená
Kranéa
Métsovo
Ioánnina
Igoumenítsa
Párga
Préveza
Árta
Amfilochía
Agrínio
Thérmo
Messolóngi
Náfpaktos
Pátra
Káto Achaía
Aígio
Lecheó
Lechainá
Gastoúni
Amaliáda

Gulf of Corinth
Corinth (Kórinthos)
Corinth Canal
Xylokastro
Neméa
Tripoli

Peloponnese (Pelopónnisos)

Ionian Islands (Iónioi Nísoi)

Corfu (Kérkyra)
Sidári
Kassiópi
Lefkáda
Lefkáda
Vasilikí
Kefaloniá (Kefalliniá)
Lixoúri
Argostóli
Póros
Keri
Zákynthos

Ionian Sea

GREEK WEDDING

0 km   100   100   50
0 miles   100   50   50

Ukraine, Moldova & Romania

THROUGHOUT MUCH OF THE last century, Ukraine and Moldova formed part of the Soviet Union, while Romania was ruled for 20 years by the dictator Nicolae Ceausescu. In 1989 Ceausescu was overthrown, while Ukraine and Moldova became independent in 1991. Today the three countries are struggling to come to terms with their communist inheritance and transform themselves into modern democracies. All three lack modern technology and face serious economic and environmental problems arising from outdated industry. They also face increasing ethnic tensions with their minority populations – Hungarians in Romania, as well as Russians left behind in Ukraine and Moldova after the collapse of the Soviet Union.

CITY LIFE

Romania has many cities and towns with a mix of old and new buildings. Sibiu (left) was founded in the 12th century and, at one time, had 19 guilds – each representing a different craft – within its city walls. Much remains from this colourful history, especially in the painted buildings of the old town.

FOLK CUSTOMS

Despite years of communist rule, folk customs thrived in the rural areas of Romania and Ukraine. In Ukraine, singers perform *dumas*, historical epics that tell of slavery under the Turks. One of the traditional instruments is a *bandura* (left), a stringed instrument that sounds like a harpsichord.

DRACULA'S CASTLE

Situated in Transylvania – and a favourite tourist destination – lies Bran Castle. This is where author Bram Stoker's fictional blood-drinking Count Dracula lived. The story is probably based on 15th-century Romanian prince Vlad Dracul who reigned for less than 10 years but caused more than 50,000 deaths.

Did you know?

▶ The word Transylvania means "land beyond the forests".

▶ Russia's famous beetroot soup – *borscht* – comes from Ukraine.

▶ Built entirely underground, Crivoca winery north of Chisinau, Moldova, stretches over 60 km (37 miles).

EASTER BREAD

In Romania, Easter is celebrated with a meal of roast lamb served with a bread called *cozonac*. This is made by pounding nuts, raisins, and even cocoa, into the dough.

BELARUS

Pripet
Pripet Marshes

POLAND

Kovel'
Styr
Sarny

Volodymyr Volyns'kyy
Kivertsi
Olevs'k
Ovruch

Luts'k   Rivne
Novohrad-Volyns'kyy
Korosten'

Sokal'
Dubno
Radom

Zhovkva
Chervonohrad
Shepetivka
Zhytomyr

Yavoriv
L'viv
Kremenets'
Izyaslav
Polonne

Horodok
Zolochiv
Zbarazh
Starokostyantyniv
Berdychiv

Sambir
Khodoriv
Berezhany
Kozyatyn

Boryslav
Ternopil'
UK

Stryy
Khmel'nyts'kyy

Dolyna
Kalush
Chortkiv
Vinnytsya   Lypo

Uzhhorod
Ivano-Frankivs'k
Kam'yanets'-Podil's'kyy
Zhmerynka

Nadvirna
Podil's'ka Vysoch

Mukacheve
Kolomyya
Chernivtsi
Mohyliv-Podil's'kyy
Hay

Berehove
Khust
Dniester
Tul

Vynohradiv
Negreşti-Oaş
Hora Hoverla 2061m

Satu Mare
Carpathian Mountains
Darabani
Soroca

Baia Mare
Borşa
Rădăuţi
Dorohoi

Carei
Sight
Suceava
Botoşani
Bălţi

Marghita
Năsăud
Fălticeni
Rîbniţa
Kotovs

Şimleu Silvaniei
Zălău
Dej
Paşcani   Ungheni
MOLDOVA
Călăraşi

Oradea
Bistriţa
Topliţa
Bicaz
Roman
Iaşi
Dubăsari

Aleşd
Cluj-Napoca
CHIŞINĂU

Salonta
Transylvania
Turda
Târgu Mureş
Piatra-Neamţ
Hînceşti
Tighina

Beiuş
Muntii Apuseni
Bacău
Vaslui
Tiraşp

Curtici
Cristuru Secuiesc
Miercurea-Ciuc
Basarabeasca

Arad
Lipova
Alba Iulia
Mediaş
Târgu Ocna
Bârlad
Giadîr-

Jimbolia
Mureş
Deva
ROMANIA
Artsyz

Timişoara
Lugoj
Hunedoara
Sibiu
Făgăraş
Sfântu Gheorghe
Bolhrad
Ozero Yalpu

Oţelu Roşu
Haţeg
Vârful Moldoveanu 2544m
Tecuci
Reni
Ki

Bocşa
Petroşani
Transylvanian Alps
Braşov
Focşani
Cahul

Oraviţa
Reşiţa
Câmpulung
Sinaia
Râmnicu Sărat
Galaţi
Izmayi

Orşova
Motru
Târgu Jiu
Râmnicu Vâlcea
Câmpina
Mizil
Brăila
Mācin
Tulcea

Drobeta-Turnu Severin
Strehaia
Târgovişte
Buzău
Babadag
Lacul Raz

Filiaşi
Piteşti
Titu
Ploieşti
Urziceni
Hârşova
Lacul Sinoi

Craiova
Slatina
Buftea
Ialomiţa
Tăndărei

Calafat
Băileşti
Caracal
BUCHAREST (BUCUREŞTI)
Feteşti
Medgidia
Constanţa

Roşiori de Vede
Corabia
Alexandria
Călăraşi
Eforie Sud

Danube (Dunărea)
Zimnicea
Giurgiu
Olteniţa
Mangalia

BULGARIA

SLOVAKIA
HUNGARY
SERBIA
Timiş
Olt
Jiu
Prut

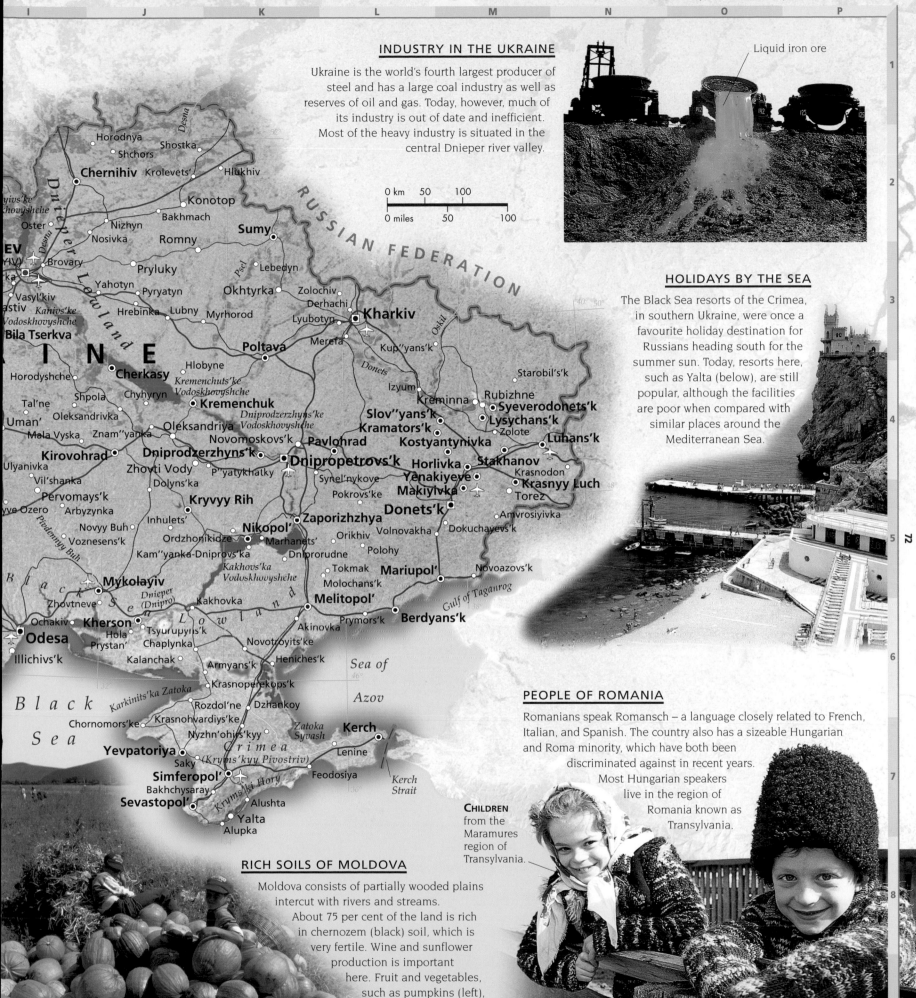

INDUSTRY IN THE UKRAINE

Ukraine is the world's fourth largest producer of steel and has a large coal industry as well as reserves of oil and gas. Today, however, much of its industry is out of date and inefficient. Most of the heavy industry is situated in the central Dnieper river valley.

Liquid iron ore

HOLIDAYS BY THE SEA

The Black Sea resorts of the Crimea, in southern Ukraine, were once a favourite holiday destination for Russians heading south for the summer sun. Today, resorts here, such as Yalta (below), are still popular, although the facilities are poor when compared with similar places around the Mediterranean Sea.

PEOPLE OF ROMANIA

Romanians speak Romansch – a language closely related to French, Italian, and Spanish. The country also has a sizeable Hungarian and Roma minority, which have both been discriminated against in recent years. Most Hungarian speakers live in the region of Romania known as Transylvania.

CHILDREN from the Maramures region of Transylvania.

RICH SOILS OF MOLDOVA

Moldova consists of partially wooded plains intercut with rivers and streams. About 75 per cent of the land is rich in chernozem (black) soil, which is very fertile. Wine and sunflower production is important here. Fruit and vegetables, such as pumpkins (left), also grow well.

Baltic States & Belarus

THE THREE BALTIC STATES, Estonia, Latvia, and Lithuania, all share a small stretch of coast on the Baltic Sea. Belarus lies between Poland, Ukraine, and the Russian Federation. Following independence from the Soviet Union in 1991, all these countries faced problems such as price rises, food shortages, and pollution. However, the Baltic States have since tried to reform their societies and economies along western lines. Belarus has kept close links with Russia and has been the slowest to reform. This mainly rural country remains isolated from the rest of Europe and, with few natural resources, remains one of its poorest nations.

SINGING REVOLUTION

Estonia is known for its classical music tradition – most notably its choirs. This love of music was most powerful when people raised their voices during the Singing Revolution in 1988 (right), part of their move towards indpendence.

POLITICAL RALLY IN TALLINN

TALLINN OLD TOWN

With its colourful buildings, turreted walls, and gabled roofs Tallinn is one of the best-preserved capital cities in Europe. All the winding, cobbled streets lead to the Town Hall Square (left).

AMBER

Two-thirds of the world's amber, the fossilized resin of pine trees, is washed up from the seabed along the Baltic coast. Amber is used to make jewellery, among other things.

Did you know?

▶ Riga, the capital of Latvia, is often ice-bound from December to April.

▶ Rubbing amber with a cloth will make it electrically charged, attracting bits of paper.

▶ Belarus used to be known as Belorussia, a name that means "White Russia".

▶ Lithuania is the only one of the Baltic countries whose respect for animals means that they have no zoos or circuses.

RUSSIAN FEDERATION

Gulf of Finland

Baltic Sea

Gulf of Riga

ESTONIA

Tallinn, Maardu, Loksa, Aegviidu, Kunda, Rakvere, Rakke, Kohtla-Järve, Sillamäe, Narva, Narva Bay, Narva Reservoir, Lake Peipus, Lake Pskov, Rapina, Võnnu, Tartu, Põlva, Võru, Otepää, Valga, Tõrva, Rõngu, Elva, Puurmani, Pajamuse, Kallaste, Viljandi, Mõisaküla, Suure-Jaani, Kilingi-Nõmme, Pärnu, Sindi, Audru, Virtsu, Lihula, Haapsalu, Risti, Rapla, Paide, Tapa, Raasiku, Keila, Paldiski, Hiiumaa, Kärdla, Vormsi, Emmaste, Väinameri, Saaremaa, Orissaare, Kuressaare, Sääre

LATVIA

Rīga, Jūrmala, Saulkrasti, Ainaži, Salacgrīva, Mērsrags, Kolka, Roja, Kolkasrags, Ventspils, Mazirbe, Ugāle, Talsi, Kuldīga, Dundaga, Kandava, Saldus, Broceni, Jelgava, Dobele, Bauska, Iecava, Baldone, Ogre, Aizkraukle, Pļaviņas, Madona, Gulbene, Balvi, Alūksne, Ape, Valka, Valmiera, Cēsis, Smiltene, Jaunpiebalga, Sigulda, Līgatne, Viesīte, Jēkabpils, Līvāni, Krustpils, Varakļāni, Rēzekne, Ludza, Kārsava, Malta, Dagda, Krāslava, Daugavpils, Spogi, Western Dvina, Lubāns Ezers, Gaujiena

LITHUANIA

Vilnius, Kaunas, Šiauliai, Panevėžys, Klaipėda, Mažeikiai, Telšiai, Plungė, Kretinga, Gargždai, Šilutė, Šilalė, Tauragė, Jurbarkas, Raseiniai, Kelmė, Kuršėnai, Radviliškis, Joniškis, Pakruojis, Pasvalys, Biržai, Kupiškis, Rokiškis, Obeliai, Zarasai, Anykščiai, Utena, Ukmergė, Jonava, Kėdainiai, Kaišiadorys, Dotnuva, Naujamiestis, Subačius, Visaginas, Vidzy, Giedraičiai, Širvintos, Elektrėnai, Trakai, Prienai, Vilkaviškis, Marijampolė, Kalvarija, Alytus, Merkinė, Varėna, Druskininkai, Veisiejai, Lazdijai, Rudiškės, Neris, Neman

KALININGRAD (to Russian Federation)

Kaliningrad, Pionerskiy, Zelenogradsk, Neringa, Primorsk, Svetlogorsk, Gvardeysk, Chernyakhovsk, Gusev, Cherniakhovsk, Zheleznodorozhny, Mamonovo, Bagrationovsk, Courland Lagoon

BELARUS (RUSSIAN FEDERATION area)

Navapolatsk, Polatsk, Yezyaryshcha, Harany, Vyerkhnyadzvinsk, Drysa, Bihosava, Pastavy, Vyetryna, Myadzel, Hlybokaye, Myory, Vyetryna

POLAND

TALLINN

RĪGA

VILNIUS

KAUNAS

Panevėžys

Šiauliai

Liepāja

Ventspils

Klaipėda

Kaliningrad

MINSK CITY

The capital of Belarus, Minsk, was destroyed during World War II and then rebuilt in a starkly modern style. Minsk is the country's economic centre.: Cars, trucks and tractors, chemicals, timber products, and a range of high-tech goods are all produced here. Farm produce (above) is also sold in the markets.

FORESTS AND LAKES

All four countries are low-lying with many moors, bogs, unspoiled lakes, and fir and pine forests. Forestry is an important industry, providing wood pulp for paper making, and timber for furniture and houses.

FERNS THRIVE in this Latvian forest.

GYMNASTICS

The former Soviet Union worked its young athletes and gymnasts extremely hard in order to win Olympic medals and thus national glory. Many of the most famous gymnasts came from Belarus, notably Olga Korbut and, more recently, Svetlana Boginskya (right), who has won 3 gold, 1 silver, and 1 bronze Olympic medals.

FARMING

The fertile soils and flat landscapes make this region good for farming. The Baltic States, particularly Latvia (left), have large dairy farms. Belarus is a major producer of flax – used to make linen and other products. Potatoes – used to make vodka – sugar beet and other root crops are also grown here.

LITHUANIAN COSTUME

In some Lithuanian villages people still wear traditional folk costume, especially for festive occasions. Women's clothing is generally colourful (left) and might include a white linen shirt, a skirt, and an apron. The decoration and style of the costume shows which region of Lithuania the wearer comes from.

TEXTILES

Development of the textile industry (above) in these countries is strong, with foreign investment from Sweden (for Latvia) and Indonesia (for Lithuania) helping growth. Clothes, bedlinen, curtains, and towels are just some of the items made for export.

Scale:
0 km   50   100
0 miles   50   100

RUSSIAN FEDERATION

B E L A R U S

POLAND

U K R A I N E

Pripet Marshes

European Russia

SEPARATED FROM ASIAN RUSSIA by the Ural Mountains, European Russia is so large that it spans four time zones. The climate and landscape range from cold desert and frozen tundra in the north to the warm coast of the Black Sea in the southwest. Forests and grassy steppes cover huge areas of the country. More than 100 million people – two-thirds of the total Russian population – live in European Russia, most of them in cities such as the capital, Moscow. Since the collapse of communism in 1991, many Russians have experienced a fall in their standard of living. There are shortages of food and manufactured goods, crime rates have risen, and so has unemployment. As a result, Russia is the only European country in which life expectancy has fallen in the last decade.

ST PETERSBURG

Once Russia's capital, St Petersburg was built in the 18th century by Csar Peter the Great as a "Window on the West". Today, it is a popular tourist destination, full of grand palaces and extravagant architecture (left). The city spreads over some 40 islands, linked by a network of canals and rivers.

THE CHURCH ON SPILLED BLOOD marks the spot where Tsar Alexander II was murdered in 1881.

BALLET

Russia is famous for its ballet companies, such as the Bolshoi Ballet of Moscow and the Kirov Ballet of St Petersburg. Most of the ballets performed are classics, such as Swan Lake or Sleeping Beauty. Developed in Europe in the 19th century, ballet became a popular entertainment in the 20th century.

SLEEPING BEAUTY is performed here by dancers from the Kirov Ballet.

EDUCATION

Children have to attend school here from the age of 7 through to 17. Although the state system is free, education has declined since the fall of communism due to chronic underfunding. Private schools are now becoming increasingly popular.

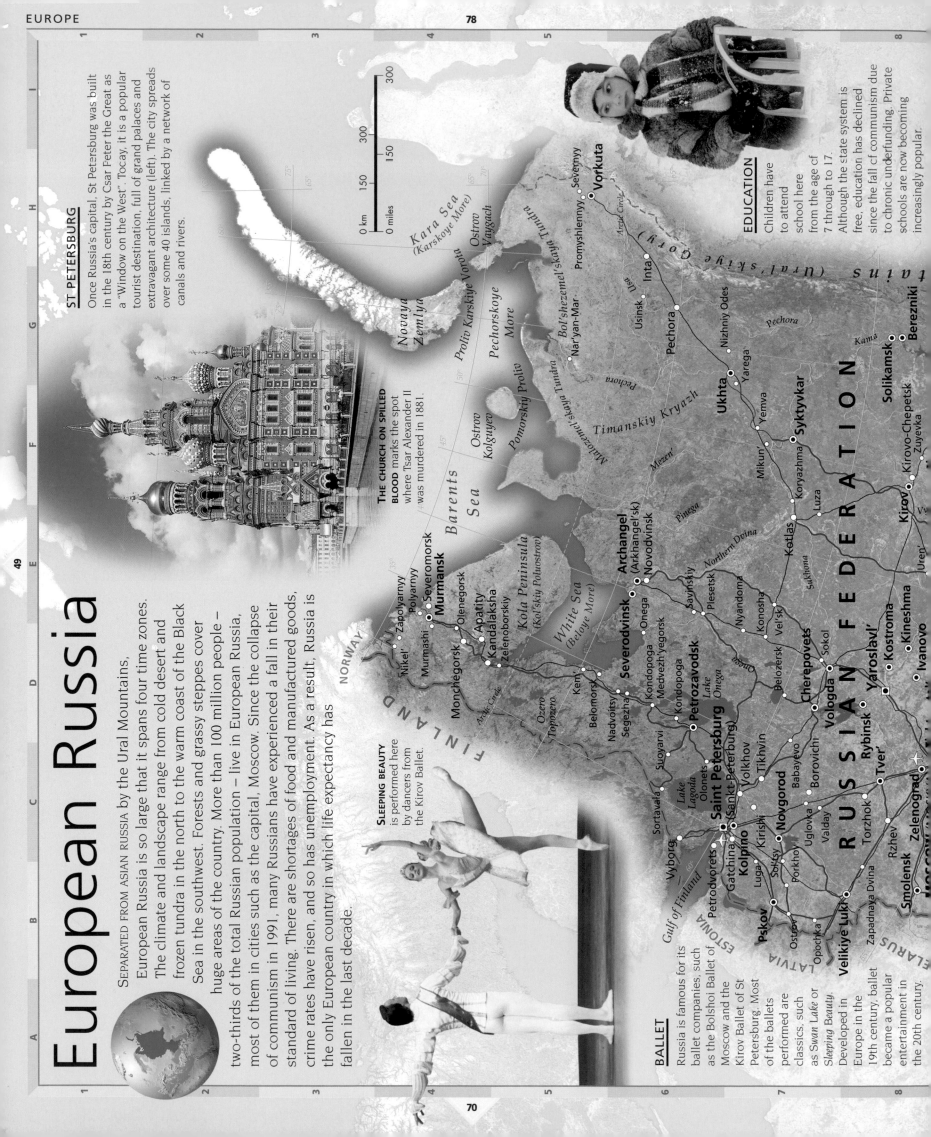

INDUSTRIAL SMOG casts a haze over Moscow.

RURAL LIFE

Rural life has become extremely tough since the economic collapse of large-scale farms in the 1990s, with many people living in poverty. Smaller co-operatives and farms (above) have sprung up, and the agricultural industry is going through a painful period of reform. Because of the harsh climate, only 10 per cent of the land is suitable for agriculture.

RUSSIAN icons show religious scenes painted on wood.

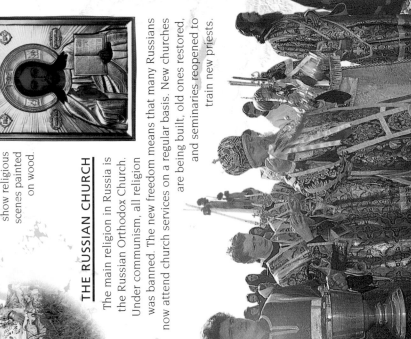

THE RUSSIAN CHURCH

The main religion in Russia is the Russian Orthodox Church. Under communism, all religion was banned. The new freedom means that many Russians now attend church services on a regular basis. New churches are being built, old ones restored, and seminaries reopened to train new priests.

THE TARTARS

Russia's largest ethnic minority, the Tartars (below), are an Islamic people descended from the Mongols. They live in the Tatarstan Republic, midway between Moscow and the Urals.

POLLUTION

The communists invested heavily in industry, but their outdated methods of production have affected the environment. Rivers such as the Volga are badly polluted, and many cities are covered in a permanent and poisonous smog. Chest infections and other diseases related to air pollution are common.

Did you know?

▲ Ice cream is popular in Russia, even in winter. It can be bought from places marked *morozhenoe*.

▲ The title csar, or tzar, once used for Russian rulers, is a word meaning "emperor".

▲ During the 20th century, St Petersburg went through three revolutions as well as a 900-day siege.

MOSCOW METRO

Not many underground railways can claim to be tourist attractions, but Moscow's metro can. Built in the 1930s, many of its stations are decorated with beautiful chandeliers, mosaics, paintings and sculptures. One of the busiest, most efficient metros in the world, it is used by over seven million people daily.

Map labels

Chaykovskiy, Neftekamsk, Naberezhnyye Chelny, Al'met'yevsk, Ufa, Oktyabr'skiy, Sterlitamak, Salavat, Birsk, Kumertau, Sibay, Baymak, Saraktash, Orsk, Novotroitsk, Beloretsk

Cheboksary, Kazan', Kanash, Nizhnekamsk, Kuybyshevskoye Vodokhranilishche, Tol'yatti, Buguruslan, Buzuluk, Samara, Orenburg, Sol'-Iletsk, Novocheboksarsk, Saransk, Ul'yanovsk, Dimitrovgrad, Syzran', Chapayevsk

Ural M

KAZAKHSTAN

Penza, Kuznetsk, Vol'sk, Balakovo, Saratov, Krasnyy Kut, Sasovo, Balashov, Kamyshin, Volzhskiy, Akhtubinsk

Tambov, Michurinsk, Ryazan', Novomoskovsk, Tovarkovskiy, Yefremov, Gryazi, Voronezh, Liski, Borisoglebsk, Krasnoarmeysk, Mikhaylovka, Volgograd, Caspian Sea, Volga, Ilovlya

Tula, Orël, Yelets, Lipetsk, Kursk, Staryy Oskol, Belgorod, Gubkin, Shebekino, Rossosh', Kantemirovka, Millerovo, Kamensk-Shakhtinskiy, Volgodonsk, Zimovniki, Elista, Astrakhan', Kaspiyskoye More

Shchëkino, Zheleznogorsk, Bryansk, Don, Donets, UKRAINE, Sal'sk, Svetlograd, Nevinnomyssk, Stavropol', Cherkessk, Pyatigorsk, Prokhladnyy, Groznyy, Khasavyurt, Makhachkala, Kaspiysk, Derbent, AZERB.

Sea of Azov, Novoshakhtinsk, Taganrog, Rostov-na-Donu, Novocherkassk, Tikhoretsk, Starominskaya, Kropotkin, Maykop, Nal'chik, Vladikavkaz, Buynaksk, GEORGIA, Caucasus Mts

Black Sea, Novorossiysk, Tuapse, Sochi, Krasnodar, Kislovodsk

ASIA

ASIA IS THE BIGGEST CONTINENT in the world. From east to west it stretches

almost half way around the globe, from north

to south it spreads from the frozen Arctic to the

sweltering, tropical heat of Southeast Asia. All 17 of the world's

 mountains over 8,000 m (26,246 ft) can be found in

Asia, as well as the largest and deepest lakes – the

Caspian Sea and Lake Baikal. The world's first civilizations started here,

many of the most important inventions were made here, and all the

world's major religions began here. Much of Asia is uninhabited, yet

its 48 countries are home to 3,672,342,000 people –

more than half the world's population. The discovery

 of oil in countries such as Saudi Arabia has made

some people very rich, while many of those who live

on the Indian subcontinent live in rural areas and are extremely poor.

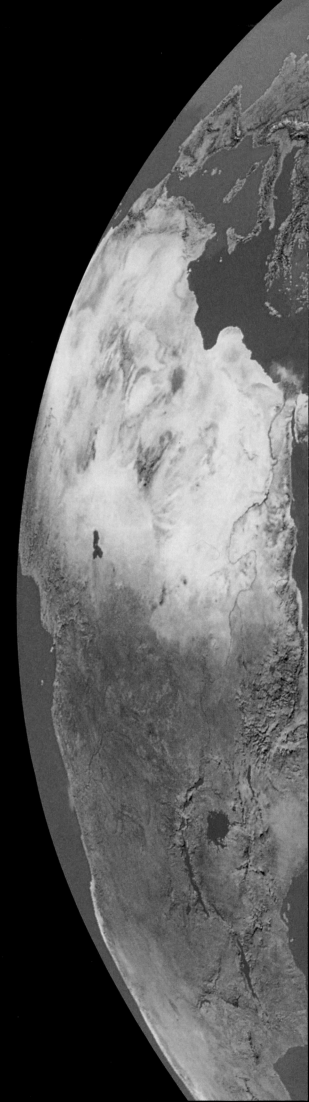

Turkey and the Caucasus

TURKEY LIES IN BOTH ASIA and Europe – separated by the Bosporus – and was once part of the powerful Ottoman Empire. Although the Turks are 99 per cent Muslim, modern Turkey is a country with no official religion. Western Turkey is relatively industrialized, with a tourist industry along the Mediterranean coast that brings in considerable income. Many farmers and herders in the centre and east, however, struggle to make a living in the harsh environment. To the northeast lie the Caucasus countries of Georgia, Azerbaijan, and Armenia. Once part of the USSR, they are now independent.

ISTANBUL

The different faces of Turkey can seen in its former capital, Istanb which lies on both sides of the Bosporus waterway. Churches, mosques, and ancient buildings both European and Islamic style sit side by side with modern sho and offices. Bridges link the two parts of the city. In 1923, Ankara became the new capital.

TURKISH FOOD

Turkey is self-sufficient in food, and grows specialized crops such as aubergines, peppers, figs, and dates. A typical Turkish meal might consist of spiced lamb, often grilled on a skewer with onion and tomato to make a *shish kebab*. This would be served with rice or cracked wheat.

EPHESUS

Tourism is one of Turkey's major industries. As well as beach resorts, the country has many ancient sites. One of these is the old Greek city of Ephesus, which lies 56 km (35 miles) south of modern-day Izmir on the Aegean coast. The city was famous for its Temple of Artemis, which was considered one of the seven wonders of the world.

VISITORS to Ephesus admire the remains of the Library of Celsus.

FATHER OF THE TURKS

Mustafa Kemal Atatürk (1881–1939), founder of the modern Turkish state, became its first president in 1923. He introduced many reforms, including more equality for women and better education for all. He also declared that Islam was no longer to be the official religion.

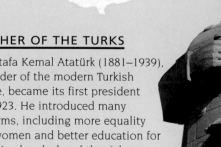

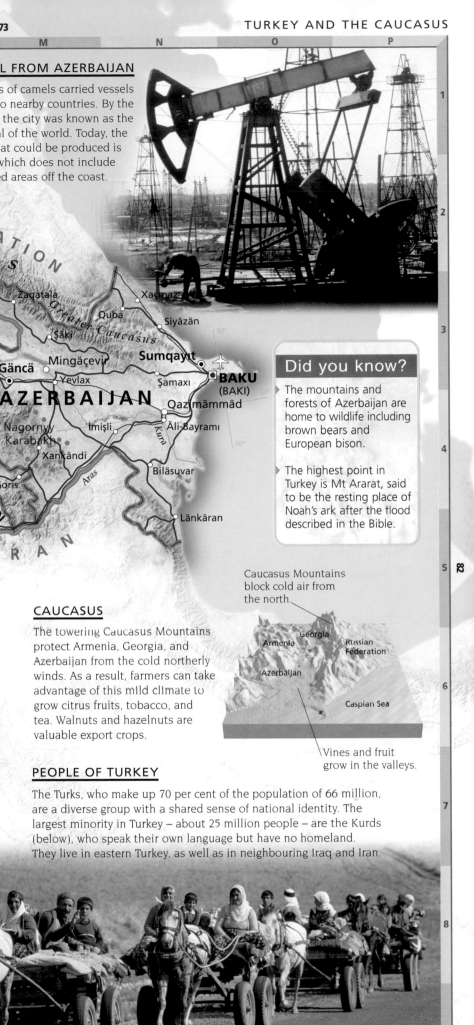

OIL FROM AZERBAIJAN

Many years ago, caravans of camels carried vessels loaded with oil from Baku to nearby countries. By the end of the 19th century, the city was known as the "black gold" capital of the world. Today, the total amount of oil that could be produced is 1 billion tonnes, which does not include undeveloped areas off the coast.

Did you know?

▸ The mountains and forests of Azerbaijan are home to wildlife including brown bears and European bison.

▸ The highest point in Turkey is Mt Ararat, said to be the resting place of Noah's ark after the flood described in the Bible.

CAUCASUS

The towering Caucasus Mountains protect Armenia, Georgia, and Azerbaijan from the cold northerly winds. As a result, farmers can take advantage of this mild climate to grow citrus fruits, tobacco, and tea. Walnuts and hazelnuts are valuable export crops.

Caucasus Mountains block cold air from the north.

Vines and fruit grow in the valleys.

CARPET MARKET

Turkey is world-famous for its knotted-pile carpets, known as kilims, woven by skilled craftworkers. Each region of Turkey produces carpets with different designs and colours. Every worker incorporates into the designs symbols that tell the maker's own family history or origins.

CARPETS are made in centres such as Malatya and Kayseri.

PEOPLE OF TURKEY

The Turks, who make up 70 per cent of the population of 66 million, are a diverse group with a shared sense of national identity. The largest minority in Turkey – about 25 million people – are the Kurds (below), who speak their own language but have no homeland. They live in eastern Turkey, as well as in neighbouring Iraq and Iran.

Russia and Kazakhstan

THE RUSSIAN FEDERATION is the biggest country in the world, almost twice as big as either the USA or China. It extends halfway around the world, crosses two continents, and spans 11 time zones. The vast region of Siberia alone is larger than Canada. Kazakhstan lies to its south and is a large but sparsely populated country. From 1917 to 1991, both countries were part of the Union of Soviet Socialist Republics (USSR), the world's first communist state. When the USSR collapsed, Russia, Kazakhstan, and the 13 other member republics gained independence. Since then, Russia and Kazakhstan have begun to transform themselves from communist states into democratic nations. Both countries have a lot of fertile land, huge mineral deposits, and many other natural resources. However, Russia still has the lowest life expectancy rate of all the industrialized countries.

Did you know?

▶ The Chukchi people of Siberia get their name from the Chukchi word *Chauchu*, meaning "rich in reindeer".

▶ Lake Baikal is up to 1,940 m (6,367 ft) deep. It is the world's largest freshwater lake, containing more than 20 per cent of the world's supply of fresh water.

▶ The traditional home of the Kazakh is called the *yurt*. This is made of felt stretched over a collapsible framework.

▶ The native populations of Siberia are bilingual. They speak their own native languages as well as Russian.

A KAZAKH man hunts with a trained golden eagle.

KAZAKH CULTURE

The majority of people in Kazakhstan are Kazakh Muslims. They were once a nomadic people who travelled around on horseback, herding their sheep. Now the Kazakhs mainly live in the rural areas of the country, retaining a strong loyalty to their clan and family.

COAL MINERS IN SIBERIA

NATURAL WEALTH

Siberia contains one-third of the world's natural gas reserves and has vast deposits of oil, as well as abundant minerals such as coal, and precious metals, including gold. However, many of these resources are inaccessible or in remote places, and the extreme winters make it difficult to extract them.

0 km 400 800
0 miles 400 800

Franz Josef Land

ARCTIC

Barents Sea

North Cape (Nordkapp)

Novaya Zemlya

Kara Sea (Karskoye More)

Ostrov Kolguyev

Ostrov Bely

Diks

FINLAND

Murmansk

Kandalaksha

Kola Peninsula

White Sea

Arctic Circle

Gulf of Finland

EST.

LAT.

BELARUS

Saint Petersburg (Sankt-Peterburg)

Lake Lagoda

Pskov

Novgorod

Petrozavodsk

Lake Onega

Severodvinsk

Arkhangel'sk

Nar'yan-Mar

Pechora

Severnaya Dvina

Vel'sk

Smolensk

Cherepovets

MOSCOW (MOSKVA)

Tver'

Vologda

Yaroslavl'

Kotlas

Ukhta

Vorkuta

Talna

UKRAINE

Bryansk

Tula

Vladimir

Kineshma

Syktyvkar

Salekhard

Noril'

Belgorod

Ryazan

Nizhniy Novgorod

Kirov

Glazov

Solikamsk

Nyagan'

Nadym

Igarka

Voronezh

Tambov

Penza

Kazan'

Izhevsk

Perm'

Serov

Khanty-Mansiysk

West Siberian Plain

Yenisei

Rostov-na-Donu

Saratov

Ul'yanovsk

Naberezhnyye Chelny

Yekaterinburg

Surgut

Nizhnevartovsk

Black Sea

Krasnodar

Volgograd

Stavropol'

Tol'yatti

Samara

Sterlitamak

Ufa

Ural

Tyumen'

Tobol'sk

RUSSIAN

Sochi

Elbrus 5642m

Ural'sk

Orenburg

Magnitogorsk

Chelyabinsk

Ishim

GEORGIA

Nal'chik

Astrakhan'

Aktobe

Orsk

Kostanay

Ob'

Vladikavkaz

Groznyy

Makhachkala

Atyrau

Alga

Rudnyy

Petropavlovsk

Omsk

Tomsk

Str

Fort-Shevchenko

Emba

Kokshetau

Atbasar

Shchuchinsk

Novosibirsk

Krasnoyar

Caspian Sea

Aktau

Zhanaozen

Chelkar

KAZAKHSTAN

ASTANA

Kulunda Steppe

Barnaul

Kemerovo

AZERBAIJAN

Ustyurt Plateau

Aral Sea

Aral'sk

Novokazalinsk

Temirtau

Pavlodar

Novokuznetsk

Abak

TURKMENISTAN

Syr Darya

Saran'

Karaganda

Semipalatinsk

Zhezkazgan

Kazakh Uplands

Shar

Leninogorsk

Zyryanovsk

Napa

Dzhusaly

Kyzylorda

Ust'-Kamenogorsk

Gora Belukha 4506m

UZBEKISTAN

Kyzyl Kum

Balkhash

Ayaguz

Ozero Zaysan

Altai Mountain

Turkestan

Kentau

Lake Balkhash

Karataw

Arys

Karatau

Shu

Taldykorgan

Tekeli

CHINA

Shymkent

Taraz

Kirghiz Range

Almaty (Alma-Ata)

KYRGYZSTAN

Taiga forest

Russia's forests cover more than two-fifths of the country's territory. The Taiga forest region extends across the Urals to cover much of Siberia. This type of forest is characterized by small, widely spaced trees, with large areas of poorly drained marsh grasses.

NENET man guiding a sled and reindeer

NATIVE PEOPLES

During the winter months, temperatures in Siberia regularly drop to below −43°C (−45°F). The native people who live here, such as the Nenet people of the Yamal Peninsula region, have adapted well to their environment and survive by herding reindeer, hunting, and fishing.

RUSSIAN LANGUAGE

Russian is the official language of the Russian Federation, but many of the 152 other nationalities inside the federation speak their own language as well. The Russian language uses the Cyrillic alphabet, which was devised by Greek missionaries.

OLD CUSTOMS

The communists tried to impose a Russian national culture on the native peoples of Siberia, but many of their customs survived in remote areas. Today, traditional costume, music, and dance are all flourishing throughout Siberia.

RUSSIAN dancer in traditional dress

SIBERIAN WILDLIFE

Siberia is home to a huge range of wildlife, including the rare Siberian tiger – the biggest in the world – wolves, reindeer, and black and brown bears. The Baikal seal – found only in Lake Baikal – is the world's only freshwater seal.

SIBERIAN TIGER

TRANS-SIBERIAN RAILWAY TRAIN

TRANS-SIBERIAN RAILWAY

The longest railway in the world runs 9,310 km (5,785 miles) from Moscow's Yaroslavl Station in the west, across Siberia to the Pacific port of Vladivostok in the east. The railway was started in 1891 and took 14 years to finish. Trains take eight days to complete the journey and cross eight time zones.

The Near East

ISRAEL, JORDAN, SYRIA, AND LEBANON are the countries collectively known as the Near East. This is a land that is dominated by desert but also has fertile coastal plains. Lack of water is a constant problem here, although Israel has introduced computerized irrigation systems to extend the land suitable for agriculture. The creation of the Jewish state of Israel in 1948, in what was previously Arab-dominated Palestine, has led to almost continuous conflict in the region. Arabs and Israelis have fought four major wars, which have cost many lives. The Mediterranean island of Cyprus has also suffered a violent recent history.

LEBANON REBUILT

Beirut, the capital of Lebanon, was once the commercial and banking centre of the Arab world, but was devastated by the civil war that ravaged the country from 1975 to 1989. Today, the country is largely at peace and Beirut is regaining much of its former glory. Lebanon remains dominated, however, by its two powerful neighbours – Syria and Israel.

SYRIAN MARKET

Damascus is one of the oldest inhabited cities in the world. At its centre is a massive souk (bazaar) where the streets are full of stalls and small shops selling everything from carpets, textiles, and jewellery to household goods and fresh produce.

DAILY LIFE

Even in a war-torn country such as Israel, people continue to live as normal a life as possible. Children listen to pop music and watch their favourite sports stars, either live or on TV. In a peaceful break, these Palestinian boys play soccer in a Jerusalem street.

CYPRUS

Cyprus became independent from Britain in 1960. However, conflict between Greeks and Turks caused Turkey to invade the island in 1974. Since then, Cyprus has been split between a Turkish Cypriot north and a Greek Cypriot south. Most Cypriots make a living from farming grapes, citrus fruit, and olives. Women often sell hand-made lace items to tourists.

Map labels

TURKEY

IRAQ

IRAN

SYRIA

Al Mālikiyah
A Qāmishlī
Al Ḥasakah
Al Jazīrah
Ash Shaddādah
Al Manāṣif
Aş Şuwār
Sucaykhān
Abū Ḥajdān
Abū Kamāl
Ra's al 'Ayn
Jabal 'Abd al 'Azīz
Al Mayādīn
Al 'Ashārah
Buşayrah
Dayr az Zawr
Euphrates
At Tibnī
As ṣabkhah
Ar Raqqah
Jabal Bishrī
As Sukhnah
At Tall al Abyaḍ
Nahr Balīkh
Madīnat ath Thawrah
Lake Assad (Buḥayrat al Asad)
Tudmur (Palmyra)
Ar Rāmī
Manbij
Sabkhat al Jabbūl
Jarābulus
Euphrates
A'zāz
Al Bāb
Aleppo (Ḥalab)
Abū aḍ Ḍuhūr
Salamīyah
Ma'arrat an Nu'mān
Ḥamāh
Ḥimş
Afrin
Idlib
Ḥārim
Arīḥā
Orantes
Jibāl as Sāḥiliyah
Al Qubşayr
Al Bāridah
Mazyaf
Tall Kalakh
Qoubaiyāt
Jabal Tripoli
Jablah
Bāniyās
Ţarţūs
El Mina
Tripoli
Batroūn
Al Lādhiqīyah

Mediterranean Sea

CYPRUS
Agialousa (Yenierenköy)
TURKISH REPUBLIC OF NORTHERN CYPRUS (recognized only by Turkey)
Ammóchostos (Gazimağusa) (Famagusta)
Sovereign Base Area (to UK)
Kerýneia (Girne)
Kythréa (Değirmenlik)
NICOSIA
Dekelia
Lárnaca
Sovereign Base Area (to UK)
Lápithos (Lapta)
Mórfou (Güzelyurt)
Pólis
Páfos
Lemesós
Limassol
CYPRUS

Scale

0 km 50 100
0 miles 50 100

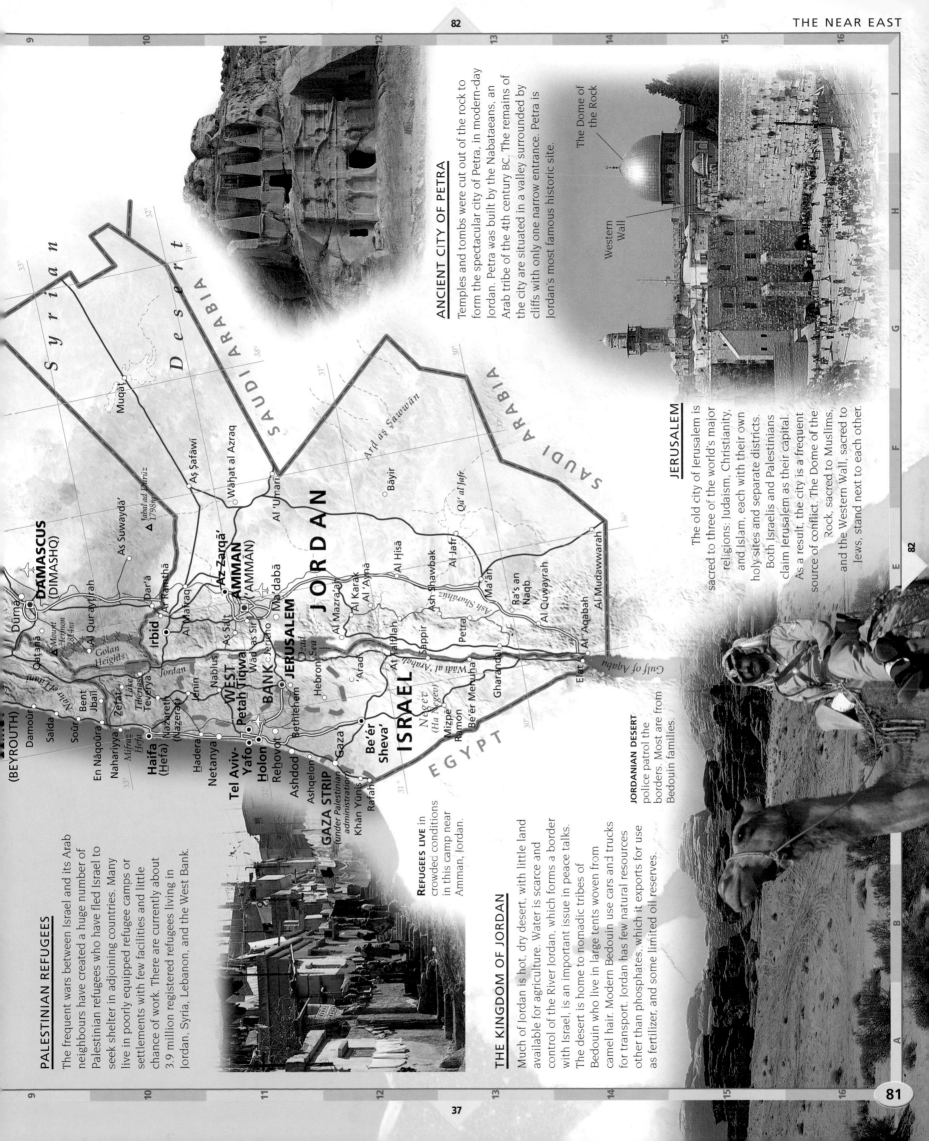

ANCIENT CITY OF PETRA

Temples and tombs were cut out of the rock to form the spectacular city of Petra, in modern-day Jordan. Petra was built by the Nabataeans, an Arab tribe of the 4th century BC. The remains of the city are situated in a valley surrounded by cliffs with only one narrow entrance. Petra is Jordan's most famous historic site.

The Dome of the Rock

Western Wall

JERUSALEM

The old city of Jerusalem is sacred to three of the world's major religions: Judaism, Christianity, and Islam, each with their own holy sites and separate districts. Both Israelis and Palestinians claim Jerusalem as their capital. As a result, the city is a frequent source of conflict. The Dome of the Rock, sacred to Muslims, and the Western Wall, sacred to Jews, stand next to each other.

JORDANIAN DESERT police patrol the borders. Most are from Bedouin families.

PALESTINIAN REFUGEES

The frequent wars between Israel and its Arab neighbours have created a huge number of Palestinian refugees who have fled Israel to seek shelter in adjoining countries. Many live in poorly equipped refugee camps or settlements with few facilities and little chance of work. There are currently about 3.9 million registered refugees living in Jordan, Syria, Lebanon, and the West Bank.

REFUGEES LIVE in crowded conditions in this camp near Amman, Jordan.

THE KINGDOM OF JORDAN

Much of Jordan is hot, dry desert, with little land available for agriculture. Water is scarce and control of the River Jordan, which forms a border with Israel, is an important issue in peace talks. The desert is home to nomadic tribes of Bedouin who live in large tents woven from camel hair. Modern Bedouin use cars and trucks for transport. Jordan has few natural resources other than phosphates, which it exports for use as fertilizer, and some limited oil reserves.

Map labels

S y r i a n   D e s e r t

SAUDI ARABIA

SAUDI ARABIA

JORDAN

ISRAEL

Negev (Ha Negev)

EGYPT

DAMASCUS (DIMASHQ)

(BEYROUTH)

Nahr al Liṭāni

Golan Heights

Mount Hermon 2814m

Jabal ad Durūz 1798m

Muqāṭ

Aş Şafāwī

Waḥat al Azraq

Al 'Umarī

Bāyir

Arḍ aş Şawwān

Qaʿ al Jafr

As Suwaydā'

Al Quraytayah

Ḍará

Al Ramthā

Irbid

AMMAN ('AMMĀN)

Az-Zarqa'

Al Mafraq

As Salt

Mādabā

Wādī as Sīr

JERUSALEM

WEST BANK

Petaḥ Tiqwa

Jenin

Nablus

Zefat (Zefaṭ)

Nazareth (Nazerat)

Lake Tiberias

Teverya

Bent Jbail

Soûr

Saïda

Damoûr

Douma

Qaṭana

Jordan

Mizraʿ Ḥefa

Haifa (Ḥefa)

En Nāqoūra

Nahariyya

Hadera

Netanya

Tel Aviv-Yafo

Holon

Rehovot

Ashdod

Ashqelon

GAZA STRIP (under Palestinian administration)

Gaza

Khān Yūnis

Rafaḥ

Be'ér Sheva'

'Arad

Hebron

Bethlehem

Dead Sea

Al Mazraʿah

Al Karak

Al 'Aynā

Aş Ṣāfī

At Ṭafīlah

Al Ḥisā

Ash Shawbak

Al Jafr

 Maʿān

Ash Sharāḥah

Ra's an Naqb

Al Quwayrah

Al Mudawwarah

Petra

Mizpe Ramon

Be'ér Menuha

Gharandal

Wādī al 'Arabah

Eilat Al 'Aqabah

Gulf of Aqaba

76

The Middle East

THE MIDDLE EAST IS HOME to the world's oldest civilizations, which grew up in the Tigris and Euphrates river valleys of present-day Iraq more than 6,000 years ago. The world's first towns and cities were built here. Since then, many powerful empires have dominated the region, all leaving a wealth of buildings and monuments behind them. Today, the Middle East is at the centre of the Islamic world. The population of every country is Arab and speaks Arabic, except Iran, where half the population are Farsi-speaking Persians.

DESERT WARS

Most international boundaries in the Middle East are just lines drawn in the sand by the former European colonial powers, and have often caused conflict. Iraq and Iran fought a bitter eight-year war along their common border from 1980. Since then, further conflicts between Iraq and international forces have caused much suffering.

ROLE OF WOMEN

Family life is important throughout the Muslim world. The role of women varies from country to country – traditionally, women stay at home and look after the family, but some now work. In public, many cover their head, or whole body, with a burqa.

THE IRANIANS

About half the total population of Iran are Persians, who live in the centre and north of the country. Large numbers of Azeris live in the northwest, while Kurds live in the west and Baluchis in the southeast. The official language of Iran is Farsi, but many other languages are also spoken.

The Persian language is written in Arabic script.

OIL PRODUCTION

The Middle East is the world's major oil producer – Saudi Arabia alone produces 10 per cent of the world's supply. Oil has brought great wealth to the region, in particular to Saudi Arabia and the Gulf States.

80

86

A WEALTH OF FISH

The Arabian Sea, south of Yemen and Oman, is rich in fish, providing a valuable source of both income and food for local people. The fishermen use traditional sailboats equipped with outboard motors for greater speed, landing large catches of sardines, tuna, anchovies, cuttlefish, cod, and other fish.

MIDDLE EASTERN FOOD

A typical Middle Eastern meal consists of pita bread, hummus made from chickpeas, bulgur wheat, lentils, spiced meat – usually lamb or goat, and fruit. Most Muslims do not drink alcohol, preferring water, mint tea, or coffee from Yemen, producer of some of the world's finest coffee beans.

AN IRANIAN BAKERY

WATER

Much of the Middle East is covered with a hot desert. Water is scarce, although there are some oases where animals can be watered and crops irrigated. On the coastline, desalination plants, such as this one in Oman (left), remove salt from seawater to make it suitable for domestic consumption and agriculture.

Socotra (Suqutrā) (to Yemen)

0 km   150   300
0 miles   150   300

ISLAM

The Islamic religion began in the 7th century in the holy cities of Mecca and Medina in Saudi Arabia. Minarets, the tall thin towers of mosques, dominate the skyline of every town and city in the region. From these, devout Muslims are summoned to pray five times a day. Muslims are also required to make a hajj, or pilgrimage, to Mecca (above) at least once in their lifetime.

THE KORAN is the book of sacred writings of Islam.

Did you know?

Saudi Arabia is the only country in the world to be named after its royal family – the house of al-Sa'ud.

What is now Iraq used to be called Mesopotamia, a Greek word for "the land between rivers" – the Tigris and Euphrates.

Saudi Arabia is so hot and dry that it has no permanent rivers. Months can pass without rainfall.

Map labels

Makran Coast
Gulf of Oman
Ash Shāriqah
MUSCAT (MASQAȚ)
Şūr
Ar Rustāq
Suḥār
Al Ḥajar al Gharbī
Dubai (Dubayy)
ABU DHABI (ABU ẒABY)
UNITED ARAB EMIRATES
DOHA (AD DAWḤAH)
QATAR
MANAMA (AL MANĀMAH)
Al Ḥufūf
Jazīrat Maşīrah
Ramlat Al Waḥībah
Khalīj Maşīrah
Al Ghābah
Duqm
Ramlat
Şawqirah
Jūzur al Ḥalānīyāt
Thamarit
Şalālah
OMAN
Damqawt
Al Mahrah
Sayḥūt
Ash Shiḥr
Al Mukallā
Ḥaḍramaut
Sanāw
Tarīm
Say'ūn
Wudayʻah
SAUDI ARABIA
Ar Rubʻ al Khālī (Empty Quarter)
Arabian Peninsula
Jabal Ṭuwayq
Dahnā'
(Al Majma'ah)
Al Majma'ah
RIYADH (AR RIYĀḌ)
Shaqrā'
Laylā
As Sulayyil
Zalim
Turaban
Qalʻat Bīshah
Tathlīth
Najrān
Khamīs Mushayt
Abhā
Saʻdah
Şaʻdah
Jīzān
Şabyā
Wādī Bīshah
Mecca (Makkah)
Aṭ Ṭāʼif
Al Līth
Al Bāḥah
Zabid
Hodeida (Al Ḥudaydah)
Medina (Al Madīnah)
Harrat Rahaṭ
Jedda (Jiddah)
Red Sea
Yanbuʻ al Baḥr
Wādī al Ḥamd
Shaqrā'
Wādī ar Rimah
Tropic of Cancer
Tropic of Cancer
Najrān
Şanʻā'
SANA (ṢANʻĀ')
Ta'izz
Aden ('Adan)
Gulf of Aden
Bab el Mandeb
Shuqrah
Ramlat as Sabʻatayn
Ramlat Dahm
YEMEN
Arabian Sea
Straits of Hormuz

Central Asia

THE FIVE CENTRAL ASIAN NATIONS rise up from hot deserts in the west and south to cold, high mountain ranges in the east. The area has oil, gas, and mineral reserves, as well as other natural resources, but water is often scarce and agriculture is limited. The four northern nations were once part of the Soviet Union, and are now independent nations. Afghanistan is a landlocked country with three-quarters of its land being inaccessible terrain. It was invaded by the Soviet Union in 1979, prompting a civil war that has lasted for more than 20 years. In 2002, American and other western forces overthrew a fundamentalist Islamic regime in Afghanistan because of its support for international terrorism. The country, however, has been wrecked by these years of continuous warfare, making it one of the poorest and most deprived nations on Earth.

Did you know?

▶ Almost 90 per cent of Turkmenistan consists of the Garagumy Desert, meaning "black sands" in Turkic.

▶ Tashkent in Uzbekistan is known as the "city of fountains" because it has so many water features.

▶ About 10 million land mines are buried in Afghanistan, making it one of the most heavily mined countries in the world. More than 90 people are maimed or killed every month.

▶ The world's largest gold mine is at Murantau in the Kyzyl Kum desert in Uzbekistan.

CHILDREN IN KABUL, Afghanistan, who have been made homeless by war.

FESTIVALS IN AFGHANISTAN

Despite the horrors of recent years, the Afghans still celebrate important Islamic festivals, notably Eid ul-Fitr, which marks the end of the holy month of Ramadan. People visit friends and family and eat a festive meal together. The art of storytelling still flourishes in Afghanistan, as does the *attan*, the national dance.

AN AFGHAN REFUGEE carries bread with which to break the Ramadan fast.

LIFE EXPECTANCY

As a result of war, drought, and poverty, people in Afghanistan can expect to live an average of only 46 years, one of the lowest life expectancy rates in the world. Infant mortality is extremely high. Health services have almost completely collapsed and few trained doctors and nurses are available to help the sick. Sadly, there are not enough orphanages to cope with the increasing number of children made homeless by war.

ARAL SEA

The vast inland Aral Sea, between Uzbekistan and Kazakhstan, was once a thriving freshwater lake full of fish. Over the years, the rivers flowing into it were diverted or drained to provide irrigation for crops. The sea has now shrunk to half its original size, reducing the numbers of fish, and leaving former fishing villages stranded inland.

The fishing village of Muynoq is now over 48 km (30 miles) away from the Aral Sea.

A MAN in front of his home, called a *yurt*, in western Pamir, Tajikistan

MOUNTAIN LIFE

The two small eastern republics of Kyrgyzstan and Tajikistan are both very mountainous and are subject to earthquakes and landslides. Only about six per cent of Tajikistan can be used for agriculture, whereas Kyrgyzstan is more fertile.

LOCAL WEALTH

Uzbekistan, Turkmenistan, and Kyrgyzstan all grow considerable crops of cotton – Uzbekistan is the world's fourth largest producer – as well as fruit and vegetables. The three countries are also rich in mineral deposits, such as gold, mercury, sulphur, and uranium, and have reserves of coal, oil, and natural gas.

HARVESTING cotton in Uzbekistan

THE TAJIKS

The majority of people of Tajikistan are Iranian in origin and speak Tajik, which is related to Farsi. The minority Uzbeks are made up mainly of descendents of Turkic-speaking (related to Turkish) nomads. This division has led to ethnic tension between the two groups. Civil war between the government and Islamic rebels in the east of the country during the 1990s led to an exodus of Uzbeks and Russians, who had moved into the country when it was part of the Soviet Union.

TAJIK HORSEMEN, in Pamir, Tajikistan

TILLA-KARI, a 17th-century Islamic religious school in Samarqand, Uzbekistan

THE SILK ROAD

The Silk Road is the ancient trading route that brought silks and other fine goods from China through central Asia and the Middle East to Europe. Many cities were built along its route, including Bukhoro, an important place of pilgrimage for Muslims, and Samarqand (right), which contains some of the finest Islamic architecture in the world. Many of these cities are now UNESCO-designated World Heritage Sites.

0 km 100 200

0 miles 100 200

Map labels

KAZAKHSTAN

BISHKEK
Kara-Balta
Tokmak
Tyup
Dzhergalan
Kemin
Balykchy
Ozero Issyk-Kul'
Karakol
Kyzyl-Suu
Talas
Leninpol'
Kadzhi-Say
Pik Pobedy 7439m
Gora Manas 4482m
Chatkal Range
Kirgiz Range
Khrebet Moldo-Too
Kara-Say

KYRGYZSTAN

TASHKENT (TOSHKENT)
Chirchiq
Tash-Kumyr
Naryn
Kara-Say
Angren
Yangiyül
Namangan
Dzhalal-Abad
Karakol
Olmaliq
Andijon
Chatyr-Tash
Guliston
Quqon
Osh
Bekobod
Kek-Art
Jizzakh
Farghona
Kok-Art
Kattaqürghon
Sulyukta
Samarqand
Üroteppa
Khaydarkan
Sary-Tash
Urgut
Kitob
Daroot-Korgon
Qarokul
arshi
Zarafshon
Sirkhob
DUSHANBE
TAJIKISTAN
Ghudara
Denow
Norak
Qalaikhum
Murghob
Boysun
Danghara
Qürghonteppa
Külob
CHINA
Jarqürghon
Moskva
Dzhelandy
Dūstī
Farkhor
Qizilrabot
Termiz
Khorugh
qchah
Feyzäbäd
Ishkoshim
Balkh
Kunduz
Kholm
Talogän
Mazär-e Sharif
Khänäbäd
Bulunkul Pass 4177m
erghän
Baghlan
Pol-e Khomri
Hindu Kush
Charikar
Barikowt
Mahmud-e Räqi
Daryā-ye Kahmard
Kühe Bäba
KÄBUL
Mehtarläm
Maydän Shahr
Jaläläbäd
Asadäbäd
Khyber Pass 1080m
STAN
Ghaznī
Gardez
Khowst
Daryā-ye Arghandäb
PAKISTAN
Zarghün Shahr
Kalät
in Buldak

Indian Subcontinent

SEPARATED FROM THE rest of Asia by the Himalayas, the Indian subcontinent is home to more than one-fifth of the world's population – a staggering one billion people. They have a long and complex history, form many different ethnic groups, speak a wide variety of languages, and worship many different gods. Some of these countries are relatively wealthy, but many people live in poverty. Tensions between and within countries in this region have sometimes erupted in warfare. The Indian subcontinent is often affected by natural disasters, notably cyclones in the Bay of Bengal, and earthquakes. However, India, the most heavily populated state and once prone to famine, is now more than self-sufficient in food. All but Nepal and Bhutan were once ruled by the British, whose legacy can be seen in the common language of English, in the architecture, the vast railway system, and in sport – most notably cricket.

Monsoon

From May/June to September, warm, moist southerly winds sweep up from the Indian Ocean and the Bay of Bengal across the subcontinent. Once these winds meet dry land, moisture falls as monsoon rainfall. Although this irrigates the land and replenishes the water supply, it can also cause severe flooding.

FAMILY LIFE IN PAKISTAN

Pakistanis have strong ties to their extended families, and often many generations live and work together in family-run businesses. Smaller family units, however, are becoming more common in urban areas. Although some women hold prominent positions in public and commercial life – Benazir Bhutto has twice been prime minister – most women do not work outside the home.

SCHOOLCHILD in Sri Lanka

SRI LANKA

In 1983, civil war erupted in Sri Lanka between the Buddhist majority Sinhalese, who dominate the government, and the Hindu minority Tamils, who want to establish their own independent state in the north of the island. The civil war has cost many lives and disrupted the island's economy, yet Sri Lanka still has one of the highest literacy rates in the world and high levels of health care.

Hindu Kush
Indus
Mingāora
Mardān
Khyber Pass
1080m
Peshāwar
Wāh
ISLĀMĀBĀD
Rāwalpindi
AFGHANISTAN
Jhelum
Jammu
Sargodha Gujrāt
Gujrānwa
Chaman
Toba Kākar Range
Indus
Lahore
Amri
Faisalābād
Ludhiā
Quetta Dera Ghāzi Khān
Multān Okāra
Chand
Kālat
Sibi
Bathinda
Haryāna
Chāgai Hills
PAKISTAN
Bahāwalpur
Kar
Baluchistān
Jacobābād
Rahīmyār
Del
Shikārpur
Sukkur
Khān
NEW DE
Lārkāna
Khairpur
Bīkāner
IRAN
Central Makrān Range
Alwar
Turbat
Jaisalmer
Jodhpur
Jaipur
Gwādar
Pasni
Nawābshāh
Udaipur
Kota
Hyderābād Mīrpur Khās
Pāli
Beāwar
Karāchi
R ā j a s t h ā n Shi
Sind
Sujāwal
Mounts of the Indus
Tropic of Cancer
Rann of Kachchh
Pālanpur
Gūjarat
Gulf of
Kachchh
Gāndhīdhām
Ahmadābād
Ratlām
Godhra
Vindhya
Bh
Jāmnagar
Rājkot
Indore
Porbandar
Bhāvnagar
Vadodara
Satpura R
Gulf of
Khambhāt
Surat
Bhusāwal
Damān
Manmād
Nāshik
Aurangāb
Kalyān
Golāvari
Mumbai
Pune
Nānde
(Bombay)
Mahārāshtra
Arabian
Bārāmati
Sea
Solāpur
Gulba
Kolhāpur
Rāi
Karnātaka
Belgaum
Gadag
Panaji
Hubli
Dāvang
Shimoga
Udupi
Mangalore
Bangalore
Kāsargod
Mysore
Cannanore
Ero
Calicut
Coimbatore
Ernāk
Cochin
Quilon
Trivandrum
Nāgerco

0 km   150   300
0 miles   150   300

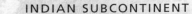

THE HIMALAYAS

The highest chain of mountains in the world, the Himalayas have eight peaks that are more than 8,000 m (26,247 ft) high. Everest, the world's highest mountain at 8,850 m (29,035 ft), is on the border of Nepal and Tibet. Mountaineers come from far and wide to scale these massive peaks.

BHUTANESE PEOPLE

ARUNACHAL PRADESH (claimed by China)

BHUTAN

Hidden away in the Himalayas, the people of Bhutan are devoutly Buddhist and have little contact with the outside world. A minority of the population are Nepalese Hindus who came to the country in the first half of the last century. Most Bhutanese live in the fertile river valleys of the centre and south of the country. Traditional dress – the *kira* for women and the *gho* for men – is widely worn.

Did you know?

▶ The name Bhutan means "Land of the Thunder Dragon" in Dzongkha, the country's official language.

▶ India has the second largest population in the world after China, officially passing the one billion mark (1,000 million) in the year 2000.

RELIGION

Two of the world's great religions – Hinduism and Buddhism – began in India more than 2,500 years ago. Most Pakistanis and Bangladeshis are Muslim, most Indians and Nepalese are Hindu, and most Sri Lankans and Bhutanese are Buddhist.

HINDUS BATHE in the River Ganges, considered sacred.

BOLLYWOOD

More films are produced in Mumbai (Bombay) – more than 800 a year – than in the whole USA, turning "Bollywood", as it is known; into a major cultural centre. Bollywood films generally have historical, religious, or social themes, and are famous for their song and dance routines and glamorous stars. These films are an important export to central Asia, the Middle East, and Africa.

TEA IN SRI LANKA

Sri Lanka is the world's largest exporter of tea. The plantations are located mainly in the centre of the island, and employ women to pick the delicate, green shoots of the bushes.

Map labels

DEMCHOK/ DÊMQOG (administered by China, claimed by India)

AKSAI CHIN (istered by China, ...ned by India)

NEPAL

CHINA

MYANMAR (BURMA)

BANGLADESH

SRI LANKA

Bay of Bengal

INDIAN OCEAN

Andaman Sea

North Andaman
Middle Andaman
Port Blair
South Andaman
Little Andaman
Andaman Islands (to India)
Nicobar Islands (to India)
Car Nicobar
Katchall Island
Little Nicobar
Great Nicobar
Indira Point

Tropic of Cancer

Mouths of the Ganges

Dibrugarh
Jorhât
Kohima
Imphâl
Silchar
Guwâhâti
Bongaigaon
Shiliguri
Darjiling
Sylhet
Rangpur
Dinajpur
Chhapra
Jamalpur
Pabna
DHAKA
Comilla
Rajshahi
Jessore
Khulna
Barisal
Chittagong
THIMPHU
BHUTAN
Bhaktapur
Lalitpur
KATHMANDU
Biratnagar
Faizâbâd
Gorakhpur
Salyan
Pokhara
Annapurna 8091m
Mount Everest 8850m
Kula Kangri 7554m
Brahmaputra
Assam
Bihar
Ganges
Jhârkhand
West Bengal
Orissa
Mahânadi
Andhra Pradesh
Eastern Ghats
Chota Nâgpur
Chhattisgarh
Bareilly
Lucknow
Kânpur
Allahâbâd
Jhânsi
Varânasi
Patna
Gaya
Sâgar
Murwâra
Jabalpur
Dhanbâd
Asânsol
Rânchi
Jamshedpur
Bilâspur
Korba
Râulakela
Kharagpur
Kolkata (Calcutta)
Sambalpur
Bâleshwar
Cuttack
Bhubaneshwar
Puri
Brahmapur
Jagdalpur
Gondia
Raipur
Vizianagaram
Visâkhapatnam
Râjahmundry
Vijayawâda
Chîrâla
Ongole
Kâvali
Nellore
Chennai (Madras)
Kânchîpuram
Pondicherry
Tiruchchirâppalli
Madurai
Jaffna
Mannar
Trincomalee
Puttalam
Batticaloa
Kandy
COLOMBO
Kalutara
Galle
Matara
Palk Strait
Meerut
Gwalior
Warangal
Hyderabad
Karimnagar
Chandrapur

Western China and Mongolia

CHINA IS A LAND of great geographical diversity and amazing landscapes. More than 90 per cent of the population is Han Chinese – descendants of people who settled here more than 5,000 years ago. This region includes Western China, Mongolia, and Tibet. Mongolia gained its independence from China in 1911, and is now an independent democracy. Tibet is currently governed by China. Compared with Eastern China, this region is sparsely populated and characterized by vast deserts, remote mountains, and extreme temperatures.

DESERT LANDS

The cold, rocky Gobi Desert (right) stretches for more than 1,000,000 sq km (400,000 sq miles) through Mongolia and northeast China. Many dinosaur bones and eggs have been found here, making it one of the richest dinosaur fossil regions in the world.

THE MONGOLIANS

Most of the people living in Mongolia are Khalkh Mongols. About half of these people now live in urban areas, but some still lead traditional lives as nomadic herders. They live in large felt tents, called yurts. Smoke from the central iron stove escapes through a chimney in the roof.

Did you know?

▶ In traditional Mongolian *khoomi* singing, male singers produce harmonic overtones deep in their throats. They are able to sing several notes at once.

▶ Prayer flags are a Tibetan tradition symbolizing the Buddhist faith. Before the Chinese occupation, they flew from every home as a symbol of good luck.

CHINESE WRITING

The Chinese alphabet is not made up of letters. Instead, separate symbols stand for individual words or parts of words. There are more than 40,000 characters in the Chinese language. The same symbols are used everywhere in China, and no matter what Chinese language or dialect people speak, they can all read the same script.

THE STROKES in each symbol have to be written in a certain order.

MONASTERIES IN MONGOLIA

Under communism, Mongolians were forbidden to practise their traditional Buddhist faith, which w[as] viewed as superstitious and unscientific. Since [a] democratic government was set up in 1990, a[bout] 100 monasteries have reopened. Most peopl[e,] however, no longer follow any religion.

0 km   200   400

0 miles   200   400

RUSSIAN FEDERATION

RUSS. FED.

Mohe
Tahe

Ergun
Zuoqi   Jagdaqi

Argun (Ergun He)

Amur (Heilong Jiang)

Yichun

Bei'an   Nancha   Hegang

Manzhouli

Yakeshi

Hailar

HEILONGJIANG   Jiamusi

Hulun
Nur   Great Khingan Range
(Da Hinggan Ling)   Qiqihar   Tonghe   Jixi

Sühbaatar

Darhan   Choybalsan

Onon Gol

elenga   Harbin   Shangzhi   Lake
Khanka

Ulan   ULAN BATOR
(ULAANBAATAR)   Menengiyn
Tal   Songyuan   Mudanjiang

Erdenet

Öndörhaan   Baruun-Urt   Changchun   Jilin   Yanji

Dzuunmod   Kerulen   JILIN   Sea
of
Japan

Xi Ujimqin Qi   Tongliao   Siping   Liaoyuan

OLIA   Xilinhot   Baishan

Saynshand   MONGOLIA
(Nei Mongol Zizhiqu)   Manzhouli

Erenhot   LIAONING   Liao He   NORTH
KOREA

Dalandzadgad   Gobi
Desert   Chifeng

'i Altayn Nuruu   INNER

b i   Lang Shan   Jining

Qi   HEBEI

Wuhai   Hohhot

Yellow River
(Huang He)   Baotou

Yabrai Shan   Mu Us
Shamo   SHANXI

Tengger
Shamo   Yinchuan

A   NINGXIA   Great Wall of China

Tongxin

Xining   Lanzhou

GANSU   Pingliang

han   Luqu   Tianshui

Zhugqu

CHUAN   Wenxian   SHAANXI

FESTIVAL OF NADAAM

Each July, people all over Mongolia
celebrate the sports festival of Naadam.
Three sports – wrestling (above), archery,
and horse-riding – are the focus of the
festivities. The skills needed to take part in
these activities are those that would have helped
people survive the traditional nomadic lifestyle.

PEOPLE OF TIBET

Most Tibetans live in the
valleys of the Tibetan
plateau, high in
the Himalayas and
surrounded by the world's
tallest mountains. They
have their own language
and culture. Recently,
many Han Chinese have
moved to this region
looking for a better life.

**TIBETAN VILLAGE
CHILDREN**

GREAT WALL OF CHINA

About 2,200 years ago, approximately
300,000 slaves began to build China's
enormous Great Wall. Originally built
to protect China's northern borders,
it is the longest human-made
structure ever built, and stretches
from central Asia to the Yellow Sea,
a distance of 6,400 km (3,980 miles).

TRADITIONAL MEDICINE

As well as modern medicine, many
Chinese still use alternative remedies.
Traditional medicine is based on the
belief that health is achieved by
balancing a person's mind and body –
their yin and yang. Any imbalance is
treated with medicines made from
dried plant materials (left). Some
animals, including Asiatic bears, are
now endangered due to the demand
for parts used in traditional medicine.

BUDDHIST PRAYER FLAGS

BUDDHIST TIBET

Many Tibetans are devout Buddhists. Their religious
leader, the Dalai Lama, used to live in Lhasa. In 1951, however, Tibet became part of
China and the government restricted the people's religious freedom and
lifestyle. This resulted in tension between the Tibetans and the Chinese
government. The Dalai Lama now lives in exile in India.

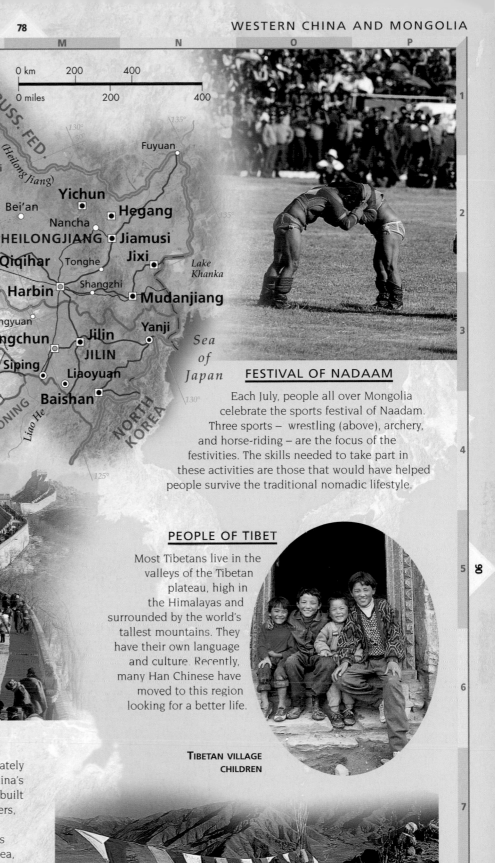

Eastern China and Korea

CHINA HAS A LARGE population of 1.3 billion, with two-thirds living in Eastern China. For thousands of years, powerful emperors ruled China. During this period, Chinese civilization was very advanced, but much of the population lived in poverty. In 1949, after a communist revolution, the People's Republic of China was established. Food, education, and healthcare became available to more people, but there was also a loss of freedom. Today, Chinese people have more freedom, but the government still has tight control over their lives. The Korean peninsula is divided politically into north and south, and attempts are being made to restore peace between the two governments. Since 1949, Taiwan has been in dispute with China over who governs this mountainous island.

NEW YEAR CELEBRATIONS

Chinese New Year, also known as the Spring Festival, is the country's most important festival. It is usually held in January or February. Good-luck messages decorate buildings and there are feasts, fireworks, fairs, and processions. People wear red clothes for good luck and give gifts of coins to symbolize wealth.

CHINESE NEW YEAR PARADE

HONG KONG

For 100 years, Hong Kong was a British colony. Then, in 1997, it was returned to China. These small islands are some of the most densely populated parts of the world. Most people live and work in high-rise buildings. Hong Kong has a prosperous economy and the people have one of the world's highest life expectancies.

THE SKYLINE OF HONG KONG with a Chinese junk in the foreground

ONE-CHILD FAMILIES

Many Chinese children do not have brothers or sisters. This is due to policies brought in by the Chinese goverment in 1979. To try and control the rising population, the government offers special benefits to couples with only one child. Although this has slowed down the rate of growth, China's population still grows by millions each year.

PADDY FIELDS

Rice forms the basis of most Chinese meals. It grows in paddy fields in the southeast of the country. During the growing season, fields are flooded so farmers can grow more rice more quickly. In the drier regions, wheat is grown and used to make noodles, buns, and dumplings. Rice or wheat is combined with local vegetables, meats, and spices to create regional dishes.

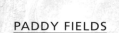

NINGXIA

Bayan Har Shan QINGHAI

GANSU

Tongchua

Baoji Xiany

Xi'an

Hanzhong SHAAN

Hongyuan

Guangyuan

Wan

Yalong Jiang

Luhuo

SICHUAN

Mianyang

Nanchong

Litang

Chengdu Sichuan Pendi

Wan

TIBET

Ya'an

Neijiang

Lichuan

Leshan

CHONGQING

Zigong

Chongqing

Hengduan Shan

Xichang

Zhongdian

Tongzi

Zunyi

Hua

Zhoatong

GUIZHOU

Panzhihua

Guiyang

MYANMAR (BURMA)

Dali

Anshun

Guanling

Kaili Duyun

Baoshan

Dushan

Salween

Kunming

Xingxi

YUNNAN

Yuxi

Liuzho

Kaiyuan

Bose

GUANGX

Tropic of Cancer

Gejiu

Wenshan

Mekong

Nanning

Jinghong

VIETNAM

Qinzhou

LAOS

Beihai

0 km   150   300

0 miles   150   300

Gulf of Tongking

Danzho

Dongfang

HAIN

NORTH KOREA

North Korea is an independent communist country, but since the breakup of the Soviet Union it has lost many of its trading partners and is now very poor. However, the country has a good education system and a high literacy rate. Schooling is free and compulsory for all children for 10 years.

SOUTH KOREA

South Korea is a democratic nation with a thriving electronics and machinery industry. A quarter of the population lives in or near the capital city, Seoul. The Internet has developed quickly in South Korea and plays an important role in work and leisure. The children below are using computers at an internet cafe in the central city of Taejon.

INNER MONGOLIA

JILIN

Najin

Ch'ŏngjin

Sea of Japan

Shenyang
Fuxin
Fushun
Chaoyang
Kanggye
Hyesan
LIAONING
Anshan
Kimch'aek
Chengde
Jinzhou
Haicheng
Zhangjiakou
Fengcheng
Sinŭiju
NORTH
Huailai
Qinhuangdao
Dandong
KOREA
Datong
BEIJING
Chŏngju
Hamhŭng
(PEKING)
Tangshan
P'YŎNGYANG
Wŏnsan
East
Shouzhou
Langfang
Tianjin
Dalian
Korea
Rengiu
TIANJIN SHI
Bo Hai
Sariwŏn
Bay
Shijiazhuang
HEBEI
Haeju
taiyuan
Botou
Cangzhou
Korea
Ch'unch'ŏn
Yuci
Dezhou
Binzhou
Yantai
Bay
SEOUL
SOUTH
SHANXI
Zibo
(SÔUL)
KOREA
Handan
Jinan
Weifang
Inch'ŏn
SHANDONG
Taejŏn
Taegu
Anyang
Qingdao
(North and South Korea
Chŏnju
Ulsan
Changzhi
Xinxiang
Jining
have been divided
by a ceasefire
Pusan
hmenxia
Kaifeng
Zaozhuang
agreement since 1953)
Kwangju
Chinju
Luoyang
Zhengzhou
Lianyungang
Yellow
Yŏsu
Pingdingshan
Xuzhou
Sea
Mokp'o
Cheju Strait
Korea Strait
HENAN
JIANGSU
Nanyang
Suzhou
Cheju-do
Xiangfang
Huainan
Bengbu
Xinyang
Nanjing
Yangzhou
Hefei
Yangtze
Wuxi
Suzhou
HUBEI
ANHUI
Wuhu
Shanghai
Yichang
Wuhan
Anqing
Jiaxing
Jingzhou
Huangshi
Hangzhou
Jiujiang
Ningbo
Yueyang
Jingdezhen
Quzhou
Jinhua
Changde
Nanchang
ZHEJIANG
Wenzhou
Changsha
Loudi
Xiangtan
Linchuan
Shangrao
HUNAN
JIANGXI
FUJIAN
Fu'an
jiang
Hengyang
Nanfeng
Nanping
East China Sea
Lengshuitan
Sanming
anzhou
Ganzhou
Yong'an
Fuzhou
Chenzhou
Longyan
Chilung
iilin
Shaoguan
Quanzhou
Taiwan Strait
TAIPEI
Zhangzhou
(China and Taiwan
claim all of each
other's territory)
T'aichung
GUANGDONG
Xiamen
Hualien
Guangzhou
Chaozhou
Chiai
Tropic of Cancer
Shantou
haoqing
Dongguan
T'ainan
TAIWAN
Jiangmen
South China
Sea
Maoming
Hong Kong
Kaohsiung
(Xianggang)
Macao
(Aomen)
(Huang He)
Hainan Dao

Did you know?

> Many of the world's inventions and technological advances originally came from China, including paper, money, compasses, fireworks, and silk.

> North Korean students are required to work for the government during part of their summer holidays as payment for their free education.

> The majority of the Chinese population lives in just 15 per cent of the total land area.

MODERN SHANGHAI

China's largest city is Shanghai. More than eight million people live in this wealthy east coast port. International trade has recently transformed Shanghai's skyline, which is now crowded with high-rise buildings and modern shopping malls. The centre of town still has some old western-style buildings that have survived from the days before the revolution.

CHINESE INDUSTRY

After the revolutionary leader Mao Zedong died in 1976, China's economy opened up. New industry is now encouraged, and many people are moving from the country to cities where there are relatively well-paid jobs.

BICYCLE FACTORY

BEAUTY OF TAIWAN

Taiwan's mountainous countryside is famous for its natural beauty, scenic lakes, and many ornate Buddhist temples. This peaceful environment contrasts sharply with Taiwan's capital city, Taipei, which is one of the fastest growing cities in Asia.

Japan

JAPAN IS SITUATED in the north Pacific Ocean off the coast of the Asian continent. It is made up of four main islands and more than 3,000 smaller ones. The Japanese people have a distinctive culture based on traditions built up over thousands of years. They have their own language and script. Schoolchildren all learn to read and write both in the traditional script and using letters. Social rules in Japan are strict, and respect and politeness are considered very important. Most people bow when greeting one another, for example. Japan is a very modern country, however, with one of the world's most technologically advanced societies. Its economy is based on the development and production of cutting-edge electronics and vehicles, and most families have the latest consumer goods.

RELIGIONS OF JAPAN

Many Japanese people follow a mix of the Shinto and Buddhist religions, attending wedding blessings in Shinto shrines and funerals in Buddhist temples. Buddhism originated in India, and arrived in Japan in the 6th century, whereas the Shinto faith is native to Japan. Respect for nature is especially important in the Shinto religion. Many natural locations, such as Mount Fuji, are considered sacred.

MOUNT FUJI is a dormant volcano.

JAPANESE TEMPLE

Earthquakes

The islands of Japan are situated in an area where four of the Earth's tectonic plates meet. This causes frequent earthquakes. Japanese schoolchildren are taught how to keep safe during an earthquake by sheltering in a doorway or under a table.

OVERCROWDING

Most of the country's 126 million people live in cities in the flatter, coastal areas. Tokyo and Osaka are very crowded, and homes here are usually very small and are designed to make the most of the limited space.

FASHION IN JAPAN

On ordinary days, Japanese people usually wear western-style clothes. Most children have a school uniform. On festival days, such as Children's Day, many people prefer to wear the traditional kimono. Women's kimonos are often made of colourful silk, decorated with beautiful designs.

Traditional and modern dress side-by-side

Map labels

Kuril'sk
Ostrov Iturup
Kurile Islands
Ostrov Shikotan
Ostrov Kunashir

(Kurile Islands administered by Russian Federation, claimed by Japan)

Sea of Okhotsk

Nemuro
Akkeshi
Bekkai
Shari
Kushiro
Kitami
Abashiri
Shintoku
Asan-dake 2290m
Obihiro
Hiroo
Hokkaidō
Monbetsu
Hiroshiri-dake 2051m
Shirataki
Nakagawa
Shibetsu
Nayoro
Chitose
Ebetsu
Tomakomai
Noboribetsu
Takikawa
Asahikawa
Muroran
Uchiura-wan
Wakkanai
Rebun-tō
Rishiri-tō
Iwanai
Otaru
Sapporo
Ishikari-wan
Esashi
Setana
Hakodate
Fukushima
Okushiri-tō
Tsugaru-kaikyō

La Perouse Strait

Mutsu
Mutsu-wan
Towada
Aomori
Goshogawara
Kuroishi
Hirosaki
Noshiro
Ōdate
Gojōme
Akita
Honjō
Yuzawa
Sakata
Tsuruoka
Shinjō

Kuji
Fudi
Hachinohe
Iwate
Miyako
Morioka
Hanamaki
Kesennuma
Yokote
Shizugawa
Ishinomaki
Furukawa

Scale

0 km 100 200
0 miles 100 200

BASEBALL

Baseball, known as *yakyu*, is fast becoming Japan's most popular sport. As well as two professional leagues, the game is played at universities and high schools. It was introduced to Japan in the late 1800s.

A HEALTHY DIET

Rice is the major crop grown on the small amount of flat land in Japan. Along with rice, fish is an important part of most meals, and Japan has one of the world's largest fishing fleets. This healthy diet may be part of the reason why Japanese people have the world's longest life expectancy.

A **DISH** of raw fish and rice, known as sushi

BULLET TRAIN

One of the fastest ways to travel around Japan is on their high-speed train system, known as the bullet trains, or Shinkansen. This network connects Tokyo with most of the country's other major cities, such as Sapporo and Nagasaki. The trains reach speeds of over 300 kmh (186 mph). Japan ran the world's first high-speed train in 1964.

MODERN TECHNOLOGY

Japan's economy is based on high-tech research, development, and production. The country has built up a reputation for providing the latest technology in vehicles and electronic goods, such as televisions, computers, and stereo systems. Their products are usually of a high quality but are still affordable.

A **PROTOTYPE** of a Mazda car produced in Hiroshima.

MARTIAL ARTS

Kendo is a popular martial art in Japan. It was developed (in its modern form) about 200 years ago, and teaches the art of Japanese Samurai swordsmanship. Children train using bamboo swords (above).

Map labels

JAPAN

Honshū

Chōshi, Chiba, Yokohama, TŌKYŌ, Kawasaki, Fujisawa, Narita, Oyama, Kawagoe, Utsunomiya, Mito, Takasaki, Maebashi, Matsumoto, Kōfu, Fuji, Shizuoka, Toyota, Okazaki, Nagoya, Gifu, Ōgaki, Ise, Tsu, Wakayama, Tanabe, Gobō, Shingū, Owase

Hitachi, Iwaki, Kōriyama, Sukagawa, Fukushima, Aizu, Niitsu, Niigata, Nagaoka, Jōetsu, Nagano, Takaoka, Kanazawa, Komatsu, Fukui, Tsuruga, Ōtsu, Kyōto, Kōbe, Ōsaka, Sakai, Himeji, Okayama, Kurashiki, Fukuyama, Kure, Tottori, Yonago, Matsue, Izumo, Gōtsu, Hamada, Masuda

Ōyama, Kashiwazaki, Itoigawa

Maizuru, Hiroshima, Iwakuni, Hōfu, Ube, Nagato, Yamaguchi, Shimonoseki, Kitakyūshū, Fukuoka, Karatsu, Sasebo, Nagasaki, Kumamoto, Yatsushiro, Akune, Sendai, Kagoshima, Kanoya, Miyakonojō, Miyazaki, Nobeoka, Saiki, Ōita, Nakarura, Sukumo, Uwajima, Matsuyama, Niihama, Tokushima, Kōchi, Mugi

Shikoku

Kyūshū

Ōmuta, Kurume, Hitoyoshi

PACIFIC OCEAN

Sea of Japan

East China Sea

Korea Strait

Tsushima, Kō-saki, Iki

Oki-shotō, Dōgo, Dōzen

Sado, Shinano-gawa, Inawashiro-ko, Kasumiga-ura, Bōsō-hantō

Izu-shotō, Izu-hantō, Sagami-nada, Sagami-wan, Suruga-wan, Kōzu-shima, Ō-shima, Nii-jima, Miyake-jima, Mikura-shima, Hachijō-jima

Biwa-ko, Awaji-shima, Kii-suidō, Harima-nada, Wadayama

Hida, Kiso-sammyaku, Iida, Ina, Nakatsugawa, Mount Fuji 3776m, Kaga, Toyama-wan, Chūgoku-sanchi

Tosa-wan, Iyo-nada, Bungo-suidō, Shibushi-wan, Tanega-shima, Yaku-shima, Ōsumi-shotō, Ōsumi-hantō

Amakusa-nada, Koshikijima-rettō, Gotō-rettō

Hamamatsu

Ryūkyū Islands (Nansei-shotō)

Kyūshū, Ōsumi-shotō, Satsunan-shotō, Kagoshima-wan, Amami-guntō, Amami-ō-shima, Naze, Okinawa, Naha, Oki-no-erabu-jima, Okinawa-shotō

0 km 100
0 miles 100

Mainland SE Asia

THE PENINSULA of Southeast Asia lies directly below India and China, between the Pacific and Indian oceans. It is made up of Myanmar (Burma), Thailand, Vietnam, Cambodia, and Laos. Over thousands of years, the influence of people from nearby Indian, Chinese, and Arabian cultures has helped to give this region a diverse mix of cultures and religions. Much of the land here is mountainous, with half the region covered in forest. Most people live in coastal or lowland regions, where they can grow crops such as rice, raise cattle, and catch fish. In recent years, the electronics industry has also become an important part of Southeast Asian economies, especially in Thailand.

ORPHANS IN CAMBODIA

Cambodia has the highest percentage of widows and orphans of any country in the world. Many men were killed in civil wars in recent decades.

CAMBODIAN ORPHANAGE

GROWING RICE

Rice is the most important crop in Southeast Asia. It grows well in wet lowland areas, such as the Mekong River delta in Vietnam, where the plants can be grown in paddy fields. Most rice is planted and harvested by women.

RURAL LIVING

Most people in Southeast Asia live in rural areas rather than cities, and farming is the most common occupation. The steep mountainous regions are often unsuitable for growing crops or raising cattle, however, and many farming communities are based in the fertile river valleys and deltas. There are over 200 villages on and around this lake (right) in Myanmar.

KAREN TRIBE

PADAUNG women, who are part of the Karen tribe, wear distinctive gold neck rings.

There are 600,000 tribespeople living in the northeastern hills of Thailand. The Karen are the largest hill tribe. They originated from Myanmar, but moved into Thailand to escape political unrest

Gulf of Tongking

Tropic of Cancer

CHINA

BANGLADESH

Bay of Bengal

Ramree Island
Cheduba Island

Sandoway

MYANMAR (BURMA)

INDIA

Kumon Range

Hkakabo Razi

Hengduan Shan

Myitkyina
Mogaung
Maingkwan
Katha
Bhamo
Banmauk
Tamu
Palam
Monywa
Shwebo
Sagaing
Mandalay
Amarapura
Myingyan
Kyaukse
Meiktila
Pakokku
Chauk
Yenangyaung
Myinmu
Minbu
Magwe
Pyechin
Pyu
Thayetmyo
Allanmyo
Prome
Taungdwingyi
Myanaung
Letpadan
Henzada
Pegu
Nyaunglebin
Pyuntaza
Pyinmana
Toungoo
Paungde

Shan Plateau

Taunggyi
Loi-Kaw
Keng Tung
Lashio

Arakan Yoma

Chin Hills

Irrawaddy

Salween

Sittang

Pawn

THAILAND

Fang
Chiang Rai
Chiang Mai
Lampang
Lamphun
Phrae
Phayao
Nan

Mae Nam Ping
Nam Yom

LAOS

CHINA

Lai Chau
Lao Cai
Ha Giang
Cao Bang
Lang Son
Bac Giang
Dien Bien
Muang Namo
Xam Nua
Sop Hao
Phongsali
Nam Qu
Louangnamtha
Muang Sing
Muang Xiang Ngeum
Louangphabang
Viangphoukha
Houayxay
Nam Ou

Hoang Lien Son

Black River

Mekong

VIETNAM

Thai Nguyen
Viet Tri
HA NOI
Ha Dong
Ha Bình
Hoa Binh
Nam Dinh
Thanh Hoa
Tuong Duong
Vinh
Dong Hoi

Hong Gai
Cam Pha
Hai Phong
Thai Binh

Chaine Annamitique

Xaignabouri
Ang Nam Nguin
Pek
Pakxan
Bao Hin Heup
VIENTIANE (VIANGCHAN)
Nong Khai
Loei
Nan
Nam Ngum

Sirikit Reservoir

Khorat

Thakhek
Nakhon

Tropic of Cancer

ANGKOR WAT

The impressive temple complex of Angkor Wat in Cambodia attracts visitors interested in its history and architecture. This combination of temples and palaces was built in AD 1113 by the Khmer king Suryavarman II. The buildings are made of stone and brick and are decorated with relief sculptures showing mythical scenes of Hindu gods and great royal processions. The complex was uncovered in 1861 by French naturalist Henri Mouhot, following stories of a "lost city" in the jungle.

TEMPLE AT ANGKOR WAT

MONASTIC LIFE

The main religion in mainland Southeast Asia is Buddhism. Nearly all Thai villages have their own temple, or *wat*, which is the centre of village life. Most young men spend some time in a monastery, where they have few possessions and spend much of their time in meditation.

FLOATING MARKET

The capital of Thailand, Bangkok, is a busy, crowded city with about six million inhabitants. The city was built on an island in the river, and has many canals. Boats, known as *sampans*, (above) act as floating markets from which traders sell fresh fruit and vegetables.

Did you know?

- A traditional greeting in Thailand is the "wai". The hands are placed together in prayer position and slightly raised, as the head is bowed.

- A large, previously unknown mammal, the vu quang ox, was only recently discovered in the forests of northern Vietnam.

THAI BEACHES

Tourism is now a major industry for Thailand. Popular destinations include the country's lively capital, Bangkok, and the beautiful island beach resorts (below). Phuket, Thailand's largest island, is often referred to as the "Pearl of the South".

Maritime SE Asia

To the south of the Asian mainland lies maritime Southeast Asia. It includes Malaysia, Indonesia, East Timor, Singapore, and the Philippines. Part of Malaysia is connected to the mainland, but the rest of the region is made up of more than 20,000 islands that stretch across the Pacific and Indian Oceans. Lying near the Equator, the climate is mostly hot, wet, and humid. Most of the larger islands are mountainous and covered in dense forest, and many people live in villages near rivers or on the coast. Like the rest of Southeast Asia, the population is made up of people from many different cultural backgrounds and hundreds of different languages are spoken. The most common religion is Islam, except in the Philippines, where most people are Roman Catholic.

GREAT APES

The orangutans are great apes that only live in Borneo and the northern corner of Sumatra. They spend most of their time in the trees, even building treetop nests in which to sleep. Sadly, the orangutan is endangered because of deforestation.

PEOPLE OF MALAYSIA

Ethnic Malaysians make up 59 per cent of the population, and are known as *bumiputera*, meaning "sons of the soil". Most Malaysians are Muslim. Ethnic Chinese form 26 per cent of the population.

Ubadiah mosque, Malaysia

THE SULTAN OF BRUNEI

SULTAN OF BRUNEI

Brunei is ruled by a sultan who lives in the world's largest palace. The sultan is one of the wealthiest men in the world.

SINGAPORE

As the financial and industrial centre of Southeast Asia, Singapore is one of the wealthiest countries in this region. It has a thriving high-tech industry and a high standard of living. There are strictly enforced laws forbidding littering and other small crimes. The death penalty is imposed for drug smuggling. The government also controls the press and restricts the Internet.

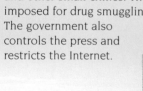

SKYSCRAPERS in Singapore's financial district

KITE-FLYING

After the harvest, the people of Malaysia celebrate with the Wau-flying (kite-flying) Festival. Here, skilled people demonstrate the traditional Malaysian sport.

Map labels

Andaman Sea
South China Sea
THAILAND
Bandaaceh
Sigli
Langsa
Meulaboh
George Town
Butterworth
Pulau Pinang
Taiping
Ipoh
Kota Bharu
Kuala Terengganu
Dungun
Cukai
Kuala Lipis
Kuantan
Medan
Tebingtinggi
Klang
KUALA LUMPUR
Pulau Simeulue
Pematangsiantar
PUTRAJAYA
Seremban
M A L A Y S I A
Kepulauan Banyak
Sibolga
Danau Toba
Melaka
Muar
Keluang
Batu Pahat
Johor Bahru
SINGAPORE
Pulau Nias
Panyabungan
Pekanbaru
Singkawang
Kepulauan Natuna
Miri
Bintulu
Kota Kinabalu
BANDAR SERI BEGAWAN
BRUNEI
Gunung Kin
Bal
INDIAN OCEAN
Equator
Solok
Rengat
Kepulauan Lingga
Pontianak
Sidas
Sungai Kapuas
Kuching
Sri Aman
Sibu
Batang Rajang
Sarawak
Sungai K
Pegunungan Muller
Sungai Mahu
B o r n e o
Padang
Pulau Siberut
Kualatungkal
Selat Karimata
Balikpap
Kalimantan
Sungai Barito
Amu
Batang Hari
Jambi
Bangka
Pangkalpinang
Sumatra (Sumatera)
Palembang
Sampit
Kandangan
Banjarmasin
Kepulauan Mentawai
Sungaipenuh
Pegunungan Barisan
Lahat
Pulau Belitung
I N D O
Bengkulu
Kotabumi
Pu
La
Bandarlampung
Cirebon
Java Sea
JAKARTA
Serang
Tegal
Pekalongan
Semarang
Pulau Madura
Bogor
Kudus
Sukabumi
Selat Sunda
Bandung
Tasikmalaya
Java (Jawa)
Surabaya
Probolinggo
Jember
Bali
Mataram
Cilacap
Magelang
Malang
Kediri
Denpa
Yogyakarta
Madiun
Pula
Lomb
Surakarta
Strait of Malacca
Selat Serasan

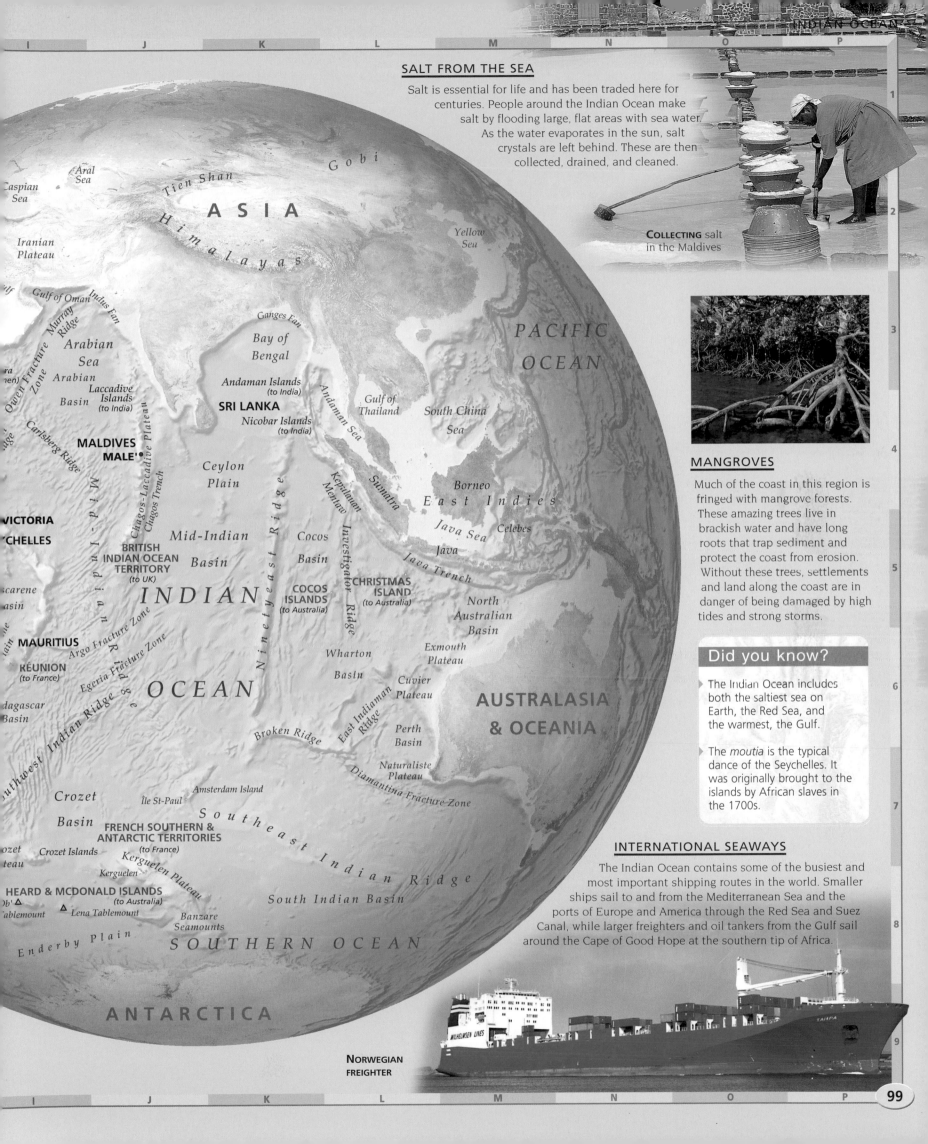

SALT FROM THE SEA

Salt is essential for life and has been traded here for centuries. People around the Indian Ocean make salt by flooding large, flat areas with sea water. As the water evaporates in the sun, salt crystals are left behind. These are then collected, drained, and cleaned.

COLLECTING salt in the Maldives

MANGROVES

Much of the coast in this region is fringed with mangrove forests. These amazing trees live in brackish water and have long roots that trap sediment and protect the coast from erosion. Without these trees, settlements and land along the coast are in danger of being damaged by high tides and strong storms.

Did you know?

▸ The Indian Ocean includes both the saltiest sea on Earth, the Red Sea, and the warmest, the Gulf.

▸ The *moutia* is the typical dance of the Seychelles. It was originally brought to the islands by African slaves in the 1700s.

INTERNATIONAL SEAWAYS

The Indian Ocean contains some of the busiest and most important shipping routes in the world. Smaller ships sail to and from the Mediterranean Sea and the ports of Europe and America through the Red Sea and Suez Canal, while larger freighters and oil tankers from the Gulf sail around the Cape of Good Hope at the southern tip of Africa.

NORWEGIAN FREIGHTER

Map labels:

Caspian Sea, Aral Sea, Tien Shan, Gobi, ASIA, Himalayas, Yellow Sea, Iranian Plateau, Gulf of Oman, Indus Fan, Murray Ridge, Qwen Fracture Zone, Arabian Sea, Arabian Basin, Laccadive Islands (to India), Carlsberg Ridge, Ganges Fan, Bay of Bengal, Andaman Islands (to India), SRI LANKA, Nicobar Islands (to India), Andaman Sea, Sumatra, Gulf of Thailand, South China Sea, PACIFIC OCEAN, MALDIVES, MALE', Chagos-Laccadive Plateau, Chagos Trench, Ceylon Plain, Kepulauan Mentawi, Investigator Ridge, Borneo, East Indies, Java Sea, Celebes, VICTORIA, SEYCHELLES, Mid-Indian Ridge, BRITISH INDIAN OCEAN TERRITORY (to UK), Mid-Indian Basin, Cocos Basin, Java, Java Trench, INDIAN, COCOS ISLANDS (to Australia), CHRISTMAS ISLAND (to Australia), North Australian Basin, scarene asin, MAURITIUS, Argo Fracture Zone, Egeria Fracture Zone, Ninetyeast Ridge, Wharton Basin, Exmouth Plateau, RÉUNION (to France), OCEAN, Cuvier Plateau, AUSTRALASIA & OCEANIA, dagascar Basin, Southwest Indian Ridge, East Indiaman Ridge, Perth Basin, Broken Ridge, Naturaliste Plateau, Diamantina Fracture Zone, Crozet Basin, Amsterdam Island, Île St-Paul, Southeast Indian Ridge, FRENCH SOUTHERN & ANTARCTIC TERRITORIES (to France), Crozet Islands, ozet teau, Kerguelen Plateau, Kerguelen, HEARD & MCDONALD ISLANDS (to Australia), South Indian Basin, ablemount, Lena Tablemount, Banzare Seamounts, Enderby Plain, SOUTHERN OCEAN, ANTARCTICA

AUSTRALASIA & OCEANIA

THE CONTINENT OF AUSTRALIA – the smallest of the

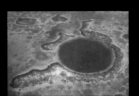

world's seven continents – lies between the Indian

and Pacific oceans. It forms part of a much larger region known

as Oceania that includes numerous small islands

and stretches across the southern half of the Pacific,

the world's deepest and biggest ocean. Australia is by far the biggest

island in Oceania. Nine out of every ten Australians live next

to the coast, as the interior is hot, inhospitable

desert. New Zealand is mountainous and temperate

in climate, while Papua New Guinea is largely

rainforest. The rest of Oceania consists of thousands

of small coral atolls and island outcrops of solid rock. In all, the region

comprises 14 countries with a population of almost 31 million people.

SW Pacific

THE ISLANDS OF THE southwest Pacific are home to people of many different cultures and languages. The islands are divided into three general groups based on their location and the similarities between their peoples. The Polynesian islands to the east include Tonga, Samoa, the Cook Islands, and Tahiti. Melanesia includes Fiji, the Solomon Islands, and Vanuatu. The smallest group, Micronesia, includes the Marshall, Kiribati, and Caroline Islands. The first Europeans came to the southwest Pacific in the 1600s, several thousand years after Melanesians, Micronesians, and Polynesians first settled there.

MEN from Papua New Guinea wearing traditional make-up

Beads, shells, and feathers form part of the decoration.

ISLAND HOLIDAYS

White sandy beaches and warm water makes this region ideal for tourists.

NORTHERN MARIANA ISLANDS (to US)

Tinian
Saipan
Rota

GUAM ✈ **HAGÅTÑA**
(to US)

Mi c r o n e s i a

Enewetak Atoll Bikini Atoll Rongelap Atoll

MARSHA

Ujelang Atoll *Ratak Ch* *Ralik Ch* Rata

Yap

Kwajalein Atoll
Namu Atoll

MICRONESIA

Ailinglaplap Atoll

Babeldaob
OREOR ✈

Chuuk Islands
PALIKIR ✈ Pohnpei

C a r o l i n e   I s l a n d s

Jaluit At

Kosrae

Ebo
Ato

PALAU

Did you know?

On some Melanesian Islands, people have overcome the problems caused by having so many languages by learning an additional language – Pidgin English. This language is a mixture of English and some common words from island languages.

M i c r o n e s

NAURU

M e l a

Equator

LAND OF MANY LANGUAGES

Historically, the mountainous landscape of Papua New Guinea made contact between the villages difficult. As a result of many years of isolation, some villages developed their own individual languages. Nationwide, about 750 different languages evolved.

Admiralty Islands
St. Matthias Group

Bismarck Archipelago
Bismarck Sea
New Ireland

INDONESIA

Madang
Central Range
△ Mount Wilhelm 4509m
Owen Stanley Range
Lae

PAPUA NEW GUINEA

New Guinea

Bougainville Island

New Britain

Solomon Sea

Choiseul

Santa Isabel

Bougainville

New Georgia Islands
Malaita

HONIARA ✈

Guadalcanal

San Cristobal

Rennell

SOLOMON

ISLANDS

Santa Cr
Islands

PORT MORESBY ✈

Gulf of Papua

D'Entrecasteaux Islands

Louisiade Archipelago

A MIX OF RELIGIONS

Christianity is the dominant religion on most southwest Pacific islands, however Islam and Hinduism are also practised. Many people also retain beliefs from traditional religions that existed before the islands were colonized by people from Europe and Asia.

C o r a l   S e a

CORAL SEA ISLANDS
(to Australia)

Bank
Islan

VANUATU

Espiritu Santo

Ma
Pe

Malekula

PORT-VILA ✈

E

NEW CALEDONIA
(to France)

Erromango
Tanna
Ane

Ouvéa
Iles Loyauté
Lifou
Ma

New Caledonia

NOUMÉA

Tropic of Capricorn

VANUATU tribespeople dance at a religious ceremony.

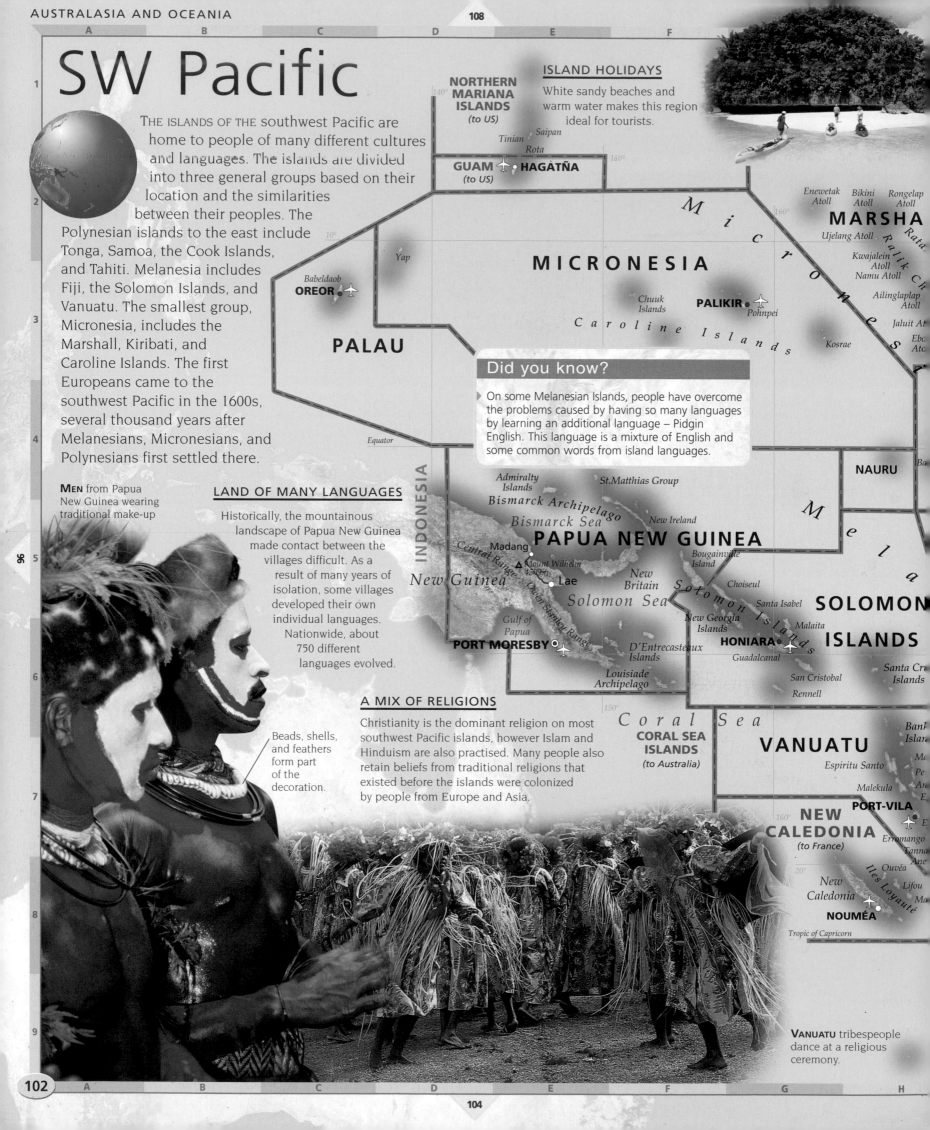

FOOD CROPS

Most Pacific islanders live in small villages near the sea. Inland areas are often mountainous, making farming difficult. Instead, people grow foods such as sweet potatoes, bananas, and coconuts in lowland areas. As well as providing milk, the coconut meat is used to produce copra, a substance for making soap and cosmetics.

COPRA WORKER in Fiji scooping coconut kernels

THE KINGDOM OF TONGA

Tonga is the only Pacific nation never fully brought under foreign rule. Instead, it is run in the traditional way by its own king. All land is owned by the royal family and is allotted to households for their use. Now, some young, westernized Tongans have started calling for more democracy.

THE ROYAL PALACE IN TONGA

FAMILY LIFE

Many Pacific people live in extended family groups. Recently, however, some islanders have migrated to countries such as New Zealand and the United States in order to look for work.

COOK ISLAND FAMILY

KINGMAN REEF

PALMYRA ATOLL (to US)

BAKER & HOWLAND ISLANDS (to US)

JARVIS ISLAND (to US)

Teraina
Tabuaeran

Kiritimati (Christmas Island)

International Dateline

BAIRIKI

Tungaru

Beru
Nikunau
Tamana
Arorae

PACIFIC OCEAN

KIRIBATI

Kanton
Birnie Island
Enderbury Island
McKean Island
Orona
Manra
Nikumaruro

Phoenix Islands

Malden Island

Starbuck Island

Line Islands

Nuku Hiva

Marquesas Islands

Hiva Oa
Fatu Hiva

Nanumea Atoll
Niutao
Nanumaga
Nui Atoll
Nukufetau
Funafuti **FONGAFALE**
Atoll

UVALU

Nukulaelae

Niulakita

Atafu Atoll
Nukunonu Atoll
Fakaofo Atoll

TOKELAU (to New Zealand)

Penrhyn
Rakahanga

Vostok Island
Millennium Island

Polynesia

Flint Island

Polynesia

WALLIS & FUTUNA (to France)

Rotuma

Île Uvea
MATĀ'UTU
Île Futuna

SAMOA

Savai'i
Upolu

ĀPIA

AMERICAN SAMOA (to US)

PAGO PAGO
Ta'ū
Tutuila

Manihiki

Northern Cook Islands

Tikehau
Takaroa

Fakarava

Makemo

Tuamotu Islands

FIJI

Cikobia
Vanua Levu

Nadi
Viti Levu
SUVA

Kadavu

Lau Group

Niuatoputapu

TONGA

Vava'u Group
Tofua
Ha'apai Group

International Dateline

COOK ISLANDS (to New Zealand)

Palmerston

NIUE (to New Zealand)

ALOFI

Manuae

Raiatea
PAPEETE
Tahiti

Archipel de la Société

Amanu
Tatakoto

Ahunui

NUKU'ALOFA
Tongatapu
'Eua

Tongatapu Group

Southern Cook Islands

Takutea

AVARUA
Rarotonga
Mangaia

FRENCH POLYNESIA (to France)

Vanavana
Marutea

Rurutu
Tubuai

Tureia

Îles Australes

Raevavae

Tropic of Capricorn

Fangataufa

OUTRIGGER CANOES

Transport between many islands has traditionally been by outrigger canoes. Floats attached to the side provide extra stability, particularly useful for the fishermen who stand in the boats to cast their nets.

ISLANDERS netfishing in an outrigger off the coast of Ifalik, Micronesia.

| 0 km | 300 | 600 |
| 0 miles | 300 | 600 |

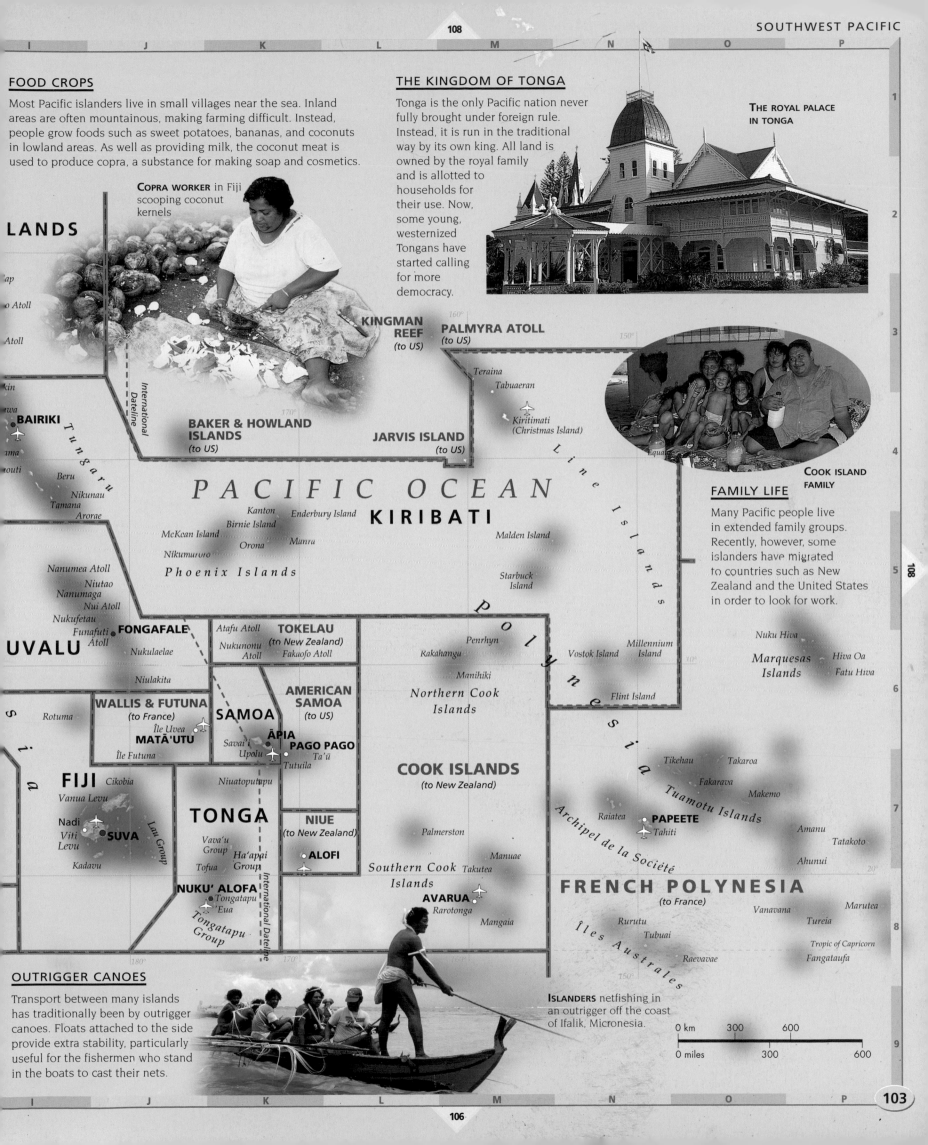

Australia

A HUGE, GENERALLY FLAT COUNTRY, Australia has relatively few inhabitants. This is mainly because most of the land is hot, semi-arid desert – known as the outback – unsuitable for towns or farms. In places where there is some vegetation, or the land has been irrigated, sheep and cattle are grazed. Wheat is grown in the fertile south. The first people to live here were the Aboriginals, who arrived from Asia at least 50,000 years ago. Today, most Australians are descendants of European immigrants, with a more recent addition of Asians.

FLYING DOCTOR

For anyone living in the remote Australian outback, the nearest doctor can be many hours away. When emergency help is needed, the Royal Flying Doctor Services can get to the scene to treat a patient or fly them to hospital.

AUSTRALIAN ABORIGINALS

The original inhabitants of Australia had an intimate understanding of their environment. This connection to the land, and its plants and animals, affects every aspect of their culture. When Europeans started arriving in the late 18th century, only the Aboriginals in remote areas escaped contact with the diseases they brought. Today, Aboriginals rarely live off the land, but work in factories or farms.

MINING

Australia has one of the world's most important mining industries, with resources including gold (left), coal, natural gas, iron ore, copper, and opals. However, damage to the environment, and Aboriginal claims over land used for mining, still need to be faced.

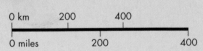

0 km   200   400

0 miles   200   400

AUSTRALIAN FOOTBALL

A popular sport here is Australian Rules Football. One of the rules is that players can kick or punch the ball but they must not throw it. Many Australians either play the game themselves or support their favourite team. As the name implies, the game originated in Australia, but it now has leagues in other countries, such as Great Britain and the USA.

OUTDOOR SPORTS

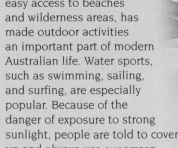

A warm climate, with easy access to beaches and wilderness areas, has made outdoor activities an important part of modern Australian life. Water sports, such as swimming, sailing, and surfing, are especially popular. Because of the danger of exposure to strong sunlight, people are told to cover up and always use sunscreen.

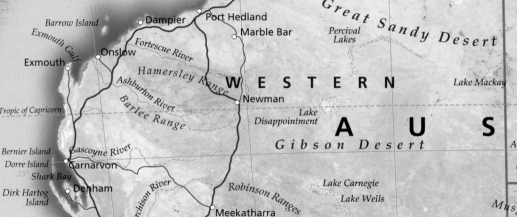

Melville Island
Bathurst Island
Darwin
Cape Londonderry   Joseph Bonaparte Gulf   Pine
Bonaparte
Bigge Island   Victoria Ri
Archipelago
Heywood   Wyndham
Islands   Kununurra   Top Sp
Roadh
Kimberley
King Sound   Plateau   Fitzroy
Broome   Crossing   Halls Creek   Tan
De
Fitzroy River
INDIAN OCEAN   Eighty Mile Beach
N
Barrow Island   Dampier   Port Hedland   Great Sandy Desert
Exmouth Gulf   Marble Bar   Percival   TE
Onslow   Fortescue River   Lakes   Lake Mackay   Mad
Exmouth   Hamersley Range   W E S T E R N
Ashburton River   Newman   A U S T
Tropic of Capricorn   Barlee Range   Lake
Disappointment   Lake
Amadeus
Gibson Desert   Uluru
Bernier Island   Gascoyne River   (Ayers Rock)
Dorre Island   Carnarvon   867m
Shark Bay   Denham   A U S T R A L I A   Musgrave Ra
Dirk Hartog   Murchison River   Lake Carnegie
Island   Robinson Ranges   Lake Wells
Meekatharra   A U S T R A L I A
Kalbarri   Mount Magnet   Great Victoria
Lake Carey   Desert
Geraldton   Lake Barlee
Lake Moore   Lake Rebecca
Moora   Kalgoorlie   Zanthus   Reid
Southern Cross   Coolgardie   Nullarbor Plain
Gingin   Merredin   Lake Cowan   Eucla
Perth   Northam   Norseman
Fremantle   Brookton   Balladonia
Mandurah   Narrogin
Bunbury   Wagin   Esperance
Collie   Katanning
Busselton   Great Australian Big
Manjimup
Augusta
Albany

UNIQUE WILDLIFE

Animal parks and refuges allow "townies" and tourists to get close to Australia's unique wildlife. They can see marsupials, such as koalas and wallabies (left), as well as crocodiles, snakes, and the world's only egg-laying mammals – the platypus and the echidna.

Did you know?

▶ Voting in government elections in Australia is compulsory. Citizens who fail to vote can be fined.

▶ July and August are the coldest months, when some Australians like to go skiing.

▶ The deadly blue-ringed octopus lives in the waters off the Australian coast.

TOURIST ATTRACTIONS

Tourism is important to Australia's economy, and there is plenty to attract visitors. Popular destinations include the tropical waters around the Great Barrier Reef (above), the modern cities of Sydney and Melbourne, and the impressive sight of Uluru (Ayers Rock), a mountainous rock sacred to the Aboriginals.

VINEYARDS

Australia boasts an impressive range of high-quality wine-growing regions, specializing in different grapes. Wines are exported to more than 90 countries.

LIFE IN THE CITIES

Most Australians live in the coastal towns and cities of southeastern Australia where the climate is cooler. Although Canberra is the capital, Sydney is the largest and oldest city, and is beautifully situated around Sydney Harbour. One of the world's most famous landmarks is the Sydney Opera House (below) which has five separate halls for concerts, operas, and plays. The design echoes the sails of a ship.

Arafura Sea

Gulf of Carpentaria

Coral Sea

Great Barrier Reef

QUEENSLAND

NORTHERN TERRITORY

SOUTH AUSTRALIA

NEW SOUTH WALES

VICTORIA

AUSTRALIAN CAPITAL TERRITORY

Tasman Sea

Bass Strait

TASMANIA

New Zealand

MADE UP OF TWO MAIN ISLANDS and several smaller islands, New Zealand is one of the most isolated countries in the world. Located in the southern Pacific, the country has a mild climate, with warm summers and cool, wet winters. Both islands have mountains, short, swift-flowing rivers, forests, and fertile farmland. Until the Europeans arrived, most of the landscape was covered in dense forest, known as native bush. Today, although forests remain, much has been cleared for farming. Most New Zealanders live on North Island, which is warmer and less mountainous. Although New Zealanders are of mainly British descent, the Maoris – a people of Polynesian origin – were the first to arrive about 1,000 years ago. Today, non-Maori Polynesians and Asians are adding to the ethnic mix. The country has a liberal, clean, green image and a high standard of living.

AUCKLAND

With its safe harbour and nearby scenic islands, Auckland is known as the City of Sails. It boasts more pleasure boats per person than anywhere else in the world. The water that separates the bigger islands is home to dolphins, families of blue penguins, and the occasional whale.

Did you know?

▶ The Maori name for New Zealand is Aotearoa, meaning "land of the long white cloud".

▶ In 1893, New Zealand was the first country to grant women the vote.

▶ There is only one poisonous animal here, the katipo spider.

MAORI CULTURE

Maoris make up almost16 per cent of the population, with most living on North Island. Before the coming of the *Pakeha* (white man) Maori history was passed on orally to succeeding generations. This included many legends and *waiata* (song). Their carvings in wood (left) and stone (right) were another way they recorded and remembered events. In recent years, interest in Maori culture has increased, and school children are now taught the Maori language.

GREENSTONE (jade) carving is an example of Maori art.

PACIFIC OCEAN

Tasman Sea

North Island

Three Kings Islands
Cape Reinga
North Cape
Te Kao
Ninety Mile Beach
Great Exhibition Bay
Kaitaia
Okaihau
Kaikohe
Hokianga Harbour
Kerikeri
Paihia
Bay of Islands
Hikurangi
Whangarei
Ruawai
Wairoa
Dargaville
Kaipara Harbour
Wellsford
Helensville
Waikworth
Waiuku
Takapuna
Manurewa
Auckland
Papakura
Pukekohe
Waiuku
Huntly
Morrinsville
Hamilton
Cambridge
Otorohanga
Te Kuiti
Taumarunui
Ohura
Stratford
New Plymouth
Waitara
Cape Egmont
Mount Taranaki (Mount Egmont) 2518m
Hawera
Patea
Wanganui
North Taranaki Bight
South Taranaki Bight
Little Barrier Island
Great Barrier Island
Coville Channel
Hauraki Gulf
Coromandel
Whitianga
Thames
Paeroa
Katikati
Tauranga
Matamata
Mayor Island
Whakatane
Opotiki
Bay of Plenty
Kawerau
Rotorua
Lake Rotorua
Lake Rotoiti
Tokoroa
Lake Taupo
Taupo
Turangi
Waiouru
Taihape
Raetihi
Mount Ruapehu 2797m
Marton
Feilding
Rangitikei
Kaimanawa Range
Wairoa
Lake Waikaremoana
Murupara
Gisborne
Poverty Bay
East Cape
Ruatoria
Raukumara Range
Mahia Peninsula
Hawke Bay
Napier
Hastings
Havelock North
Waipawa
Waipukurau
Dannevirke

100
50
100
0 km   50
0 miles

38°
40°
176°
178°

AN AGRICULTURAL NATION

Agriculture is of prime importance, and accounts for more than half of national export earnings. Orchards produce a vast range of fruit from apples (above) to kiwi fruit (below). Cereal and other crops, such as sunflowers, add colour and variety to the landscape. Traditional sheep and cattle farming has expanded to include deer, goats, and even ostriches.

FLIGHTLESS KIWI BIRD

UNIQUE WILDLIFE

New Zealand has many unique and endangered animal species, especially birds. Because there were no mammal predators before humans introduced them, many species have few means of defence, and some birds, such as the kiwi (above) cannot fly. Conservation schemes are now in place to protect endangered species.

GREEN ENERGY

Most of the country's electricity comes from hydro-electric power. It is generated by river water gushing through turbines inside dams at power stations (left). New Zealand also has geothermal energy using heat from inside the Earth.

VOLCANIC ACTIVITY

A fault line runs through New Zealand where two major tectonic plates meet. It has caused devastating earthquakes, but has also helped create breathtaking scenery. This includes South Island's Southern Alps, and many smaller volcanic mountains, hot springs, and geysers in North Island.

LADY KNOX geyser, North Island

FILM INDUSTRY

New Zealand has a well-established film industry. Today, thanks to the acclaimed Tolkien trilogy, *Lord of the Rings* (above), the country has become increasingly popular with international studios for location work. The country offers an unusually wide range of scenery as well as technical experts.

ADVENTURE SPORTS PARADISE

New Zealand offers a huge range of adventure sports and outdoor activities, from whitewater rafting (below) to bungy jumping. The latter originated in Queenstown in South Island. The town is billed as the country's top adventure tourism destination because its surrounding lakes, mountains, and rivers, and its mostly dry climate, are ideal for outdoor pursuits.

Map labels

NEW ZEALAND

WELLINGTON
Porirua
Lower Hutt
Cape Palliser
Cape Campbell
Cook Str.
Blenheim
Seddon
Clarence
Picton
Nelson
Motueka
Richmond
Richmond Range
Wairau
Cuthenue
Kaikoura
Hanmer Springs
Waipara
Pegasus Bay
Rangiora
Kaiapoi
Lyttelton
Christchurch
Lyttelton
Banks Peninsula
Lake Ellesmere
Canterbury Bight
Springs Junction
Mount Owen 1875m△
Reefton
Otira
Arthur's Pass
Oxford
Darfield
Ashburton
Canterbury Plains
Hinds
Geraldine
Temuka
Timaru
Seddonville
Karamea Bight
Westport
Cape Foulwind
Runanga
Greymouth
Hokitika
Ross
Lake Brunner
Rakaia
Mayfield
Fairlie
Studholme
Waimate
Oamaru
Hampden
Mount Cook/Aoraki 3744m△
Fox Glacier
Abut Head
Whataroa
Haast
Lake Mapourika
Lake Wanaka
Lake Hawea
Wanaka
Cromwell
Alexandra
Clutha
Waitaki
Otago Peninsula
Dunedin
Mosgiel
Milton
Balclutha
South Island
Southern Alps
Queenstown
Lake Wakatipu
Lake Te Anau
Te Anau
Lake Manapouri
Eyre Mts
Lumsden
Mataura
Gore
Mataura
Tokanui
Toetoes Bay
Ruapuke Island
Invercargill
Winton
Riverton
Foveaux Strait
Stewart Island
Milford Sound
George Sound
Caswell Sound
Lake Te Anau
Livingstone Mts
Waiau
Codfish Island
Halfmoon Bay
Te Wae Wae Bay
Muttonbird Islands
Fiordland
Resolution Island
West Cape
South West Cape
Lake Hauroko

Pacific Ocean

THE LARGEST OCEAN ON EARTH, the Pacific covers one-third of the Earth's surface. The island nations of Japan, Indonesia, Australia, New Zealand, and many others are completely surrounded by this enormous ocean, which stretches from the Arctic in the north to the Antarctic in the south. The Pacific is also the world's deepest ocean – its greatest known depth is in the Mariana Trench, off Guam, which plunges steeply for 11,033 m (36,198 ft). Within the Pacific, there are many smaller seas that lie near land. These include the Tasman Sea, the South China Sea, and the Bering Sea. There are more than 30,000 islands in the Pacific. Most are too small or barren to be inhabited, but others are home to people of many different cultures and religions. The native island peoples fall into three main groups – Polynesians, Melanesians, and Micronesians. Although the word pacific means peaceful, strong currents, tropical storms, and tsunamis can all make this ocean far from peaceful.

HAWAII
This chain of eight volcanic islands and 124 islets forms the 50th state of the United States of America and was admitted to the union in 1959. The dramatic landscape and palm-fringed beaches make Hawaii a popular destination for tourists. Today, native Hawaiians are a minority in their own land.

HAWAIIAN conch shells were once blown to sound a warning.

MARINE iguana on the black volcanic rocks of the Galápagos Islands

Tsunami

Earthquakes beneath the sea may cause giant waves called tsunamis. These can travel great distances across the ocean, building into a huge wall of water as they approach the coast. They can leave immense damage in their wake.

GALÁPAGOS ISLANDS
When British naturalist Charles Darwin (1809–82) went to the Galápagos Islands, he found many unusual animals. He also noticed differences between animals of the same species living elsewhere. This led him to believe that, over time, animals adapt, or evolve, to suit their habitats.

Black smoker chimneys

Large red tube worms

SURFING
The Hawaiian sport of surfing ranks as the oldest sport in the USA. It was first practised by the nobility as a form of religious ceremony until the 1820s when missionaries, who thought it immoral, tried to ban it. Today, surfing is one of the most popular watersports and can be seen from Australia and New Zealand to Mexico.

DEEP-SEA VENTS
Underwater exploration has revealed some amazing places deep in the Pacific. Large vents, formed by solidified minerals, act as chimneys for superhot steam and gas that stream up from the seabed. These are known as black smokers. Scientists have found a host of new creatures living in this hostile environment.

Did you know?

▶ The Pacific is larger than Earth's entire land surface.

▶ The Pacific is surrounded by a zone of violent volcanic and earthquake activity, known as the Pacific Ring of Fire.

ASIA

Sea of Japan

Yellow Sea

Japan

East China Sea

Emperor Seamounts

Shikoku Basin

Ryukyu Trench

Taiwan

Philippine Sea

Philippine Basin

NORTHERN MARIANA ISLANDS (to US)

GUAM (to US)

South China Basin

Philippines

▽ Challenger Deep 11,034m

PALAU

Caroline Isle

South China Sea

Celebes Sea

MICR

Borneo

Celebes

M

East Indies

Java Sea

Banda Sea

New Guinea

Java

Timor

Timor Sea

Arafura Sea

Torres Strait

Great Barrier Reef

INDIAN OCEAN

AUSTRALASIA & OCEANIA

Great Australian Bight

South Australian Basin

Bass

Tasm

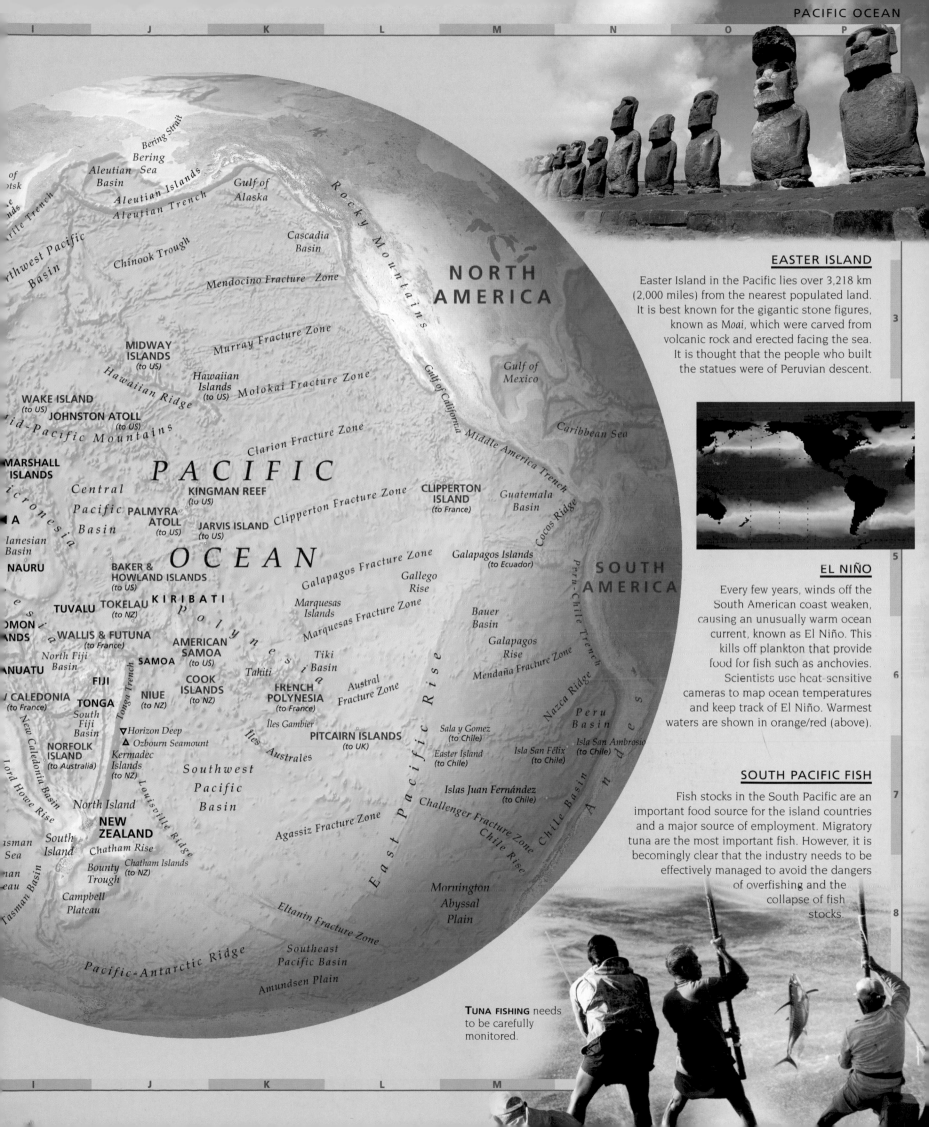

NORTH AMERICA

PACIFIC OCEAN

Bering Strait
Bering Sea
Aleutian Basin
Aleutian Islands
Aleutian Trench
Gulf of Alaska

Rocky Mountains

Chinook Trough

Cascadia Basin

Mendocino Fracture Zone

Northwest Pacific Basin

Kurile Trench

MIDWAY ISLANDS
(to US)

Murray Fracture Zone

Hawaiian Ridge

Hawaiian Islands
(to US)

Molokai Fracture Zone

Gulf of California

Gulf of Mexico

WAKE ISLAND
(to US)

JOHNSTON ATOLL
(to US)

Mid-Pacific Mountains

MARSHALL ISLANDS

Micronesia

Central Pacific Basin

KINGMAN REEF
(to US)

PALMYRA ATOLL
(to US)

Clarion Fracture Zone

JARVIS ISLAND
(to US)

Clipperton Fracture Zone

Middle America Trench

Caribbean Sea

CLIPPERTON ISLAND
(to France)

Guatemala Basin

Cocos Ridge

Melanesian Basin

NAURU

BAKER & HOWLAND ISLANDS
(to US)

Galapagos Fracture Zone

Gallego Rise

Galapagos Islands
(to Ecuador)

SOUTH AMERICA

Peru-Chile Trench

TUVALU

TOKELAU
(to NZ)

KIRIBATI

Polynesia

Marquesas Islands

Marquesas Fracture Zone

Bauer Basin

SOLOMON ISLANDS

WALLIS & FUTUNA
(to France)

North Fiji Basin

AMERICAN SAMOA
(to US)

SAMOA

Tiki Basin

Tahiti

Galapagos Rise

Mendaña Fracture Zone

VANUATU

FIJI

NEW CALEDONIA
(to France)

TONGA

South Fiji Basin

Tonga Trench

NIUE
(to NZ)

COOK ISLANDS
(to NZ)

FRENCH POLYNESIA
(to France)

Austral Fracture Zone

East Pacific Rise

Nazca Ridge

Peru Basin

Andes

NORFOLK ISLAND
(to Australia)

▽ *Horizon Deep*
△ *Ozbourn Seamount*

Kermadec Islands
(to NZ)

Îles Gambier

Îles Australes

PITCAIRN ISLANDS
(to UK)

Sala y Gomez
(to Chile)

Easter Island
(to Chile)

Isla San Félix
(to Chile)

Isla San Ambrosio
(to Chile)

Lord Howe Basin

New Caledonia Basin

Lord Howe Rise

Louisville Ridge

Southwest Pacific Basin

North Island

NEW ZEALAND

Islas Juan Fernández
(to Chile)

Challenger Fracture Zone

Chile Basin

Chile Rise

Tasman Sea

South Island

Chatham Rise

Chatham Islands
(to NZ)

Bounty Trough

Tasman Basin

Campbell Plateau

Agassiz Fracture Zone

Eltanin Fracture Zone

Mornington Abyssal Plain

Pacific-Antarctic Ridge

Southeast Pacific Basin

Amundsen Plain

EASTER ISLAND

Easter Island in the Pacific lies over 3,218 km (2,000 miles) from the nearest populated land. It is best known for the gigantic stone figures, known as *Moai*, which were carved from volcanic rock and erected facing the sea. It is thought that the people who built the statues were of Peruvian descent.

EL NIÑO

Every few years, winds off the South American coast weaken, causing an unusually warm ocean current, known as El Niño. This kills off plankton that provide food for fish such as anchovies. Scientists use heat-sensitive cameras to map ocean temperatures and keep track of El Niño. Warmest waters are shown in orange/red (above).

SOUTH PACIFIC FISH

Fish stocks in the South Pacific are an important food source for the island countries and a major source of employment. Migratory tuna are the most important fish. However, it is becoming clear that the industry needs to be effectively managed to avoid the dangers of overfishing and the collapse of fish stocks.

TUNA FISHING needs to be carefully monitored.

Antarctica

THE FROZEN CONTINENT OF ANTARCTICA is covered by a vast icecap, many thousands of years old, and surrounded by the freezing seas of the Southern Ocean. It is the only continent with no permanent inhabitants – the only people who come here are scientists or tourists. Although the land is rich in oil and minerals, mining is prohibited under the laws of the Antarctic Treaty. This Treaty, agreed by 45 countries, made Antarctica a "continent for science" to be used for peaceful purposes only.

DAY TRIPPERS

Tourists visit Antarctica in summer. There are no resorts, so visitors generally stay on small cruise ships. When they come ashore, people have to wear insulated clothing and goggles to protect their eyes from glare off the ice.

LONG DAYS

Seasons at the poles are extreme. Polar summers are short but there can be sunshine 24 hours a "day". This is because Earth rotates at an angle to the Sun.

RESEARCH

The only people who stay in Antarctica are scientists. They come to study the climate, weather, and geology. By taking ice samples, for example, they can learn about changes in the world's climate over the years.

SCIENTISTS check an ice core.

KRILL

Tiny, shrimp-like creatures, krill are the primary food source for a great number of Antarctic animals. These include whales, seals, penguins, squid, and fish.

EMPEROR PENGUINS huddle for warmth.

FLOATING ICE

Icebergs are giant chunks of floating ice that break away, or calve, from ice sheets or glaciers. Most of their mass lies hidden below sea level.

Did you know?

➤ Antarctica is actually a desert – a barren region, incapable of supporting people or vegetation.

PENGUINS

Penguins walk awkwardly on land, but can swim swiftly to catch fish. Waterproof feathers and a thick layer of fat help keep them warm.

Map labels: Orcadas (Argentina), South Orkney Islands, Signy (UK), South Shetland Islands, Esperanza (Argentina), Capitán Arturo Prat (Chile), Palmer (US), Rothera (UK), San Martin (Argentina), Drake Passage, Antarctic Peninsula, Graham Land, Palmer Land, Weddell Sea, Ronne Ice Shelf, Berkner Island, Belgrano II (Argentina), Coats Land, Halley (UK), Sanae (South Africa), Georg von Neumayer (Germany), Novolazarevskaya (Russian Federation), Dronning Maud Land, Lützow Holmbukta, Syowa (Japan), Molodezhnaya (Russian Federation), Enderby Land, Mawson (Australia), Cape Darnley, Mackenzie Bay, Prydz Bay, Princess Elizabeth Land, Davis (Australia), Greater Antarctica, Mirny (Russ. Fed.), Shackleton Ice Shelf, Casey (Australia), Cape Poinsett, Wilkes Land, Vostok (Russian Federation), Terre Adélie, Dumont d'Urville (France), South Geomagnetic Pole, George V Land, Leningradskaya (Russian Federation), Cape Adare, Balleny Islands, Antarctic Circle, Victoria Land, Scott Base (NZ), McMurdo Base (US), Mount Erebus 3794m, Ross Sea, Ross Ice Shelf, Roosevelt Island, Transantarctic Mountains, Mount Markham 4351m, Mount Kirkpatrick 4528m, Amundsen-Scott (US), South Pole, ANTARCTICA, Mount Sidley 4181m, Mount Siple 3100m, Marie Byrd Land, Lesser Antarctica, Ellsworth Land, Vinson Massif 4897m, Amundsen Sea, Bellingshausen Sea, PETER I ISLAND (to Norway), SOUTHERN OCEAN, SOUTHERN OCEAN

Arctic Ocean

THE SMALLEST OF THE world's oceans, the Arctic is almost entirely surrounded by the northern edges of North America, Europe, and Asia. For most of the year, its waters are covered by a thick sheet of ice, although warmer currents from the Pacific and Atlantic melt the ice along the continental coasts for a short time in summer. Despite the harsh conditions, the region is home to a range of wildlife, such as reindeer, musk ox, foxes, and wolves. Some people, including the Inuit of Canada and the Sami of northern Scandinavia, have also adapted to this tough environment.

OZONE HOLE

High in the atmosphere, ozone (a gas) forms a natural shield that protects us from the Sun's ultraviolet rays. Scientists (right) at both poles have found holes in the ozone layer, caused by chemicals known as CFCs, once used in aerosols, fridges, and plastic packaging.

SATELLITE image shows a hole over the Arctic.

ALASKAN OIL

Reserves of oil and gas in the Beaufort Sea, off the coast of Alaska, have attracted interest. However, the introduction of ships and oil platforms brings problems. In a bid to protect the area, several environmental organizations are actively working to prevent drilling for more oil in this area.

Did you know?

▸ The main Arctic icepack is not stationary – strong winds cause it to rotate very slowly clockwise.

▸ The Sami are an indigenous people who form an ethnic minority in Norway, Sweden, Finland, and Russia.

▸ Walruses breed off the Arctic coasts.

```
0 km   250    500
0 miles  250    500
```

ARCTIC SURVIVORS

Polar bears live along the Arctic coasts of Canada, Greenland, and Russia. They hunt seals and fish at points where the sea ice melts. The bears have an insulating layer of fat, called blubber, which helps them survive the cold. Their white fur also provides essential camouflage on the ice.

NORTHERN LIGHTS

In midwinter, the north polar skies are sometimes lit up by dramatic curtains of red and green light. Known as the Northern Lights, these special effects are caused by disturbances in the upper atmosphere. The same happens near Antarctica, where the effect is called the Southern Lights.

Map labels:

Bering Strait · Arctic Circle · 180° · 170° · 170° · Chukchi Sea · Ostrov Vrangelya · East Siberian Sea · 160° · 150° · 130° · Novosibirskiye Ostrova · Laptev Sea · RUSSIAN FEDERATION · 120° · 110° · 70° · Beaufort Sea · 75° · 80° · Amundsen Gulf · Banks Island · Victoria Island · 110° · Melville Island · 100° · CANADA · Queen Elizabeth Islands · North Geomagnetic Pole · ARCTIC · 85° · North Pole · OCEAN · Severnaya Zemlya · 100° · Kara Sea · 70° · 90° · Lancaster Sound · 80° · Ellesmere Island · Nares Strait · Lincoln Sea · Franz Josef Land · 60° · Knud Rasmussen Land · Kap Morris Jesup · 70° · Baffin Bay · 70° · Wandel Sea · 50° · 60° · Kong Frederik VIII Land · SVALBARD (to Norway) · Spitsbergen · LONGYEARBYEN · 40° · GREENLAND (to Denmark) · Greenland Sea · Bjørnøya (to Norway) · 30° · Barents Sea · NUUK · 65° · Kong Christian IX Land · Norwegian Sea · JAN MAYEN (to Norway) · 50° · 40° · 65° · Denmark Strait · ICELAND · REYKJAVÍK

Gazetteer

HOW TO USE THE GAZETTEER

This gazetteer is a selection of the names in *Children's World Atlas*, and can be used to help you find places on the maps. For example, to find the city of Lisbon in Portugal, look up its name in the gazetteer. The entry reads:

Lisbon *Capital* Portugal 58 E6

The first number, 58, tells you that Lisbon appears on the map on page 58. The second number, E6, shows that it is in square E6. Turn to page 58. Trace down from the letter E along the top of the grid (or up from the letter E on the bottom of the grid), and then across from the number 6 on the side of the grid. You will find Lisbon in the area where the letter and number meet.

A

Aachen *Town* Germany 56 B7
Aalborg *Town* Denmark 49 B11
Aalen *Town* Germany 57 E9
Aalst *Town* Belgium 53 D11
Aalter *Town* Belgium 53 C10
Äänekoski *Town* Finland 48 G8
Aba *Town* Nigeria 41 L8
Aba *Town* Democratic Republic of Congo 42 I8
Ābādān *Town* Iran 82 E7
Abakan *Town* Russian Federation 78 H7
Abbeville *Town* France 54 E5
Abéché *Town* Chad 42 F6
Abengourou *Town* Côte d'Ivoire 41 I8
Aberdeen *Town* South Dakota, USA 12 G4
Aberdeen *Town* Maryland, USA 9 H8
Aberdeen *Town* Scotland, UK 50 F5
Aberystwyth *Town* Wales, UK 51 E10
Abhā *Town* Saudi Arabia 83 C11
Abidjan *Town* Côte d'Ivoire 40 H8
Abilene *Town* Texas, USA 17 K5
Åbo *see* Turku
Abomey *Town* Benin 41 J7
Abrantes *Town* Portugal 58 F6
Abu Dhabi *Capital* United Arab Emirates 83 F9
Abu Hamed *Town* Sudan 38 E6
Abuja *Capital* Nigeria 41 L7
Abū Kamāl *Town* Syria 80 I7
Abū Ẓaby *see* Abu Dhabi
Acapulco *Town* Mexico 19 J9
Acarigua *Town* Venezuela 26 D5
Accra *Capital* Ghana 41 I8
Aconcagua, Cerro *Mountain* Argentina 30 D7
A Coruña *Town* Spain 58 E2
Açu *Town* Brazil 29 M3
Adamawa Highlands *Mountain range* Cameroon 42 D8
'Adan *see* Aden
Adana *Town* Turkey 76 G6
Adapazari *Town* Turkey 76 E4
Ad Dahnā' *Desert* Saudi Arabia 83 E9
Ad Dakhla *Town* Western Sahara 36 C7
Ad Dammān *Town* Saudi Arabia 83 E9
Ad Dawḥah *see* Doha
Addis Ababa *Capital* Ethiopia 39 F9
Adelaide *Town* South Australia, Australia 105 J7
Aden *Town* Yemen 83 D13

Aden, Gulf of Indian Ocean 83 E13
Adirondack Mountains New York, USA 8 H4
Ādīs Ābeba *see* Addis Ababa
Adiyaman *Town* Turkey 76 H6
Adrar *Town* Algeria 36 G6
Aegean Sea Greece 67 F9
Afghanistan *Country* 84 H7
Afmadow *Town* Somalia 39 G11
Afyon *Town* Turkey 76 E5
Agadez *Town* Niger 41 L4
Agadir *Town* Morocco 36 E5
Agen *Town* France 55 D10
Agialoúsa *Town* Cyprus 80 B7
Āgra *Town* India 87 I3
Ağri *Town* Turkey 77 K4
Agrigento *Town* Sicily, Italy 61 E13
Agropoli *Town* Italy 61 F10
Aguachica *Town* Colombia 26 C5
Agua Prieta *Town* Mexico 18 F3
Aguascalientes *Town* Mexico 19 I7
Aguaytía *Town* Peru 27 B10
Aguilas *Town* Spain 59 J8
Aguililla *Town* Mexico 19 I8
Ahaggar *Mountain range* Algeria 37 I7
Ahlen *Town* Germany 56 C7
Ahmadābād *Town* India 86 G4
Ahuachapán *Town* El Salvador 22 E5
Ahvāz *Town* Iran 82 E7
Aiken *Town* South Carolina, USA 11 J4
Ailigandí *Town* Panama 23 N7
'Aïn Ben Tili *Town* Mauritania 40 G2
Aiquile *Town* Bolivia 27 E12
Aïr, Massif de l' *Mountain range* Niger 41 L4
Aix-en-Provence *Town* France 55 G11
Aizu *Town* Japan 93 G9
Ajaccio *Town* France 55 I13
Ajo *Town* Arizona, USA 16 E5
Akchâr *Desert* Mauritania 40 E3
Akhalts'ikhe *Town* Georgia 77 K3
Akhisar *Town* Turkey 76 C5
Akhtubinsk *Town* Russian Federation 73 D11
Akita *Town* Japan 92 F8
Akjoujt *Town* Mauritania 40 E3
Akkeshi *Town* Japan 92 H5
Akron *Town* Ohio, USA 13 M6
Akrotírion *Town* Cyprus 80 A8
Aksai Chin *Administrative region* China 88 D6
Aksaray *Town* Turkey 76 F5
Akşehir *Town* Turkey 76 E5
Aktau *Town* Kazakhstan 78 D6
Aktobe *Town* Kazakhstan 78 E6
Aktsyabrski *Town* Belarus 71 F11
Akula *Town* Democratic Republic of Congo 43 F9
Akune *Town* Japan 93 B14
Alabama *State* USA 10 G5
Alabama River Alabama, USA 10 G6
Al 'Amārah *Town* Iraq 82 D7
Alamo *Town* Nevada, USA 14 H7
Alamogordo *Town* New Mexico, USA 16 H5
Åland *Island group* Finland 49 F9
Alanya *Town* Turkey 76 E7
Al 'Aqabah *Town* Jordan 81 D14
Alaşehir *Town* Turkey 76 D5
Alaska *Province* Canada 4 E5
Alaska, Gulf of Alaska, USA 4 E6
Alaska Range *Mountain Range* Alaska, USA 4 E5
Albacete *Town* Spain 59 J6
Alba Iulia *Town* Romania 68 E6
Albania *Country* 65 F12
Albany *River* Ontario, Canada 6 F5
Albany *Town* Western Australia, Australia 104 E7
Albany *Town* Georgia, USA 10 H6
Albany *Town* New York, USA 9 I5
Al Bāridah *Town* Syria 80 F8
Al Baṣrah *Town* Iraq 82 D7
Alberta *Province* Canada 4 H7
Albert, Lake Democratic Republic of Congo 43 I9
Albuquerque *Town* New Mexico, USA 16 H4
Alcañiz *Town* Spain 59 K5
Alcoy *Town* Spain 59 K7
Alderney *Island* Channel Islands, UK 51 G13
Aleksin *Town* Russian Federation 73 C9
Alençon *Town* France 54 D7
Alenquer *Town* Brazil 29 I2

Aleppo *Town* Syria 80 E6
Alessandria *Town* Italy 60 C5
Aleutian Islands *Island Group* Alaska, USA 4 B5
Alexander Archipelago *Island*
British Colombia, Canada 4 E7
Alexandria *Town* Louisiana, USA 10 E6
Alexandria *Town* Egypt 38 D4
Alexándria *Town* Romania 68 F7
Alexandroúpoli *Town* Greece 66 G8
Alga *Town* Kazakhstan 78 E6
Algarve *Region* Spain 58 E8
Algeciras *Town* Spain 58 G9
Alger *see* Algiers
Algeria *Country* 36 H5
Al Ghābah *Town* Oman 83 G10
Algiers *Capital* Algeria 36 H3
Algona *Town* Iowa, USA 12 H5
Al Ḥasakah *Town* Syria 80 H5
Al Ḥillah *Town* Iraq 82 D7
Al Hudaydah *see* Hodeida
Al Hufūf *Town* Saudi Arabia 83 E9
Alíartos *Town* Greece 67 E11
Alicante *Town* Spain 59 L7
Alice Springs *Town* Northern Territory, Australia 105 I4
Aliquippa *Town* Pennsylvania, USA 8 E7
Al Jafr *Town* Jordan 81 E13
Al Jaghbūb *Town* Libya 37 N5
Al Jahrā' *Town* Kuwait 82 D8
Al Jawf *Town* Saudi Arabia 82 B8
Al Jazīrah *Physical region* Syria/Iraq 80 I5
Al Karak *Town* Jordan 81 E12
Al Khufrah *Town* Libya 37 N7
Al Khums *Town* Libya 37 K4
Alkmaar *Town* Netherlands 52 E7
Al Kūt *Town* Iraq 82 D7
Al Kuwayt *see* Kuwait
Al Lādhiqīyah *Town* Syria 80 D7
Allahābād *Town* India 87 I4
Allegheny Plateau Pennsylvania/New York, USA 8 F6
Allentown *Town* Pennsylvania, USA 9 H7
Al Līth *Town* Saudi Arabia 83 B11
Alma-Ata *see* Almaty
Al Madīnah *see* Medina
Al Mafraq *Town* Jordan 81 E10
Al Majma'ah *Town* Saudi Arabia 83 D9
Al Mālikīyah *Town* Syria 80 I4
Al Manāmah *see* Manama
Almansa *Town* Spain 59 K7
Al Marj *Town* Libya 37 M4
Almaty *Town* Kazakhstan 78 G8
Al Mawṣil *Town* Iraq 82 C6
Al Mayādīn *Town* Syria 80 H6
Almelo *Town* Netherlands 52 G8
Almere *Town* Netherlands 52 F8
Almería *Town* Spain 59 J8
Al'met'yevsk *Town* Russian Federation 73 F9
Almirante *Town* Panama 23 K8
Al Mukallā *Town* Yemen 83 E13
Alofi *Capital* Niue 103 K7
Alotip *Town* Indonesia 97 N8
Alpena *Town* Michigan, USA 13 L4
Alpine *Town* Texas, USA 17 I7
Alps *Mountain range* Central Europe 57 D12
Al Qāmishlī *Town* Syria 80 I4
Al Qunayṭirah *Town* Syria 81 D9
Altai Mountains *Mountain range* Mongolia/Russian Federation 88 F4
Altamaha River Georgia, USA 11 I5
Altamira *Town* Brazil 29 J2
Altamura *Town* Italy 61 H10
Altar, Desierto de *Desert* Mexico 18 D2
Altay *Town* China 88 F3
Altay *Town* Mongolia 88 H3
Altin Köprü *Town* Iraq 82 C6
Altiplano *Physical region* Bolivia 27 E13
Altoona *Town* Pennsylvania, USA 9 F7
Altun Ha *Ancient site* Belize 22 F2
Altun Shan *Mountain range* China 88 G5
Al 'Umarī *Town* Jordan 81 F11
Al 'Uwaynāt *Town* Libya 37 J6
Alupka *Town* Ukraine 69 K7
Alva *Town* Okahoma, USA 17 L3

Al Wajh *Town* Saudi Arabia 83 A9
Alwar *Town* India 86 H3
Al Wari'ah *Town* Saudi Arabia 82 D8
Alytus *Town* Lithuania 70 D8
Amamapare *Town* Indonesia 97 N7
Amantea *Town* Italy 61 G12
Amarapura *Town* Myanmar 94 B6
Amarillo *Town* Texas, USA 17 J4
Amazon *River* Brazil 29 J2
Amazon Basin Brazil 28 G3
Ambanja *Town* Madagascar 45 M4
Ambarchik *Town* Russian Federation 78 L3
Ambato *Town* Ecuador 26 A8
Amboasary *Town* Madagascar 45 L6
Ambon *Town* Indonesia 97 K7
American Samoa *Dependent territory* USA, Pacific Ocean 103 K6
Amersfoort *Town* Netherlands 52 F8
Amfilochía *Town* Greece 67 C10
Amherst *Town* Nova Scotia, Canada 7 K7
Amiens *Town* France 54 E6
Amman *Capital* Jordan 81 E11
'Ammān *see* Amman
Ammóchostos *Town* Cyprus 80 B8
Āmol *Town* Iran 82 F5
Amos *Town* Québec, Canada 6 H6
Amritsar *Town* India 86 H2
Amstelveen *Town* Netherlands 52 F8
Amsterdam *Capital* Netherlands 52 E8
Am Timan *Town* Chad 42 F6
Amu Darya *River* Uzbekistan 84 G4
Amundsen Gulf Canada 4 H4
Amundsen-Scott *Research station* Antarctica 110 E6
Amundsen Sea Southern Ocean 110 B7
Amuntai *Town* Indonesia 96 H7
Amur *River* China 89 L2
Anadyr' *Town* Russian Federation 78 M2
Anamur *Town* Turkey 76 F7
Anápolis *Town* Brazil 29 K5
Anatolia *Plateau* Turkey 76 E6
Anchorage *Town* Alaska, Canada 4 E5
Ancona *Town* Italy 60 F7
Andalucía *Region* Spain 58 H8
Andaman Islands *Island group* India 87 M8
Andaman Sea Indian Ocean 87 M8
Anderson *Town* Indiana, USA 13 K6
Andes *Mountain range* South America 26–27, 30–31
Andijon *Town* Uzbekistan 85 K4
Andkhvoy *Town* Afghanistan 84 H5
Andorra *Country* 55 D12
Andorra la Vella *Capital* Andorra 55 D12
Andreanof Islands *Island Group* Alaska, USA 4 A4
Andrews *Town* Texas, USA 17 J5
Andria *Town* Italy 61 H10
Andros Island Bahamas 24 F2
Andros Town Bahamas 24 F2
Angarsk *Town* Russian Federation 79 I7
Angeles *Town* Philippines 97 I2
Angel Falls *Waterfall* Venezuela 26 F6
Ångermanälven *River* Sweden 48 E7
Angers *Town* France 54 C7
Angkor Wat *Ancient site* Cambodia 95 F10
Anglesey *Island* Wales, UK 51 E9
Angola *Country* 44 E3
Angola Basin *Undersea feature* Atlantic Ocean 33 M6
Angoulême *Town* France 55 D9
Angren *Town* Uzbekistan 85 J3
Anguilla *Dependent territory* UK, Atlantic Ocean 25 N5
Anhui *Administrative region* China 91 J5
Ankara *Capital* Turkey 76 F4
Annaba *Town* Algeria 37 I3
An Nafūd *Desert* Saudi Arabia 82 B8
'Annah *Town* Iraq 82 C6
An Najaf *Town* Iraq 82 C7
Annamitique, Chaîne *Mountain range* Laos 94 F8
Annapolis *Town* Maryland, USA 8 G8
Ann Arbor *Town* Michigan, USA 13 L5
An Nāṣirīyah *Town* Iraq 82 D7
Annecy *Town* France 55 G9

Muncie *Town* Indiana, USA 13 K6
Munich *Town* Germany 57 F10
Munster *Cultural region* Ireland 51 B10
Münster *Town* Germany 56 C6
Muonioälv *River* Sweden 48 F4
Muqāv *Town* Jordan 81 G10
Muqdisho *see* Mogadishu
Murcia *Town* Spain 59 K7
Murmansk *Town* Russian Federation 72 E4
Murom *Town* Russian Federation 73 D9
Muroran *Town* Japan 92 F6
Murray River *New South Wales/Victoria/South Australia, Australia 105 K8
Murska Sobota *Town* Slovenia 57 H11
Murwāra *Town* India 87 I4
Murzuq, Idhān *Desert* Libya 37 K7
Muş *Town* Turkey 77 J5
Muscat *Capital* Oman 83 H9
Musgrave Ranges *Mountain range* South Australia, Australia 104 H5
Musoma *Town* Tanzania 39 E11
Mutare *Town* Zimbabwe 45 I5
Mutsu *Town* Japan 92 G6
Muttonbird Islands *Island group* New Zealand 107 B14
Mŭynoq *Town* Uzbekistan 84 F2
Mwanza *Town* Tanzania 39 E12
Mwene-Ditu *Town* Democratic Republic of Congo 43 F12
Mweru, Lake *Democratic Republic of Congo 43 H12
Myanmar *Country* 94 B5
Myanaung *Town* Myanmar 94 B8
Myaungmya *Town* Myanmar 95 B9
Myingyan *Town* Myanmar 94 B6
Myitkyina *Town* Myanmar 94 C5
Mykolayiv *Town* Ukraine 69 J5
Myrhorod *Town* Ukraine 69 K3
Mýrina *Town* Greece 67 F9
Myrtle Beach *Town* South Carolina, USA 11 K4
Mysore *Town* India 86 H8
My Tho *Town* Vietnam 95 G11
Mzuzu *Town* Malawi 45 J3

N

Naberezhnyye Chelny *Town* Russian Federation 73 F9
Nablus *Town* Israel 81 D11
Nacala *Town* Mozambique 45 K4
Nadi *Town* Fiji 103 I7
Nadvirna *Town* Ukraine 68 F4
Nadym *Town* Russian Federation 78 G5
Naga *Town* Philippines 97 J2
Nagano *Town* Japan 93 F10
Nagaoka *Town* Japan 93 F9
Nagasaki *Town* Japan 93 B14
Nagato *Town* Japan 93 C12
Nāgercoil *Town* India 86 H9
Nagornyy Karabakh *Region* Azerbaijan 77 M4
Nagoya *Town* Japan 93 F11
Nāgpur *Town* India 87 I5
Nagqu *Town* China 88 G7
Nagykanizsa *Town* Hungary 63 D12
Nagykőrös *Town* Hungary 63 F11
Naha *Town* Ryukyu Islands 93 A16
Nā'īn *Town* Iran 82 F7
Nain *Town* Newfoundland & Labrador, Canada 7 K3
Nairobi *Capital* Kenya 39 F11
Najin *Town* North Korea 91 M2
Najrān *Town* Saudi Arabia 83 C12
Nakagawa *Town* Japan 92 F4
Nakamura *Town* Japan 93 D13
Nakatsugawa *Town* Japan 93 F11
Nakhodka *Town* Russian Federation 79 M7
Nakhon Ratchasima *Town* Thailand 95 E9
Nakhon Sawan *Town* Thailand 95 D9
Nakhon Si Thammarat *Town* Thailand 95 D12
Nakuru *Town* Kenya 39 F11
Nal'chik *Town* Russian Federation 73 C13
Nālūt *Town* Libya 37 J5
Namangan *Town* Uzbekistan 85 K3

Nam Đinh *Town* Vietnam 94 G7
Namib Desert *Namibia* 44 E5
Namibe *Town* Angola 44 D4
Namibia *Country* 44 E5
Nampa *Town* Idaho, USA 14 H4
Nampula *Town* Mozambique 45 K4
Namur *Town* Belgium 53 E12
Nanaimo *Town* British Colombia, Canada 4 G9
Nancha *Town* China 89 M2
Nanchang *Town* China 91 J6
Nanchong *Town* China 90 H6
Nancy *Town* France 54 H7
Nānded *Town* India 86 H6
Nanfeng *Town* China 91 J7
Nanjing *Town* China 91 K5
Nanning *Town* China 90 H8
Nanping *Town* China 91 K7
Nanterre *Town* France 54 E6
Nantes *Town* France 54 C8
Nantucket *Town* Massachusetts, USA 9 K6
Nantucket Island *Massachusetts, USA 9 K6
Nanyang *Town* China 91 I5
Napa *Town* California, USA 14 F6
Napier *Town* New Zealand 106 H7
Naples *Town* Italy 61 F10
Napoli *see* Naples
Napo, Río *River* Peru 26 C8
Narathiwat *Town* Thailand 95 E13
Narita *Town* Japan 93 G10
Närpes *Town* Finland 48 F8
Närpiö *see* Närpes
Narva *Town* Estonia 70 H4
Narvik *Town* Norway 48 E4
Năsăud *Town* Romania 68 F5
Nāshik *Town* India 86 G5
Nashua *Town* New Hampshire, USA 9 J5
Nashville *Town* Tennessee, USA 10 G3
Nassau *Capital* Bahamas 24 G2
Nasser *Lake* Egypt 38 E6
Nata *Town* Botswana 44 H5
Natal *Town* Brazil 29 N3
Natitingou *Town* Benin 41 J6
Nauru *Country* 102 H4
Nauta *Town* Peru 27 C9
Navapolatsk *Town* Belarus 70 G8
Navassa Island *Dependent territory* USA, Atlantic Ocean 24 H5
Navojoa *Town* Mexico 18 F5
Nawābshāh *Town* Pakistan 86 F3
Nawoiy *Town* Uzbekistan 85 I4
Nayoro *Town* Japan 92 F4
Nazareth *Town* Israel 81 D10
Nazca *Town* Peru 27 C11
Nazerat *see* Nazareth
Nazilli *Town* Turkey 76 D6
Nazrēt *Town* Ethiopia 39 G9
N'Dalatando *Town* Angola 44 E2
Ndélé *Town* Central African Republic 42 F7
Ndjamena *Capital* Chad 42 D6
Ndola *Town* Zambia 44 H3
Neagh, Lough *Lake* Northern Ireland, UK 50 D8
Neápoli *Town* Greece 67 G14
Neápoli *Town* Greece 67 C9
Near Islands *Island Group* Alaska, USA 4 A3
Nebitdag *Town* Turkmenistan 84 D4
Nebraska *State* USA 12 F5
Necochea *Town* Argentina 31 G10
Neftekamsk *Town* Russian Federation 73 F9
Negēlē *Town* Ethiopia 39 G10
Negev *Desert* Israel 81 D12
Negombo *Town* Sri Lanka 87 I9
Negotin *Town* Serbia 64 H8
Negro, Rio *River* Brazil 28 G2
Neijiang *Town* China 90 G6
Nei Mongol Zizhiqu *see* Inner Mongolia
Neiva *Town* Colombia 26 B7
Nellore *Town* India 87 I7
Nelson *Town* New Zealand 107 E9
Nemuro *Town* Japan 92 H4
Nepal *Country* 87 J3
Neringa *Town* Lithuania 70 C6
Neryungri *Town* Russian Federation 79 K6
Netanya *Town* Israel 81 D11
Netherlands *Country* 52 E7

Netherlands Antilles *Dependent territory* Netherlands, Atlantic Ocean 25 K8
Neubrandenburg *Town* Germany 56 F5
Neuchâtel *Town* Switzerland 57 C11
Neufchâteau *Town* Belgium 53 F13
Neumünster *Town* Germany 56 D4
Neunkirchen *Town* Germany 57 C9
Neuquén *Town* Argentina 31 D10
Neustadt an der Weinstrasse *Town* Germany 57 C9
Neu-Ulm *Town* Germany 57 E10
Neuwied *Town* Germany 56 C8
Nevada *State* USA 14 H6
Nevinnomyssk *Town* Russian Federation 73 C11
Nevşehir *Town* Turkey 76 G5
New Amsterdam *Town* Guyana 26 G6
Newark *Town* New Jersey, USA 9 I7
Newark *Town* New York, USA 8 G5
New Bedford *Town* Massachusetts, USA 9 K6
Newberg *Town* Oregon, USA 14 F3
New Britain *Island* Papua New Guinea 102 F5
New Caledonia *Island* New Caledonia 102 G8
New Caledonia *Dependent territory* France, Pacific Ocean 102 G7
Newcastle *Town* New South Wales, Australia 105 M7
Newcastle upon Tyne *Town* England, UK 50 F7
New Delhi *Capital* India 86 H3
Newfoundland *Island* Ontario, Canada 7 M5
Newfoundland Basin *Undersea feature* Atlantic Ocean 33 J2
New Glasgow *Town* Nova Scotia, Canada 7 L7
New Guinea *Island* Indonesia/Papua New Guinea 102 D5
New Hampshire *State* USA 9 J4
New Haven *Town* Connecticut, USA 8 I6
New Iberia *Town* Louisiana, USA 10 E6
New Jersey *State* USA 9 I7
Newman *Town* Western Australia, Australia 104 E4
New Mexico *State* USA 17 I4
New Orleans *Town* Louisiana, USA 10 F6
New Plymouth *Town* New Zealand 106 F7
Newport *Town* Vermont, USA 9 I3
Newport *Town* Wales, UK 51 F11
Newport News *Town* Virginia, USA 11 L3
New Providence *Island* Bahamas 24 G2
Newquay *Town* England, UK 51 E12
Newry *Town* Northern Ireland, UK 50 D8
New Siberian Islands *Island group* Russian Federation 79 K3
New South Wales *State* Australia 105 L7
Newtownabbey *Town* Northern Ireland, UK 50 D7
New York *State* USA 8 G5
New York *Town* New York, USA 9 I7
New Zealand *Country* 107 E9
Ngaoundéré *Town* Cameroon 42 D7
Ngo *Town* Congo 43 D10
Nguigmi *Town* Niger 41 M5
Nha Trang *Town* Vietnam 95 H10
Niagara Falls *Town* Ontario, Canada 6 G8
Niagara Falls *Town* New York, USA 8 E5
Niagara Falls *Waterfall* Canada/USA 8 E6
Niamey *Capital* Niger 41 J5
Nia-Nia *Town* Democratic Republic of Congo 43 H9
Nicaragua *Country* 22 H5
Nicaragua, Lago de *Lake* Nicaragua 23 I6
Nice *Town* France 55 H11
Nicholls Town *Town* Bahamas 24 F2
Nicobar Islands *Island group* India 87 M8
Nicosia *Capital* Cyprus 80 B8
Nicoya *Town* Costa Rica 22 H7
Nicoya, Golfo de *Gulf* Costa Rica 23 I7
Nieuw-Bergen *Town* Netherlands 53 F9
Niğde *Town* Turkey 76 G6
Niger *Country* 41 K5
Niger *River* Niger/Nigeria 41 J6
Nigeria *Country* 41 M7
Niger, Mouths of the *Coastal feature* Nigeria 41 K8
Niigata *Town* Japan 93 F9

Niihama *Town* Japan 93 D12
Niitsu *Town* Japan 93 F9
Nijmegen *Town* Netherlands 53 F9
Nikiniki *Town* Indonesia 97 J8
Nikopol' *Town* Ukraine 69 K5
Nikšić *Town* Montenegro 65 E10
Nile *River* East Africa 38 E5
Nile Delta *Egypt* 38 E4
Nîmes *Town* France 55 F11
Ninetyeast Ridge *Undersea feature* Indian Ocean 99 K4
Ninety Mile Beach *Coastal feature* New Zealand 106 E3
Ningbo *Town* China 91 L6
Ningxia *Administrative region* China 89 J6
Niort *Town* France 54 D8
Nipigon, Lake *Québec, Canada 6 E6
Niš *Town* Serbia 65 H9
Nişab *Town* Saudi Arabia 82 D8
Nitra *Town* Slovakia 63 E10
Niue *Dependent territory* New Zealand, Pacific Ocean 103 K7
Nizāmābād *Town* India 87 I6
Nizhnekamsk *Town* Russian Federation 73 F9
Nizhnevartovsk *Town* Russian Federation 78 G5
Nizhniy Novgorod *Town* Russian Federation 73 E9
Nizhniy Odes *Town* Russian Federation 72 G7
Nizhyn *Town* Ukraine 69 J2
Nkayi *Town* Congo 43 D11
Nkongsamba *Town* Cameroon 42 C8
Nobeoka *Town* Japan 93 C14
Noboribetsu *Town* Japan 92 F6
Nogales *Town* Arizona, USA 16 F6
Nogales *Town* Mexico 18 E3
Nogales *Town* Arizona, USA 16 F6
Nogales *Town* Mexico 18 F3
Nokia *Town* Finland 48 G8
Nokou *Town* Chad 42 D5
Nong Khai *Town* Thailand 94 E8
Noordwijk aan Zee *Town* Netherlands 52 D8
Norak *Town* Tajikistan 85 J5
Norderstedt *Town* Germany 56 E5
Nordhorn *Town* Germany 56 C6
Nordkapp *see* North Cape
Norfolk *Town* Nebraska, USA 12 G5
Norfolk *Town* Virginia, USA 11 L3
Norfolk Island *Dependent territory* Australia, Pacific Ocean 109 I7
Noril'sk *Town* Russian Federation 78 H4
Norman *Town* Oklahoma, USA 17 L4
Normandy *Region* France 54 D6
Norrköping *Town* Sweden 49 E10
Norrtälje *Town* Sweden 49 E10
North Albanian Alps *Mountain range* Serbia/Montenegro 65 F10
Northampton *Town* England, UK 51 G10
North Bay *Town* Ontario, Canada 6 G7
North Cape *Coastal feature* New Zealand 106 E3
North Cape *Coastal feature* Norway 48 G2
North Carolina *State* USA 11 K4
North Charleston *Town* South Carolina, USA 11 J5
North Dakota *State* USA 12 F3
Northern Cook Islands *Island group* Cook Islands 103 M6
Northern Dvina *River* Russian Federation 72 E7
Northern Ireland *Political region* UK 50 D7
Northern Mariana Islands *Dependent territory* USA, Pacific Ocean 102 D1
Northern Sporades *Island group* Greece 67 E10
Northern Territory *State* Australia 104 H4
North Island *New Zealand* 106 G7
North Korea *Country* 91 M3
North Little Rock *Town* Arkansas, USA 10 E4
North Sea *Europe* 50 G4
North West Highlands *Mountain range* Scotland, UK 50 E5
Northwest Pacific Basin *Undersea feature* Pacific Ocean 109 I3
Northwest Territories *Province* Canada 4 H6
Norway *Country* 48 B8
Norwegian Sea *Arctic Ocean* 111 M8
Norwich *Town* England, UK 51 H9
Noshiro *Town* Japan 92 F7

Pau *Town* France 55 C11
Paulatuk *Town* Northwest Territories, Canada 4 H5
Pavia *Town* Italy 60 C5
Pãvilosta *Town* Latvia 70 D5
Pavlodar *Town* Kazakhstan 78 G7
Pavlohrad *Town* Ukraine 69 L4
Pawtucket *Town* Rhode Island, USA 8 J6
Paysandú *Town* Uruguay 30 H7
Pazar *Town* Turkey 77 J3
Pazardzhik *Town* Bulgaria 66 F7
Pearl River Mississippi, USA 10 F5
Peć *Town* Serbia 65 F10
Pechora *River* Russian Federation 72 G6
Pechora *Town* Russian Federation 72 G6
Pécs *Town* Hungary 63 E12
Pedro Juan Caballero *Town* Paraguay 30 H4
Pegu *Town* Myanmar 94 B8
Peiraías *see* Piraeus
Pekalongan *Town* Indonesia 96 G7
Pekanbaru *Town* Indonesia 96 D6
Peking *see* Beijing
Peloponnese *Peninsula* Greece 67 D12
Pelopónnisos *see* Peloponnese
Pematangsiantar *Town* Indonesia 96 D5
Pemba *Town* Mozambique 45 K3
Pennines *Hills* England, UK 50 F8
Pennsylvania *State* USA 8 F7
Penonomé *Town* Panama 23 L8
Penrith *Town* England,UK 50 F7
Pensacola *Town* Florida, USA 10 G6
Penza *Town* Russian Federation 73 D10
Penzance *Town* England, UK 51 D12
Peoria *Town* Illinois, USA 13 J6
Perchtoldsdorf *Town* Austria 57 H10
Pereira *Town* Colombia 26 B6
Pergamino *Town* Argentina 30 F8
Perm' *Town* Russian Federation 73 G9
Pernik *Town* Bulgaria 66 D6
Perote *Town* Mexico 19 K7
Perpignan *Town* France 55 E12
Persian Gulf *see* Gulf, The
Perth *Town* Western Australia, Australia 104 E7
Perth *Town* Scotland,UK 50 F6
Peru *Country* 27 C10
Perugia *Town* Italy 60 E8
Pervomays'k *Town* Ukraine 69 I5
Pesaro *Town* Italy 60 F7
Pescara *Town* Italy 60 F8
Peshãwar *Town* Pakistan 86 G1
Pessac *Town* France 55 C10
Petaḥ Tiqwa *Town* Israel 81 D11
Peterborough *Town* South Australia, Australia 105 J7
Peterborough *Town* Ontario, Canada 6 H8
Peterborough *Town* England, UK 51 H10
Peterborough *Town* South Australia, Australia 105 J7
Peterhead *Town* Scotland, UK 50 F5
Peter I Island *Dependent Territory* Norway, Southern Ocean 110 B6
Petersburg *Town* Virginia, USA 11 K2
Peters Mine *Town* Guyana 26 G6
Petra *Town* Jordan 81 E13
Petrinja *Town* Croatia 64 C6
Petrodvorets *Town* Russian Federation 72 C6
Petropavlovsk *Town* Kazakhstan 78 G6
Petropavlovsk-Kamchatskiy *Town* Russian Federation 79 M5
Petrozavodsk *Town* Russian Federation 72 D6
Pevek *Town* Russian Federation 78 L2
Pforzheim *Town* Germany 57 D9
Phan Thiêt *Town* Vietnam 95 H11
Phetchaburi *Town* Thailand 95 D10
Philadelphia *Town* Pennsylvania, USA 8 H7
Philippines *Country* 97 J2
Phitsanulok *Town* Thailand 94 D8
Phnom Penh *Capital* Cambodia 95 F11
Phoenix *Town* Arizona, USA 16 E5
Phoenix Islands *Island group* Kiribati 103 J5
Phuket *Town* Thailand 95 C13
Phuket, Ko *Island* Thailand 95 C12
Piacenza *Town* Italy 60 D5
Piatra-Neamp *Town* Romania 68 G5

Picos *Town* Brazil 29 L3
Picton *Town* New Zealand 107 F9
Piedras Negras *Town* Mexico 19 J4
Pielinen *Lake* Finland 48 H7
Pierre *Town* South Dakota, USA 12 F4
Pietermaritzburg *Town* South Africa 45 I7
Pietersburg *see* Polokwane
Pikeville *Town* Kentucky, USA 11 I2
Piła *Town* Poland 62 D6
Pinar del Río *Town* Cuba 24 D3
Píndos *see* Pindus Mountains
Pindus Mountains *Mountain range* Greece 67 C10
Pine Bluff *Town* Arkansas, USA 10 E4
Pingdingshan *Town* China 91 I5
Pinsk *Town* Belarus 71 D11
Piotrków Trybunalski *Town* Poland 62 F7
Piraeus *Town* Greece 67 E11
Pirot *Town* Serbia 65 H10
Pisa *Town* Italy 60 D7
Pisco *Town* Peru 27 B11
Písek *Town* Czech Republic 63 B9
Pistoia *Town* Italy 60 D6
Pitcairn Islands *Dependent Territory* UK, Pacific Ocean 109 L6
Piteşti *Town* Romania 68 F7
Pittsburgh *Town* Pennsylvania, USA 8 E7
Pittsfield *Town* Massachusetts, USA 8 J5
Piura *Town* Peru 27 A9
Placetas *Town* Cuba 24 E3
Plano *Town* Texas, USA 17 M5
Plata, Río de la *River* Argentina 31 H9
Platinum *Town* Alaska, USA 4 D5
Platte River Nebraska, USA 12 G6
Plattsburgh *Town* New York, USA 9 I3
Plauen *Town* Germany 56 F8
Plenty, Bay of New Zealand 106 H6
Plesetsk *Town* Russian Federation 72 E7
Pleven *Town* Bulgaria 66 F5
Płock *Town* Poland 62 F6
Ploieşti *Town* Romania 68 F7
Plovdiv *Town* Bulgaria 66 F7
Plungė *Town* Lithuania 70 C6
Plymouth *Capital* Montserrat 25 N6
Plymouth *Town* England, UK 51 E12
Plzeň *Town* Czech Republic 63 B9
Po *River* Italy 60 E6
Pobedy, Pik *Mountain* China 88 E4
Pocahontas *Town* Arkansas, USA 10 F3
Podgorica *Capital* Montenegro 65 E10
Podil's'ka Vysochyna *Mountain range* Ukraine 68 H4
Podol'sk *Town* Russian Federation 72 C8
Pointe-à-Pitre *Town* Guadeloupe 25 O6
Pointe-Noire *Town* Congo 43 C11
Poitiers *Town* France 54 D8
Pokhara *Town* Nepal 87 J3
Poland *Country* 62 E7
Polatli *Town* Turkey 76 F5
Polatsk *Town* Belarus 70 G8
Pólis *Town* Cyprus 80 A8
Polokwane *Town* South Africa 45 H7
Poltava *Town* Ukraine 69 K3
Polýkastro *Town* Greece 66 D8
Polynesia *Region* Pacific Ocean 103 N6
Pomeranian Bay Poland 62 C5
Pompano Beach *Town* Florida, USA 11 J8
Ponce *Town* Puerto Rico 25 L5
Pondicherry *Town* India 87 I8
Ponferrada *Town* Spain 58 G3
Ponta Grossa *Town* Brazil 29 J7
Pontevedra *Town* Spain 58 E3
Pontiac *Town* Michigan, USA 13 L5
Pontianak *Town* Indonesia 96 F6
Poole *Town* England, UK 51 G12
Popayán *Town* Colombia 26 B7
Popocatépetl *Mountain* Mexico 19 K8
Porbandar *Town* India 86 F5
Pordenone *Town* Italy 60 F5
Poreč *Town* Croatia 64 A6
Pori *Town* Finland 49 F9
Porirua *Town* New Zealand 107 F9
Póros *Town* Greece 67 E12
Port Alfred *Town* South Africa 44 H8

Port Arthur *Town* Texas, USA 17 N7
Port Augusta *Town* South Australia, Australia 105 J7
Port-au-Prince *Capital* Haiti 25 J5
Port Blair *Town* India 87 M7
Port Elizabeth *Town* South Africa 44 H8
Port-Gentil *Town* Gabon 43 B10
Port Harcourt *Town* Nigeria 41 L8
Portland *Town* Oregon, USA 14 F3
Portland *Town* Maine, USA 8 K4
Portland *Town* Victoria, Australia 105 J8
Port Laoise *Town* Ireland 51 C9
Port Louis *Capital* Mauritius 45 O6
Port Macquarie *Town* New South Wales, Australia 105 N7
Port Moresby *Capital* Papua New Guinea 102 E6
Porto *see* Oporto
Porto Alegre *Town* Brazil 29 J9
Portobelo *Town* Panama 23 M7
Porto Torres *Town* Sardinia, Italy 61 B9
Porto Velho *Town* Brazil 28 G4
Portoviejo *Town* Ecuador 26 A8
Port Said *Town* Egypt 38 E4
Portsmouth *Town* England, UK 51 G12
Portsmouth *Town* New Hampshire, USA 9 K5
Portsmouth *Town* Virginia, USA 11 L3
Port Sudan *Town* Sudan 38 F6
Portugal *Country* 58 F5
Port-Vila *Capital* Vanuatu 102 H7
Porvoo *Town* Finland 49 G9
Posadas *Town* Argentina 30 H6
Poso *Town* Indonesia 97 J6
Potenza *Town* Italy 61 G10
P'ot'i *Town* Georgia 77 J3
Potiskum *Town* Nigeria 41 M6
Potomac River Virginia, USA 11 K2
Potosí *Town* Bolivia 27 E13
Potsdam *Town* Germany 56 F6
Po Valley Italy 60 D5
Poza Rica *Town* Mexico 19 K7
Požega *Town* Serbia 65 F9
Poznań *Town* Poland 62 D6
Pozzallo *Town* Sicily, Italy 61 F14
Prague *Capital* Czech Republic 62 B8
Praha *see* Prague
Praia *Capital* Cape Verde 33 K4
Prato *Town* Italy 60 D7
Prenzlau *Town* Germany 56 G5
Přerov *Town* Czech Republic 63 D9
Presidente Epitácio *Town* Brazil 29 J7
Prešov *Town* Slovakia 63 G9
Prespa, Lake Macedonia 65 G12
Presque Isle *Town* Maine, USA 9 L1
Preston *Town* England, UK 50 F8
Prestwick *Town* Scotland, UK 50 E7
Pretoria *see* Tshwane
Préveza *Town* Greece 67 C10
Price *Town* Utah, USA 15 J6
Prichard *Town* Alabama, USA 10 G6
Prienai *Town* Lithuania 70 D8
Prieska *Town* South Africa 44 G7
Prilep *Town* Macedonia 65 G12
Primorsk *Town* Kaliningrad 70 B6
Primorsko *Town* Bulgaria 66 H7
Prince Edward Islands *Island group* South Africa 98 H7
Prince George *Town* British Colombia, Canada 4 G8
Prinzapolka *Town* Nicaragua 23 J5
Pripet *River* Belarus 71 E11
Pripet Marshes *Wetland* Belarus/Ukraine 71 D11
Priština *Town* Serbia 65 G10
Prizren *Town* Serbia 65 G10
Probolinggo *Town* Indonesia 96 H8
Progreso *Town* Mexico 19 O6
Prokhladnyy *Town* Russian Federation 73 C13
Prokuplje *Town* Serbia 65 G9
Prome *Town* Myanmar 94 B8
Prostějov *Town* Czech Republic 63 D9
Providence *Town* Rhode Island, USA 8 J6
Provincetown *Town* Massachusetts, USA 9 K5
Provo *Town* Utah, USA 15 J5

Prudhoe Bay *Town* Alaska, USA 4 F4
Pruszków *Town* Poland 62 F7
Pryluky *Town* Ukraine 69 J3
Przemyśl *Town* Poland 63 G9
Pskov *Town* Russian Federation 72 B7
Pucallpa *Town* Peru 27 C10
Pudasjärvi *Town* Finland 48 G6
Puebla *Town* Mexico 19 K8
Pueblo *Town* Colorado, USA 15 L6
Puerto Angel *Town* Mexico 19 L9
Puerto Ayacucho *Town* Venezuela 26 E6
Puerto Barrios *Town* Guatemala 22 F3
Puerto Cortés *Town* Honduras 22 F3
Puerto Deseado *Town* Argentina 31 E12
Puerto Escondido *Town* Mexico 19 L9
Puerto La Cruz *Town* Venezuela 26 E5
Puerto Lempira *Town* Honduras 23 I3
Puertollano *Town* Spain 58 H7
Puerto López *Town* Colombia 26 D4
Puerto Maldonado *Town* Peru 27 D11
Puerto Montt *Town* Chile 31 C10
Puerto Plata *Town* Dominican Republic 25 J5
Puerto Princesa *Town* Philippines 97 I4
Puerto Rico *Dependent territory* USA, Atlantic Ocean 25 L6
Puerto Suárez *Town* Bolivia 27 G12
Puerto Vallarta *Town* Mexico 18 H7
Puerto Varas *Town* Chile 31 C10
Puget Sound *Bay* Washington, USA 14 F2
Pula *Town* Croatia 64 A6
Puławy *Town* Poland 62 G7
Pune *Town* India 86 G6
Punjab *Region* Pakistan/India 86 H2
Puno *Town* Peru 27 D12
Punta Alta *Town* Argentina 31 F10
Punta Arenas *Town* Chile 31 D14
Puntarenas *Town* Costa Rica 23 I7
Puri *Town* India 87 K5
Purmerend *Town* Netherlands 52 E8
Purus, Rio *River* Brazil 28 F4
Pusan *Town* South Korea 91 M4
Putrajaya *Capital* Malaysia 96 E5
Putumayo, Río *River* Colombia 26 C8
Puurmani *Town* Estonia 70 G5
Pyatigorsk *Town* Russian Federation 73 C11
Pyechin *Town* Myanmar 94 A7
Pyinmana *Capital* Myanmar 94 C7
Pylos *Town* Greece 67 C12
P'yŏngyang *Capital* North Korea 91 L3
Pyrenees *Mountain range* France/Spain 55 C12
Pyryatyn *Town* Ukraine 69 J3

Q

Qaidam Pendi *Basin* China 88 H6
Qal 'at Bīshah *Town* Saudi Arabia 83 C11
Qamdo *Town* China 88 H7
Qarokül *Town* Tajikistan 85 L4
Qarshi *Town* Uzbekistan 85 I5
Qasr Farâfra *Town* Egypt 38 D5
Qavanã *Town* Syria 81 D9
Qatar *Country* 83 F9
Qattara Depression *Desert basin* Egypt 38 D4
Qazimämmäd *Town* Azerbaijan 77 N4
Qazvïn *Town* Iran 82 E6
Qena *Town* Egypt 38 E5
Qilian Shan *Mountain range* China 88 H5
Qingdao *Town* China 91 K4
Qinghai *Administrative region* China 88 H6
Qingzang Gaoyuan *see* Tibet, Plateau of
Qinhuangdao *Town* China 91 K3
Qinzhou *Town* China 90 H8
Qiqihar *Town* China 89 L2
Qira *Town* China 88 D6
Qitai *Town* China 88 F4
Qizilrabot *Town* Tajikistan 85 L5
Qom *Town* Iran 82 E6
Qorveh *Town* Iran 82 D6
Quang Ngai *Town* Vietnam 95 H9
Quanzhou *Town* China 91 K7
Quartu Sant' Elena *Town* Sardinia, Italy 61 B11

Wandel Sea Arctic Ocean 111 M7
Wanxian Town China 90 H6
Wanyuan Town China 90 H5
Warangal Town India 87 I6
Warren Town Michigan, USA 13 L5
Warren Town Ohio, USA 13 L6
Warren Town Pennsylvania, USA 8 E6
Warri Town Nigeria 41 K8
Warsaw Capital Poland 62 F6
Warszawa see Warsaw
Warwick Town Rhode Island, USA 8 J6
Washington State USA 14 H2
Washington, D.C. Capital USA 8 G9
Waspam Town Nicaragua 23 I4
Waterbury Town Connecticut, USA 8 I6
Waterford Town Ireland 51 C10
Waterloo Town Iowa, USA 13 I5
Watertown Town New York, USA 8 G4
Watford Town England, UK 51 H11
Wau Town Sudan 39 D9
Waukegan Town Illinois, USA 13 J5
Waukesha Town Wisconsin, USA 13 J5
Wavre Town Belgium 53 E11
Weddell Sea Antarctica 110 C4
Weifang Town China 91 K4
Weimar Town Germany 56 E5
Welkom Town South Africa 44 H7
Wellington Capital New Zealand 107 F9
Wells Town Nevada, USA 14 H5
Wellsford Town New Zealand 106 F5
Wels Town Austria 57 G10
Wenchi Town Ghana 41 I7
Wenshan Town China 90 G8
Wenxian Town China 89 J7
Wenzhou Town China 91 K6
Weser River Germany 56 D6
West Bank Disputed region Near East 81 D11
West Cape Coastal feature
   New Zealand 107 A13
Westerland Town Germany 56 D4
Western Australia State Australia 104 G5
Western Dvina River W Europe 70 F7
West Frisian Islands Island group
   Netherlands 52 B5
Western Ghats Mountain range India 86 H6
Western Sahara Disputed territory 36 C6
Weston-super-Mare Town England, UK 51 F11
West Palm Beach Town Florida, USA 11 J8
West Siberian Plain Russian Federation 78 H5
West Virginia State USA 11 J2
Wetzlar Town Germany 56 D8
Wevok Town Alaska, USA 4 E3
Wexford Town Ireland 51 D10
Whakatane Town New Zealand 106 H6
Wheeler Peak Mountain New Mexico,
   USA 16 H3
Whitby Town England, UK 50 G8
Whitehorse Town Northwest Territories,
   Canada 4 F6
White Nile River Sudan 38 E8
White Sea Russian Federation 72 E5
White Volta River Ghana 41 I7
Whitney, Mount Mountain California,
   USA 14 G7
Wichita Town Kansas, USA 12 G8
Wichita Falls Town Texas, USA 17 L5
Wick Town Scotland, UK 50 F4
Wieliczka Town Poland 63 F9
Wien see Vienna
Wiener Neustadt Town Austria 57 H10
Wiesbaden Town Germany 56 C8
Wight, Isle of Island England, UK 51 G12
Wilcox Town Pennsylvania, USA 8 F6
Wilhelm, Mount Mountain Papua New Guinea
   102 E5
Wilhelmshaven Town Germany 56 C5
Wilkes Barre Town Pennsylvania, USA 8 H6
Willard Town New Mexico, USA 16 H4
Willemstad Capital Netherlands Antilles 25 K8
Williston Town North Dakota, USA 12 E2
Wilmington Town Delaware, USA 8 H8
Wilmington Town North Carolina, USA 11 K4
Winchester Town England, UK 51 G11
Windhoek Capital Namibia 44 E6

Windsor Town Ontario, Canada 6 F8
Windward Islands Island group Caribbean Sea
   25 P8
Windward Passage Strait Cuba/Haiti 24 H5
Winisk Town Ontario, Canada 6 F4
Winnipeg Town Manitoba, Canada 5 K9
Winnipeg, Lake Manitoba, Canada 5 J8
Winona Town Wisconsin, USA 13 I4
Winston Salem Town North Carolina, USA 11 J3
Winterthur Town Switzerland 57 D11
Wisconsin State USA 13 I4
Wismar Town Germany 56 E5
Wittstock Town Germany 56 F5
Włocławek Town Poland 62 F6
Wodzisław Śląski Town Poland 63 E9
Woking Town England, UK 51 H11
Wolfsberg Town Austria 57 H11
Wolfsburg Town Germany 56 E6
Wollongong Town New South Wales,
   Australia 105 M7
Wolverhampton Town England, UK 51 F10
Wŏnsan Town North Korea 91 M3
Woodburn Town Oregon, USA 14 F3
Woodruff Town Wisconsin, USA 13 J3
Woods, Lake of the Ontario, Canada 6 D6
Woodville Town New Zealand 106 G8
Worcester Town Massachusetts, USA 9 J5
Worcester Town England, UK 51 F10
Worms Town Germany 57 C9
Worthington Town South Dakota, USA 12 H5
Wrocław Town Poland 62 D8
Wuday'ah Town Saudi Arabia 83 D12
Wuhai Town China 89 J5
Wuhan Town China 91 J6
Wuhu Town China 91 K5
Wuliang Shan Mountain range China 90 F8
Wuppertal Town Germany 56 C7
Würzburg Town Germany 56 D8
Wuxi Town China 91 K5
Wyoming State USA 15 L4

X

Xaignabouri Town Laos 94 E7
Xal-Xal Town Mozambique 45 I6
Xalapa Town Mexico 19 L7
Xankändi Town Azerbaijan 77 M4
Xiamen Town China 91 K8
Xi'an Town China 90 H5
Xiangfang Town China 91 I5
Xianggang see Hong Kong
Xiangtan Town China 91 I7
Xianyang Town China 90 H4
Xichang Town China 90 F6
Xilinhot Town China 89 K4
Xingu, Rio River Brazil 29 J3
Xingxi Town China 90 G7
Xingxingxia Town China 88 G5
Xining Town China 89 I6
Xinjiang Administrative region China 88 F5
Xinxiang Town China 91 J4
Xinyang Town China 91 J5
Xi Ujimqin Qi Town China 89 K3
Xixon see Gijón
Xuzhou Town China 91 J5

Y

Ya'an Town China 90 G6
Yablis Town Nicaragua 23 J4
Yafran Town Libya 37 K4
Yakeshi Town China 89 L2
Yakima Town Washington, USA 14 G2
Yakutsk Town Russian Federation 79 K5
Yalova Town Turkey 76 D4
Yalta Town Ukraine 69 K7
Yamaguchi Town Japan 93 C12
Yambol Town Bulgaria 66 G6
Yamoussoukro Capital Côte d'Ivoire 40 H7

Yan'an Town China 90 H4
Yanbu'al Baīr Town Saudi Arabia 83 A9
Yangiyŭl Town Uzbekistan 85 J3
Yangon see Rangoon
Yangtze River China 90 G7
Yangzhou Town China 91 K5
Yanji Town China 89 N3
Yankton Town Iowa, USA 12 G5
Yantai Town China 91 K3
Yaoundé Capital Cameroon 42 C8
Yaroslavl' Town Russian Federation 72 D8
Yatsushiro Town Japan 93 B14
Yaviza Town Panama 23 O8
Yazd Town Iran 82 F7
Ye Town Myanmar 95 C9
Yecheng Town China 88 D5
Yefremov Town Russian Federation 73 C9
Yekaterinburg Town Russian Federation 78 F5
Yelets Town Russian Federation 73 C9
Yellowknife Town Northwest Territories,
   Canada 4 H6
Yellow River River China 91 I4
Yellow Sea Pacifc Ocean 91 L4
Yellowstone River Montana, USA 15 K3
Yel'sk Town Belarus 71 E12
Yemen Country 83 D12
Yemva Town Russian Federation 72 F7
Yenakiyeve Town Ukraine 69 M5
Yenierenköy see Agialoúsa
Yenisey River Russian Federation 78 H5
Yerevan Capital Armenia 77 L4
Yevlax Town Azerbaijan 77 M3
Yevpatoriya Town Ukraine 69 J7
Yichang Town China 91 I6
Yichun Town China 89 M2
Yildizeli Town Turkey 76 H4
Yinchuan Town China 89 J5
Yining Town China 88 E4
Yogyakarta Town Indonesia 96 G8
Yokohama Town Japan 93 G10
Yokote Town Japan 92 G8
Yonago Town Japan 93 D11
Yong'an Town China 91 K7
Yonkers Town New York, USA 9 I6
York Town England, UK 51 G8
York Town Pennsylvania, USA 9 G8
York, Cape Coastal feature Australia 105 K1
Yoro Town Honduras 22 G4
Yosemite National Park California, USA 14 G6
Yoshkar-Ola Town Russian Federation 73 E9
Yŏsu Town South Korea 91 M4
Youngstown Town Ohio, USA 13 M6
Yreka Town California, USA 14 F4
Yucatan Channel Mexico 19 O6
Yucatan Peninsula Mexico 19 O7
Yuci Town China 91 I4
Yueyang Town China 91 I6
Yukhavichy Town Belarus 70 G8
Yukon River Alaska/Yukon Territory 4 E4
Yukon Territory Province Canada 4 F5
Yulin Town China 90 H8
Yuma Town Arizona, USA 16 D5
Yumen Town China 88 H5
Yunnan Administrative region China 90 F7
Yushu Town Qinghai, China 88 H7
Yuxi Town China 90 F7
Yuzhno-Sakhalinsk Town Russian Federation
   79 M6

Z

Zaanstad Town Netherlands 52 E8
Zabaykal'sk Town Russian Federation 78 K7
Zacapa Town Guatemala 22 E4
Zacatecas Town Mexico 19 I6
Zacatepec Town Mexico 19 K8
Zadar Town Croatia 64 B7
Zafra Town Spain 58 G7
Zagazig Town Egypt 38 E4
Zagreb Capital Croatia 64 C6
Zagros Mountains Mountain range Iran 82 E7

Zāhedān Town Iran 82 H7
Záhony Town Hungary 63 H10
Zaječar Town Serbia 65 H9
Zalaegerszeg Town Hungary 63 D12
Zalău Town Romania 68 E5
Zalim Town Saudi Arabia 83 C10
Zambezi River Southern Africa 45 J4
Zambia Country 44 G3
Zamboanga Town Philippines 97 J4
Zamora Town Spain 58 G4
Zamość Town Poland 62 H8
Zanjän Town Iran 82 E5
Zanzibar Town Tanzania 39 G12
Zanzibar Island Tanzania 39 G13
Zaozhuang Town China 91 K4
Zapadnaya Dvina Town Russian Federation
   2 B8
Zapala Town Argentina 31 D10
Zapolyarnyy Town Russian Federation 72 D4
Zaporizhzhya Town Ukraine 69 K5
Zaqatala Town Azerbaijan 77 M3
Zaragoza Town Spain 59 K4
Zaranj Town Afghanistan 84 G8
Zárate Town Argentina 30 G8
Zaria Town Nigeria 41 L6
Zavidovići Town Bosnia & Herzegovina 64 E8
Zawiercie Town Poland 62 F8
Zawïlah Town Libya 37 L6
Zeebrugge Town Belgium 53 C10
Zeist Town Netherlands 52 E8
Zelenoborskiy Town Russian Federation 72 D5
Zelenograd Town Russian Federation 72 C8
Zemun Town Serbia 64 G7
Zenica Town Bosnia & Herzegovina 64 D8
Zgierz Town Poland 62 E7
Zhanaozen Town Kazakhstan 78 D6
Zhangjiakou Town China 91 J3
Zhangzhou Town China 91 K8
Zhanjiang Town China 91 I9
Zhaoqing Town China 91 I8
Zhejiang Administrative region
   China 91 K6
Zheleznogorsk Town Russian Federation
   73 B9
Zhengzhou Town China 91 I4
Zhezkazgan Town Kazakhstan 78 F7
Zhlobin Town Belarus 71 F11
Zhoatong Town China 90 G7
Zhodzina Town Belarus 71 F9
Zhongdian Town China 90 F6
Zhovti Vody Town Ukraine 69 J4
Zhytomyr Town Ukraine 68 H3
Zibo Town China 91 K4
Zielona Góra Town Poland 62 C7
Zigong Town China 90 G6
Ziguinchor Town Senegal 40 E6
Žilina Town Slovakia 63 E9
Zimbabwe Country 44 H5
Zimovniki Town Russian Federation 73 C11
Zinder Town Niger 41 L5
Zipaquira Town Colombia 26 C6
Zlín Town Czech Republic 63 D9
Zoetermeer Town Netherlands 52 E8
Zolochiv Town Ukraine 68 F3
Zomba Town Malawi 45 J4
Zonguldak Town Turkey 76 E3
Żory Town Poland 63 E9
Zouar Town Chad 42 E4
Zrenjanin Town Serbia 64 G7
Zug Town Switzerland 57 D11
Zuidhorn Town Netherlands 52 G6
Zula Town Eritrea 38 G7
Zunyi Town China 90 H7
Županja Town Croatia 64 E7
Zürich Town Switzerland 57 D11
Zutphen Town Netherlands 52 G8
Zuwārah Town Libya 37 J4
Zvishavane Town Zimbabwe 45 I5
Zwedru Town Liberia 40 G8
Zwettl Town Austria 57 H10
Zwickau Town Germany 56 F8
Zwolle Town Netherlands 52 F7
Zyryanovsk Town Kazakhstan 78 H7

Index

Credits

The publisher would like to thank the following for their kind permission to reproduce their photographs:

Abbreviations key: a=above, c=centre; b=below; l=left; r=right; t=top

Agence France Presse: 59tr; 84c; 91cra.

Alaska Stock: 4clb.

American Museum of Natural History: 12cl.

Art Directors & TRIP: 61car, T. Bognar 87tr, D. Iusupov 73c, P. Mercea 68br, D. Mossienko 69tr, T. Noorits 70tl, N & J Wiseman 69cr.

British Antarctic Survey: R. Mulvaney 110clb.

British Library: 82c.

British Museum: 27br, 37tc.

Cephas Picture Library: Fred R Palmer 6tr.

Bruce Coleman Ltd: Astrophoto iv t.

Corbis: 94cl; 96cl, Theo Allofs 99cra, Jean Pierre Amet/Corbis Sygma 49tl, Tony Arruza 11br; 30br, William A. Bake 7br, Anthony Bannister 44cl, Paul Barton 9cr, Dave Bartruff 49tr; 53bc, Morton Beebe 58bl, Niall Benvie 71cr, Yann Arthus Bertrand 28cr, Georgina Bowater 54cb, Tom Brakefield 96tr, B.S.P.I. i tr; 16br; 20br; 102tr, Dean Conger 15c; 73br; 97br, Keith Dannemiller 18tr, Tim Davis 100cla; 111bc, Carlos Dominguez 32ccr, Terry W. Eggers vii clb; 3cla, Jim Erickson vi bl, Robert Estall vii car, Macduff Everton 19tr, Owen Franken 10cbr; 52br; 53tl; 53tr, Stephen Frink ii crb; 22cl, Arvino Garg 23tcl, Bill Gentile 24cl, Philip Gould 13br, Farrell Grehan 9c, Julie Habel 13tl, John Heseltine 65cb, Ralf-Finn Hestoft/Corbis Saba 9tl, Arne Hodalic 77bl, Robert Holmes 92tl, Dave G. Houser 76br, Robbie Jack 72bc, Ray Juno vii cal; 53br; Wolfgang Kaehler vii cla; 25bc; 32br; 79bl; 100cbr; 103bc; 109tr, Bob Krist vii cra; 100car; 105cra, Frank Leather/Eye Ubiquitous viii clb, Lester Lefkowitz 15br, Danny Lehman 18br, Charles & Josette Lenars 41bl; 48tcl, George D. Lepp vii tr; 33br, Barry Lewis 69bl, Steve Liss/Corbis Sygma 108tc, Lawrence Manning 76cl, Gunter Marx Photography 4bl, Stephanie Maze 29cra; 49cla; 109br, NASA iv bc, Richard J. Nowitz 7cra, Charles O'Rear 4tcr, Christine Osborne 81crb, Douglas Peebles v br; 90car, Caroline Penn viii tl, Clay Perry 67tl, Ledru Philippe/Corbis Sygma 37bc, Perrin Pierre/Corbis Sygma 55bl, Sergio Pitamitz iii br; 22br; 105br, Richard Ransier 16tr, Steve Rayner ibr; 72tr, Roger Ressmeyer 54tl, Benjamin Rondel 6bl, Bill Ross viii b, Galen Rowell v cla; 110cal, Saba/Shepard Sherbell 111tr, Michael St. Maur Sheil 50br, Kim Sayer 55bc, Alan Schein Photography 3cra; 9br, Gregor Schmid 79crb, Flip Schulke 11c, Attal Serge/Corbis Sygma 71bl, Alex Steedman 51tr, Hans Strand 33tr, Vince Streano 11cla, Keren Su 86br, Torleif Svensson 111cr, TempSport 71tc, Tim Thompson 19tc, David Turnley 77cl; 80cal; 83cr; 85cr, Peter Turnley 25bl; 45bl; 78bc, Penny Tweedie 100clb; 104cla, Pablo Corral Vega 26cl, Francesco Venturi 19cr, Patrick Ward 59br, Nevada Wier 74cla; 85cra; 85tr; 85cb, Nik Wheeler 71tl; 77br, Staffan Widstrand 5tc; 71bc, Peter M. Wilson 3crb; 5bcr, Wildcountry 50tr, Adam Woolfitt 76tc, Michael S. Yamashita 91bc; 93bcl.

Empics Ltd: Tony Marshall 3bl; 6bc; 64bc, Phil Walter 104bc.

Getty Images: Samuel Ashfield 47crb, Paul Chesley 92cl, Jim Cummins ii cra; 13cr, Sylvain Grandadam 57tr, Frans Lemmens iii tl, Photodisc/Jeremy Woodhouse 108car, Martin Puddy 86c, Michael Rosenfeld 56bc, Andy Sacks 10cl, Jess Stock 57br, Bruce Stoddard 19tl.

Getty Images News Service: Scott Harrison 60cl, Mike Powell 55ca, Matthew Stockman 11tc.

Robert Harding Picture Library: vii crb; 12ccl; 15 tc; 28cl; 31tr; 32tr; 62tc; 66tr; 79br; 83tc; 87tl; 95bl, Max Alexander 10br, Paul Allen 34bl; 45br, Mohamed Amin 83bcl, Bildagentur Schuster GMBH 108bl, Bildagentur Schuster/Gluske 30cl, Jeremy Bright 107c, Martyn F. Chillmaid 45ccr, Neale Clark 105crb, Victor Englebert 31bl, Alain Evrard 95tr, Explorer/D. Riffet 43cra, Warren Finlay/International Stock 109cr, Nigel Francis 8bl, Robert Francis 14tc, Robert Frerck iii cl; 27cr; 31tl; 59bc, Robert Frerck/Odyssey/Chicago 18cl, Lee Frost vii cbr, Kim Hart 48tl, Gavin Hellier 89br; 3ca, D. Jacobs 104tr, Maurice Joseph 70bc, Paolo Koch 88-89; 107tl, J. Lightfoot 40cla, David Lomax 74cca; 84bl, John Miller 25tr, Louise Murray vii cbl, Nakamura 23crbl; 38ca; 110br, Mike Newton 58cla, J. Nov. iii cra; 87clb, Roy Rainford 9tr; 32ca, Geoff Renner 110tr, G. R. Richardson 65tr, R. Richardson 60br, Phil Robinson 65bl, Peter Scholey 66tl, Schuster 30tl; 44bc, Michael Short 81br, Johnny Stockshooter 67cbr, J. C. Thoret 42tr, Doug Traverso 89cr, Hardie Truesdale 12bl, Upperhall Ltd 103cal, Tony Waltham 85br, Nik Wheeler 14bl, T.D. Winter 37tl, Keith Wood/International Stock 17bl; 50tc, Adam Woolfitt 32cl; 52tl.

Hopi Learning Centre: 16bc.

Hutchison Library: 39tr; 43c; 64ca; 78bl; 81bc; 82tc; 91br; 94tl, Jon Burbank 93tl, Sarah Errington 39bc; 42bcr; 45tl; 86bl, Robert Francis 22cb; 23cbl; 104-105bc, Melanie Friend 66cb; 66br; 89bl; 90cbl, Norman Froggatt 95cr, John Fuller 25tc, Bernard Gerard 82bc, Andrew Hill 45br, John Halt 96br, Nick Haslam 68clb; 93clb; 103cra, J. Henderson 81tr, Jeremy Horner 39bl; 56tc; 87bc; 90bl; 91tl; 97c, Crispin Hughes 41cr; 41bc; 45tc, Mary Jelliffee 27tr; 36bc, Eric Lawrie 27ca, R. Ian Lloyd 96bl, Michael Macintyre 102bc; 103tr, N. Durrell McKenna 104clb, Sarah Murray 88bc, John Nowell 83cr, Trevor Page 43br; 61bc, Stephen Pem 88cla, PERN 89tr, Dr Nigel Smith 28br; 97cr, Liba Taylor 63cb; 69br; 73tl; 73bl, Isabella Tree 98tr; 110bl, David Watson 65br, Philip Wolmoth 51br, Andrey Zvoznikov vi cl; vi cla; vi clb; vi tr; 73tr; 79tl; 79tr.

Impact Photos: Rupert Connant 62tr.

Barnabas Kindersley: 40bcl; 83bcr.

Masterfile UK: Didier Dorval 56tr.

NASA: 17tr.

Natural History Museum: 43ca.

N.H.P.A.: B & C Alexander 32bl, T. Kitchin and V. Hurst 5cbr, Stephen Oliver 15bcl, Andy Rouse 5br.

Only Horses Picture Agency: 57cr.

PA Photos: European Press Agency 56tl.

Panos Pictures: David Constantine 59cr; 62cl, Neil Cooper 38tcr, Clive Shirley 41tl, Teun Voeten 40bcr.

Pictorial Press Ltd: 87crb.

Pictures Colour Library: 8ca; 16tc; 50bc; 51cr; 61cl; 68cla; 79cra; 92tc, © FMGB Guggenheim Bilbao Museoa. Photo by Charles Bowman. All rights reserved. Total or partial reproduction is prohibited. 59tl.

Pitt Rivers Museum: 73tc.

Popperfoto: 51bc, Ho/Reuters 108ccl.

Powell Cotton Museum: 42bcl.

Redferns: 10bc.

Rex Features: Stuart Clarke 82tl, Simon Runting 107bl, Enrica Scalfari 60tr, Sipa Press 12bc; 15bc; 56br; 97tr, Tim Rooke 96cr, Wilhemsen 99br.

Floyd Sayers: 39br; 45bcr.

Science Photo Library: George Bernard 15bl, Laboratory for Atmospheres, NASA/ Goddard Space Flight Center 111car, Nasa vi br, Tom Van Sant, Geosphere Project/ Planetary Visions 34–35; 46–47; 74–75, 1995 Worldsat International and J. Knighton 2–3; 20–21; 100–101.

South American Pictures: 26tl; 28bl; 31br.

Still Pictures: Julio Etchart 18bl, Roland Seitre 98cb, Annelies Van Brink viii tr; 74crb.

Marie Tharp: v tr.

Topham Picturepoint: Francis Dean/Imageworks 49crb.

V. Tunnicliffe: 108cbr.

Webphotographer.com: Denissenko 64tr.

World Pictures: i bl; i tl; 4bc; 7tl; 7tr; 20clb; 20crb; 22clb; 23tr; 24bl; 25ca; 26cr; 27bl; 29cr; 29br; 30bc; 31ca; 34car; 36cl; 36cl; 37tr; 38bc; 42tc; 44bl; 47tr; 47cla; 47clb; 48bc; 52bc; 54tc; 55tc; 61r; 63tc; 63tr; 63br; 64tl; 67tr; 67br; 67bcl; 68bl; 71br; 72cl; 74bl; 76bl; 80cla; 80cb; 80bcr; 81tc; 89c; 90cl; 91cb; 92br; 93tr; 94tc; 94tr; 95bl; 98bl; 98ccl; 98ccr; 99tr; 104cal; 106tl; 106crb; 106br; 107tr.

Jacket images

Front: Corbis: Owen Franken cra, Richard Ransier crb, Stephen Frink br, Getty Images: Keren Su ca, Robert Harding Picture Library: Lee Frost bcl, Masterfile UK: Hans Blohm cb.

Front Inside Flap: Corbis: Richard Ransier br, Owen Franken tr, Masterfile UK: Hans Blohm bl, Getty Images: Keren Su tl.

Back: Corbis: Dave Bartruff cb, B.S.P.I. cbr, Stephen Frink br, Alan Schein Photography crb, Tim Davis cbl, Robert Harding Picture Library: Lee Frost bcl, Getty Images: Kevin Morris clb.

Spine: Corbis: Owen Franken t, Richard Ransier b.

All other images © Dorling Kindersley

For further information see: **www.dkimages.com**

Dorling Kindersley would also like to thank:

Clare Shedden, Philip Letsu, Kate Bradshaw, and Neal Cobourne for the jacket design, and Chris Bernstein for the index.

NORTH AMERICA

CANADA
Pages 4–7

UNITED STATES OF AMERICA
Pages 8-17

MEXICO
Pages 18-19

CENTRAL & SOUTH AMERICA

BELIZE
Pages 22-23

COSTA RICA
Pages 22-23

EL SALVADOR
Pages 22-23

GUATEMALA
Pages 22-23

HONDURAS
Pages 22-23

GRENADA
Pages 24-25

HAITI
Pages 24-25

JAMAICA
Pages 24-25

ST KITTS & NEVIS
Pages 24-25

ST LUCIA
Pages 24-25

ST VINCENT & THE GRENADINES
Pages 24-25

TRINIDAD & TOBAGO
Pages 24-25

BOLIVIA
Pages 26-27

AFRICA

CHILE
Pages 30-31

PARAGUAY
Pages 30-31

URUGUAY
Pages 30-31

ALGERIA
Pages 36-37

LIBYA
Pages 36-37

MOROCCO
Pages 36-37

TUNISIA
Pages 36-37

BURUNDI
Pages 38-39

TANZANIA
Pages 38-39

UGANDA
Pages 38-39

BENIN
Pages 40-41

BURKINA FASO
Pages 40-41

CAPE VERDE
Pages 40-41

CÔTE D'IVOIRE (IVORY COAST)
Pages 40-41

GAMBIA
Pages 40-41

GHANA
Pages 40-41

SIERRA LEONE
Pages 40-41

TOGO
Pages 40-41

CAMEROON
Pages 42-43

CENTRAL AFRICAN REPUBLIC
Pages 42-43

CHAD
Pages 42-43

CONGO
Pages 42-43

DEM. REP. CONGO
Pages 42-43

EQUATORIAL GUINEA
Pages 42-43

EUROPE

MAURITIUS
Pages 44-45

MOZAMBIQUE
Pages 44-45

NAMIBIA
Pages 44-45

SOUTH AFRICA
Pages 44-45

SWAZILAND
Pages 44-45

ZAMBIA
Pages 44-45

ZIMBABWE
Pages 44-45

DENMARK
Pages 48-49

NETHERLANDS
Pages 52-53

ANDORRA
Pages 54-55

FRANCE
Pages 54-55

MONACO
Pages 54-55

AUSTRIA
Pages 56-57

GERMANY
Pages 56-57

LIECHTENSTEIN
Pages 56-57

SLOVENIA
Pages 56-57

HUNGARY
Pages 62-63

POLAND
Pages 62-63

SLOVAKIA
Pages 62-63

ALBANIA
Pages 64-65

BOSNIA & HERZEGOVINA
Pages 64-65

CROATIA
Pages 64-65

MACEDONIA
Pages 64-65

SERBIA
Pages 64-65

MONTENEGRO
Pages 64-65

ASIA

LITHUANIA
Pages 70-71

RUSSIAN FEDERATION
Pages 78-79

CYPRUS
Pages 80-81

ARMENIA
Pages 76-77

AZERBAIJAN
Pages 76-77

GEORGIA
Pages 76-77

TURKEY
Pages 76-77

ISRAEL
Pages 80-81

QATAR
Pages 82-83

SAUDI ARABIA
Pages 82-83

UNITED ARAB EMIRATES
Pages 82-83

YEMEN
Pages 82-83

KAZAKHSTAN
Pages 78-79

AFGHANISTAN
Pages 84-85

KYRGYZSTAN
Pages 84-85

TAJIKISTAN
Pages 84-85

MONGOLIA
Pages 88-89

NORTH KOREA
Pages 90-91

SOUTH KOREA
Pages 90-91

TAIWAN
Pages 90-91

JAPAN
Pages 92-93

CAMBODIA
Pages 94-95

LAOS
Pages 94-95

MYANMAR (BURMA)
Pages 94-95

AUSTRALASIA & OCEANIA

MALDIVES
Pages 98-99

SEYCHELLES
Pages 98-99

FIJI
Pages 102-103

KIRIBATI
Pages 102-103

MARSHALL ISLANDS
Pages 102-103

MICRONESIA
Pages 102-103

NAURU
Pages 102-103

PALAU
Pages 102-103